MARINE ECOSYSTEM

MARINE ECOSYSTEM

Editor
GOPAL BHARGAVA

KALPAZ PUBLICATIONS
DELHI-110052

MARINE ECOSYSTEM
(Environment, Ecology)

ISBN: 81-7835-059-9

Published in 2001 in India by
Kalpaz Publications
C-30, Satyawati Nagar
Ashok Vihar Phase-III
Delhi-110052
E-Mail: kalpaz@hotmail.com

Laser Typesetting at : A.S. Printers
Printed at : Mehra Offset Printers, New Delhi

Preface

The ocean water covers 70. 8 per cent of Earth's total surface area. The marine ecosystem contains a wide-range of plants and animals. It represents a stable equilibrium of various physical and biological factors. The organic continuity of the system rests on a delicate network of interdependent relationships. The marine ecosystem has a rhythm and movement of its own which depends upon a whole set of delicately balanced cycles.

Marine ecosystem studies are concerned with environmental factors and problems of organic adjustments of oceanic environment. In oceans animals are relatively more conspicuous than plants. Succession is less evident, but such ecological processes represented by chemical cycles, cooperation, and desperation, food chains, productivity, population, dynamics, niche segregation, speciation, and dispersal are fully as important as on land.

The geographic distribution of marine organisms depends on their responses to water current, temperature, and physical barriers; their local distribution is affected by waves and tides, salinity and dept. To consider the entire ocean community as a single biome is stretching the concept beyond its usefulness. Since we identify biomes by differences in the life-forms, and functional adjustments of the conspicuous dominant or predominant organisms, we may properly recognise biomes that occur in the open ocean, on eroding rocky shores on muddy and sandy beaches, and composing the coral reefs and atolls.

The marine ecosystem get polluted by man, directly or indirectly, of substances or energy into the marine environment which results or is likely to result in such deleterious effects as harm to living resources and marine ecosystems, hazards to human health, hindrance to marine activities, including fishing and other legitimate uses of the sea, impairment of quality for use of sea water and reduction of amenities. Sources of marine pollution from activities conducted on offshore fixed or mobile facilities within the limits of national jurisdiction, save to the extent that these sources are governed by appropriate international agreements. Governments have adopted appropriate bilateral, regional and multilateral agreements and national legislation for the protection of the marine environment against pollution from land-based sources.

The present book is unique amidst the existing literature of marine biology. It contains authoritative and well researched aspects of marine ecosystem. Students, researchers and teachers besides environmental scientists, environment activists will find this work informative and useful.

Editor

Contents

1

Introduction

The cycle of life in the sea, like that on land, is fuelled by the sun's visible light acting on green plants. Of every million photons of sunlight reaching the earth's surface, some 90 enter into the net production of basic food. Perhaps so of the 90 contribute to the growth of the land plants and about 40 to the growth of the single celled green plants of the sea, the photoplankton. The terrestrial and marine plants and animals arose from the same sources, through similar evolutionary sequence and by the action of the same natural laws. The analogy is substantially inaccurate, because the primary marine food production is carried out by cells dispersed widely in a dense fluid medium this fact of an initial dispersal imposes a set of profound general conditions on all forms of life in the sea.

In moderately rich areas of the sea, food is 100th times more dilute in volume and hundreds of thousands of time more dilute in relative mass. To crop this meager both a blind herbivore or a simple pore in a filtering structure would need to process a weight of water hundreds of thousands of times the weight of the cell if eventually captures. In even the densest concentrations the factor exceeds several thousands and with each further step in the food web dilution increases. Thus from the beginnings of the marine food web we see many adaptations accommodating to this dilution: eyes in microscopic herbivorous animals. Filters of exquisite design, mechanisms and behaviours for discovering local concentrations, complex search gear and, on the bottom. Attachments to elicit the aid of moving water in carrying out the task of filtration. The organisms of the sea are bore, live breathe feed, excrete, move, grow, mate, reproduce, and die within a single interconnected medium. This interactions among the marine organisms and interactions of the organisms with the chemical and physical processes of the sea range across the entire spectrum from simple, adamant constraints to complex effects of many subtle interactions.

A general discussions of a living system should consider the ways in which plants elaborate basic organic material from inorganic substances and the successive and often highly intricate stems by which organisms then return this material to the inorganic reservoir. The discussion should also slow the forms of life by which such processes are conducted.

Some organic material is carried to the sea by rivers and some is manufactured in shallow water by attached plants. More than 90% of the basic organic material that fuels and builds the life in the sea, however, is synthesized within the lighted surface layers of open water by the many varieties of phytoplankton. These sunny pastures of plant cells are grazed by the herbivorous zooplanketon and by some small fishes. These in turn are prey to various carnivorous creatures, large and small, who have their predators also. The debris from the activities in the surface layers settles into the dimly lighted and unlighted midlayers of the sea, the twilight mesopelasic zone and the mid night bathypelagic zone, to serve as one source of food for their strange inhabitants. This process depletes the surface layers of some food and particularly of vital plant nutrients, or fertilizers, that become trapped below the surface layers, where they are unavailable to the plants. Food and nutrients are also actively carried downward from the surface by vertically migrating animals.

The depleted remnants of this constant "rain" of detritus continue to the sea floor and support those animals that live just above the bottom, on the bottom and burrowed into the bottom. There filter feeding and burrowing animals and bacteria rework the remaining refractory particles.

The more active animals also find repast in mid water creatures and in the occasional falls on carcasses and other larger debris. Except in unusual small areas there is an abundance of oxygen in the deep water. And the solid bottom presents advantages that allow the support of a denser populations of larger creatures than can exist in deep mid water. In shallower water such as banks, atolls, continental shelves and shallows seas conditions associated with a solid bottom and other regional modifications of general regime enable rich populations to develop. Such areas constitute about 7% of the total area of the ocean. In some of these regions added food results from the growth of larger fixed plants and from land drainage. One common group of small phytoplankton are the coccolithophores, with calcareous plants.

A swimming ability and often an oil droplet for food storage and bouyancy. The larger microscopic phytoplankton are composed of many species belonging to several groups: naked algal cells, diatoms with complex shells of silica and activity swimming and rotating flagellates.

Very small forms of many groups are also abundant and collectively are called nannoplankton. The species composition of the phytoplankton is everywhere complex and varies from place to place, season to season and year to year.

The various regions of the ocean are typified, however, by dominant major groups and particular species, seasonal effects are often strong, with dense blooms of phytoplankton occurring when high levels of plant nutrients suddenly become usable or available, such as in high latitudes in spring or along coasts at the on set of upwelling. The concentrations of phytoplankton varies on all dimensional scales, even down to small patches. In addition the large scale circulation of the ocean continuously sweeps the pelagic plants out of the region to which they are best adapted. It is essential that some individuals be returned to renew the populations.

More mechanisms for this essential return exist for single celled plants than exist for large plants or even for any conventional spores, seeds or juveniles. Any of these can be carried by oveanec gyres or diffused by large scale motions of surface eddies and periodic counter flow, but single celled plants can also ride submerged counter currents while temporarily feeding on the food particles or perhaps dissolved organic material. Other mechanisms of distribution undoubtedly are also occasionally important. For example, living marine plant cells are carried by storm-borne spray. In bird feathers and by wellfed fish and birds in their undigested food. No large plant has solved the many problems of development, dispersla, and reproduction. There are no pelagic trees, and these several factors in concert therefore restrict the open sea in a profound way. They confine it to an initial food web composed of microscopic forms, whereas larger plants live attached only to shallow bottoms.

Attached plants, unlike free-floating plants, are not subject to the afore mentioned limitations. For attached plants all degrees of water motion enhance the exchange of nutrients and wastes.

Although species of phytoplankton will populate only regions with conditions to which they are adapted, factors other than temperature, nutrients and light levels undoubtedly are important in determining the species composition of phytoplankton populations. Little is understood of the mechanisms that give rise to an abundance of particular species under certain conditions.

Grazing herbivores may consume only a parts of the size range of cells. Allowing certain sizes and types to dominate temporarily. Little is understood of the mechanisms that give rise to an abundance of particular species under certain conditions.

Chemical by products of certain species probably exclude certain other species. Often details of individual cell behaviour are probably also important in the introduction and success of a species in a particular area. In some cases we can glimpse what the mechanisms are for example, both the larger diatoms and the larger flagellates can more at appreciable velocities through the water. The diatoms commonly sink downward, whereas the flagellates actively swim upward toward light. These are probably patterns of behaviour primarily for increasing exchange. But the interaction of such undirectional motions with random turbulence or systemic convective motions is not simple, as it is with an in active particle.

Rather, we would expect diatoms to be statistically abundant in upward moving water and to sink out of the near surface layers when turbulence or upward convection is low.

Flagellates should be statistically more abundant in down welling water and should concentrate near the surface in low turbulence and slow downward water motions. These effects seem to exist. Of some continental costs in summer flagellates may eventually collect in high concentrations. As they begin to shade one to another from the light. Each individual struggles close to the lighted surface, producing such a high density that large areas of the water are turned red or brown by their pigments.

The concentration of flagellates in these "Red Tides" sometimes becomes too great for their own survival. Several specia of flagellates also become highly foxic as they grow older. Thus they sometimes both produce and participate in a mass death of fish and invertebrates that has been on own to give rise to such a high yield of hydrogen sulfide as to blacken the white houses of coastal cities.

Large diatom cells, on the other hand, spread a disproportionately greater time in upward moving regions of the water and an unlimited time in any region where the upward motion about equals their own downward motion. Diatom cells are there statistically abundant in upwelling water, and the distribution of diatoms probably is often are flection of the turbulant convective region of the water. Sinking and the dependence of the larger diatoms on upward convection and turbulence for support aids item in reaching upwelling regions, where nutrients are high, it helps to explain their dominance in such regions and such other features of their distributions as their high proportion in rich ocean regions and their frequent inverse occurrence with flagellates. Differences in adaptations to the physical and chemical products, probably reinforce such relations. In some areas, such as parts of the equatorial current system and shallow seas. Where lateral and vertical circulation is rapid, the species composition of phytoplankton is perhaps more simply a result of the inherent ability of the species to grow, survive and reproduce under the local conditions of temperature, light, nutrients, competitors and herbivores. Elsewhere second-order effects of the detailed cell behaviour often dominate. These details of behaviour that give rise to concentration on any dimensional scale are particularly important to all subsequent steps in the food chain. The grazing of the phytoplankton it principally conducted by the herbivorous members of that zooplankton.

A heterogeneous group of small animals that carry out several steps in the food web as herbivores, carnivores and detrital feeders. Among the important members of the zooplankton are the arthopods, animals and external skeletons that belong to the same broad groups as insects, crabs and shrimps. The planktonic arthopods induce the abundant copepods, which are in a sense the maring equivalent of insects. Copepods are represented in the sea by some 10,000 or more species that act not only as herbivores. Carnivores or detrital feeders but also as external or even internal parasites' two or three thousand of these species live in the open sea. Other important arthropods are the shrimp like euphausidis, the strongest vertical migrators of the zooplankton. They compose the vast shoals of krill that occur in high latitudes and that constitute one of the principal food of the baleen whales. The zooplankton also include the strange bristle jawed chateognaths or arrow worms, carnivores or mysterious origin and affinities know only in the marine environment. Widely distributed and abundant. The chateognaths are represented by a surprisingly small number of species. Perhaps fewer than 50. Larvae of many types, worms, medusae, ctenophores, gastropods, pteropods and heteropods, salps, unpigmented flagellates and many others are also important components of this milieu. Each with its own remarkably complex and often bizarre life history, behaviour and form. The larger zooplankton are mainly carnivores, and those of herbivores habit are restricted to feeding on the larger plant cells. Much of the blood supply, however, exists in the form of very small particles such as the nanoplankton, and these appear to be available almost solely to microscopic creatures. Eyesight has developed in many minute animals to make possible selective capture.

As an ex-dense concentrations of phytoplankton are often associated with low populations of zooplankton. These are probably rapidly growing blooms that zooplankton have not yet invaded and grazed on, but it is not completely clear that this is so.

Chemical repulsion may be involved. The concentration of larger zooplankton and small fishes in the surface layers is much greater at night than during the day, because of a group of strong swimming members that share their time between the surface and the mesopelagic region. Many small zooplankton organisms also make a daily migration of some vertical extent. In addition to its primary purpose daily vertical migration undoubtedly served the (migration) migrating organisms in a number of other ways. It enables the creatures to adjust their mean temperature. So that by spending the days in cooler water the amount of food used during rest is reduced. Perhaps such processes as the rate of egg development are also controlled by these tactics. Convincing arguments have also been presented to show that vertical migration serves to maintain species so that they will be more successful under many more conditions than if they lived solely in the surface layers. This migration must also play an important part in the distribution of many species. Interaction of the daily migrants with the water motion produced by daily land sea breeze alternation can hold the migrants off store by a kind of

"Rectification" of the oscillating water motion. More generally descent into the (water) lower layers increases the influence of submerged counter currents. There by enhancing the opportunity to regions and hence to find high nutrient levels and associated high phytoplankton productivity.

Even minor details of behaviour may strongly contribute to success. Migrants spend the day at a depth corresponding to relatively constant low light, where the moment of water commonly is different from that at the surface. Most of the members rise some what even on the passage of cloud shadow.

The principal food supplies of the pelagic populations are passed on in incremental steps and rapidly depleted quantity to the larger carnivores, zooplankton, then to small fishes and squids, and ultimately to the wide range of larger carnivores of the pelagic realm. The Pelagic region contains some of the largest and most superbly designed creatures ever to inhabit this earth: the exquisitely constructed pelasic tunas. The multicolored dolphin fishes, captures of flying fishes; the conversational purposes; the shallow and deep feeding swordfishes and toothed whales, and the greatest carnivores of all, the baleen whales and some plankton eating sharks. Whose prey are entire schools of krill or small fishes. Seals and sealions feed far into the pelagic realm. In concert with these great predators, large carnivorous sharks a wait injured prey.

Marine birds, some adapted to almost continuous pelagic life, consume surprising quantities of ocean food, diving, plunging, skimming and gulping in pursuit. These larger creatures of the sea commonly move in schools, shoals, and herds. In addition to meeting the needs of mating such grouping is advantageous in both defensive and predatory strategy. Small fishes of several species commonly school together. Diverse predators also form loosely cooperative groups, and many species of marine birds depend almost wholly on prey driven to the surface by submerged predators.

The reason for the ubiquitous production of light by the micro organisms of the sea remains obscure, and suggested explanations are controversial. It has been suggested that light is a kind of inadvertent by product of life in transparent organisms. It has also been hypothesized that the emission of light on disturbance is advantageous to the plankton in making the predators of the plankton conspicuous to their predators.

The fall out of organic material into the deep dimly lighted mid water supports a sparse population of fishes and invertebrates with in the mesopelasic and bathypelagic zones are found some of the most curious and bizarre creatures of this earth. These range from the highly developed and powerfully predators intruders, toothed whales and sword fishes, at the climax of the food chain to the remarkable squids, octopuses, euphausidis, lantern fishes, gulpers and angler fishes that in habit the bathypelagic region. In the mesopelagic region, where some sunlight penetrates, fishes are often countershaded, that is, they are darker above and lighter below. As are surface fishes. Many of the creatures of this dimly lighted region participate in the daily migration. Swimming to the upper layers at evening like bath emerging from their caves. There are some much larger stronger and more active fishes and squids in this region, although they are not taken in trawls or seen from submersibles. Knowledge of their evidence comes mainly from specimens found in the stomach of sperm whales and sword fish. There is evidence that the sperm whales posses highly developed long range hunting sonar. They may locate their prey over relatively great distances. Perhaps miles, from just such an extremely sparse population of active bathypelagic animals. Although many near surface organisms are luminescent. It is the bathypelagic region that bioluminescence has reached a surprising level of development. With at least two thirds of the species producing light. Clearly bioluminescence can be valuable to higher organisms, and the creatures of the bathypelagic realm have developed light producing organs and structures to a high degree. Strong fishes may confuse predators by "target alteration" effects or by producing residual images in the predators vision. Some squids and shrimps are more direct and discharge luminous organs are arranged on some fishes so that they can be used to countershade their siltouettes against faint light coming from the surface. Lights may also be used for locating a mate. A problem of this vast, sparsely populated domain that has been solved by some angler fishes by the development of tiny males that live parasitically attached to their relatively huge mates. Light level in the bathypelagic regain can be much lower. This is most probably the primary difference that accounts for the absence of bioluminescence in higher land animals and the richness of II's development in the ocean forms. There are some 2000 species of the larger invertebrates known to inhabit the bathypelagic zone. But only 4 few of these species appear to be widespread. The barriers to distribution in this widely interconnected mid water region are not obvious. The floor of the deep sea constitutes an environment quite unlike the midwater and surface environments. There are sites for the attachment of the larger invertebrates that filter detritus from the water. Among these animals are representative of some of the earliest multicelled creature to exist on the earth glass sponges, sea littles—once thought to have been long extinct—and lamp shells.

Larger numbers of active fishes and other creatures are attracted to the bait almost immediately.

It is probably I feel that several rather independent branches of the food web coexist in support of the deep bottom creatures: one the familiar rain of fine detitus, and the other the rare, widely separate falls of large food particles that are in excess of the local feeding capacity of broadly diffuse bathypelagic population.

Benthic animals are much more abundant in the shallower mater off continents, particularly offshore from large rivers. Here there is often not only a richer near surface production and less hazardous journey of food to the sea floor but also a considerable input of food conveyed by rivers to the bottom. The deep slopes of river sediments wedges are typified by a comparatively rich population of burrowing and filtering animal that utilize this fine organic material.

The shallow regions of such wedges are highly productive of active and often valuable marine organism. The bottom is much more variable than the mid water zone is. There are as a result more environmental riches for an organism to occupy, and hence we see organisms that are of a wider range of from and habit. Aside from the wide range of form and fraction the benthic environment elicits from its inhabitants, there are more fundamental conditions that influence the nature and form of life there.

Marine ecology is concerned with environmental factors and problems of organic adjustments quite different from those in fresh water. Animals are relatively more conspicuous than plants. Succession is less evident, but such ecological processes represented by chemical cycles, co-operation, and disoperation, food chains, productivity, population, dynamics, niche segregation, speciation, and dispersal are fully as important as on land.

Distinct self-contained community units are more difficult to recognize in the sea than on land because of the apparently greater interrelation of benthic species and the free movement with circulating currents of plankton and nekton. Plankton is everywhere a basic link in food chains, but the general distribution and importance of plankton species in the sea is no more remarkable than that of soil organisms in terrestrial biomes. To consider the entire ocean community as a single biome, as has been suggested by some investigators, is stretching the concept beyond its usefulness. Since we identify biomes by differences in the life-forms, and functional adjustments of the conspicuous dominant or predominant organisms, we may properly recognize biomes that occur in the open ocean, on eroding rocky shores, on muddy and sandy beaches, and composing the coral reefs and atolls.

Marine biocycle is considered to have benthic (bottom) and pelagic (open water) divisions, the littoral zone of the ocean shore exceeds between the limits of high and low tides, the sublitoral zone covers the continental shelf to a depth of about 200 m. The approximate depth at which maximum wave action produces any effect. The average depth of the ocean is about 3800 m, but oceanic trenches (hadal zone) extend much deeper, the Marianas Trench in the Pacific Ocean to approximately 11,6000 m. The neritic biochare is above the continental shelf and is commonly 16-240 km. (10-150 mi) wide.

Tides are caused by the attraction of the moon and to a lesser, extent, the sun. When the sun's attraction is added to that of the moon, as occurs twice each month at the time of full moon and new moon, the fluctuations of the tides are unusually high and unusually low, these are called spring tides. When the tidal influences of sun and moon are opposed, as happens twice each month, the tides have the least amount of flow and ebb and are called neap tides. The level of water in the ocean rises and falls usually twice each day or at an interval of 12 hours and 26 minutes. In some parts of the world the tides are less regular or there may be but one daily. Flood-tide is the period in which the level is rising and covering more and more of the shoreline; ebb-tide is the period in which the water level is less than a meter, but the change may be much more than this on the shore, depending on its configuration, the Bay of Fundy opens broadly to the sea and tapers to a narrow head landward, and tides may be 6 to 10 or even 15 m.

On the other hand, when bodies of water have only a relatively narrow connection with the sea, as does the Gulf of Mexico with the Atlantic, the range in water level is less than 30 cm. Even lakes have seiches, but they are hardly perceptible except in the larger lakes, where it may amount to a few centimeters. Tides have their greatest effect on animals on the seashore, because of the associated pounding of waves and the alternative submergence in water and exposure to the air. However, the organisms appear well adjusted to this rhythmic submergence and exposure. For instance, as the stones on which the chiton occurs become exposed, the animals react positively to gravity and negatively to strong light, and move downward. They travel at maximum speed while the stone is still moist and become aggregated on the damp lower sides of the stones. When the stone again becomes immersed by the returning tide, the animals lose their geotactic orientation, and since illumination becomes more or less equal on all sides of the stones, they move about at random until they reach the upper surfaces again.

The pounding action of waves or rocky shore may have tremendous force, estimated in one instance at 15,000 kg/cm^2 animals occupying exposed rocky shores in the surf belt must be strongly protected and firmly attached. The conical shaped limpets present a minimum of surface to the waves. Large depressions in the rock retain water at ebb tide to form tidal pools and thus may contain the more delicate species because of the protection they afford.

The various sea weeds absorb some of the wave shock for the animals living with them. The shape, form and size of corals, sponges, and other colonial type are affected by the amount of wave action to which the animals are exposed, a shell of the Mytilus mussel may weigh 58 g where the animal is exposed to a heavy surf but only 26.5 g in more quiet waters. Sandy beaches occur only where the force of waves is reduced by being spread over a more gentle slope. Even here, especially during storms the sand makes a very unstable substratum and not many animals except mollusks and some of the echinoderms can keep from being smothered or buried. Mud bottoms occur only in relatively quiet waters. Burrows made in mud hold their form better than in sand, so large population of animals can occur in mud. Organic deposits are either calcareous or siliceous, the former being derived from the shells of foraminiferans, small pelagic mollusks, or flogellate coccolithophorids and the latter from skeletal material of diatoms and radiolarian protozoans.

There is an enormous increase in the pressure of water upon the bodies of animals at great depths, and this may effect the vertical distribution of such species as crabs and mussels. This is not, however, an important limiting factor in the vertical distribution of animals in general, as internal pressures closely counter- balance external pressures and life is known to exist at the greatest depths. Adjustments of internal pressures are not so rapid, however, to prevent injury in many species that are dredged at great depths and quickly hauled to the surface.

The temperatures of surface waters vary between the freezing point (-1.9°C) in the tropics. Seasonal variations are small in polar and tropical waters but somewhat greater in the temperate zones. Temperature varies with depth, more so in the tropics than elsewhere. At 60°N latitude in the Atlantic Ocean, the mean temperature of the warmest and coldest months beneath the surface is about 10°C. On the equator the temperature beneath the surface is approximately 26°C, at 200 m, 13°C, at 1000 m 4.51°C, and at 2000 m 3.3°C (Ekman 1943). In temperate regions, seasonal thermoclinc develops near the surface in summer and is destroyed in autumn and winter when vertical mixing creates a layer of relatively uniform temperature in the upper 20 to 300 m.

Currents moving toward the poles from the equator consist of warm water, and currents moving in the opposite direction of cold water. Surface currents make wide circular movements in opposite directions in the northern and southern hemisphere. Much of the solar radiation is reflected from the surface of absorbed in the upper layers. Even in the clearest waters and at maximum radiation; the red, orange and ultraviolet are absorbed in the first 20 m. Green, yellow and blue wavelengths penetrate further, depending on the water colour. When the sun is not at the zenith, light penetration is reduced, and the maximum penetration in the winter at higher latitudes is much less than during the summer.

The salinity of sea water varies from place to place depending largely on the amount that it is diluted by the yellow of fresh water from rivers or melting glaciers or the amount that it is concentrated by evaporation. The Red Sea, for instance has a salinity of 40% (40 g of dry salts in 1000 g of seawater) while in some polar seas the salinity is less then 30%. The average salinity of the oceans as a whole is commonly given as 35% of which the chlorideion constitutes about 19% and the sodium ion little over 10%.

The various major salts occur nearly everywhere in definite and constant proportions. As one would expect, the pH of seawater is high, averaging about 8, there is some similarity in relative proportions and concentrations of the variations in seawater and in the blood of body fluids of many invertebrate organisms. This may indicate that the sea is the habitat in which living forms first evolved. The contrast in salinity between seawater (35,000 ppm) and fresh water (15,660 ppm) requires important difference in physiological adjustment of organisms to occupy these two habitats. The problem is one of osmotic regulation. Most marine invertebrates are poikilosmotic in that they are nearly isotonic with sea water, they are highly permeable to water and gain or lose water according to concentration of the medium. A few marine segmented worms, flatworms, and crabs and all marine fish and mammals have at least some internal osmotic regulation and tend to be homoisomotic.

All except the elasmobranch fishes maintain body fluids hypotonic to seawater in various ways. The skin has decreased its permeability to the free movement of water back and forth, the necessary water is obtained by swallowing surplus salts are secreted outside the body, especially through the gills, and there is a general decreased function or atrophy of water secreting organs such as the kidneys. The practical absence of insects and amphibians from the sea is largely due to their inability to secrete salts outwardly. The high osmotic concentration found in elasmobranches is the result of huge quantities of urea retained in the body tissues and fluids. These salts keep cycling through the ecosystem, but additions to the supply some come continually from the land, being washed into the oceans by the rivers. Neritic waters are especially fertile and support a great mass and variety of animal life because of this land drainage and the pattern of water circulation on the continental shelf. Biological productivity decreases progressively from shallow waters over the continental shelf, to deeper waters, to the open ocean, but it also has high over offshore banks and in areas of upwelling substantial amounts of nitrogen salts are also swept out of the air by precipitation and there is nitrogen fixation by bacteria.

The oxygen supply of seawater comes by diffusion from the air at the surface and from photosynthesis of green plants down to the compensation point. It is continuously used at all depths in respiration of animals and plants and in the decomposition of organic matter. The oxygen content of seawater is seldom limiting for the occurrence of animals, except in the deeper waters of the brackish Black and Caspian Seas, where it is practically absent. Oxygen concentration is especially high on shores where there is splashing of waves.

Surface waters of the Atlantic Ocean commonly have 4.5 to 7.5 cc/liter and abyssal regions may run 5 cc/liter. Oxygen is somewhat less abundant in the Pacific and Indian Oceans. Oxygen may be reduced to lower concentrations between 100 to 1500 m, because of its use in animal respiration and in decomposition, that at lesser depths, where there is photosynthesis, or at greater depths, where the abundance of animals is greatly diminished. Marine animals have a variety of mechanism and adaptations for respiration. Greatest difficulties occur in shore animals at low tide when they are exposed to the air, but the needs for oxygen at this time is decreased in many forms by curtailment of activity. Some crabs, barnacle, snails, and fish have become almost amphibious in being capable of respiring in air, although at reduced rates as well as in water. Pune mud bottoms may present anaerobic conditions a short distance below the surface, but mud bottoms mixed with sand contain an abundant and diversified form.

The plankton of the sea includes a great variety of forms, even more than in fresh water. Rotifers, however, are uncommon in marine plankton and cladocerans are much less important. The nannoplankton consists mostly of protozoans, algae, bacteria, fungi, and viruses.

The bacteria are largely periphytic, in that they are attached to the surfaces of floating plants, animals and to particles of detritus. Very few occur freely suspended in the water. Bacteria, including nitrifying forms, occur at all depths but are especially abundant in or close to the bottom. They are generally more numerous in the winter than in the summer. Nitrogen-fixing organisms are chiefly blue-green algae and possibly yeasts. The green phytoplankton is composed primarily of diatoms, dinoflagellates, and small unarmored flagellates, but several other kinds of algae are present and occasionally important.

The dianoflagellates Noctiluca and Ceratium are luminescent and in some regions may give a glow at night to the entire sea. Bioluminescene is not limited to these organisms, however, but occurs also in various forms of bacteria radiolarians, sponges, coelenterates, ctenophores, nemertineans, worms crustaceans, brittlestars, mollusks, balanoglossids, tunicates, and fish. The most important groups of protozoan zooplankton, other than the green flagellates which are usually considered with the phytoplankton, are the rhizopond foraminifera, the actinopod radiolaria, and the ciliate tintinnids. They may be enormously abundant at times. The actual abundance of plankton varies greatly from place to place and from one season to the next. Smaller species tend to be more numerous than larger ones. The mean annual abundance of diatoms is commonly in the tens of thousands per litre and for shorter periods the year algal blooms may increase the population to hundreds of thousands of cell per liter, zooplankton is, however, much less abundant. Large, populations of zooplankton generally follow large populations of phytoplankton and by their grazing maintain the standing crop of phytoplankton at the size suited to prevailing conditions.

The total net zooplankton (cc per unit volume of water) is some 50 times more numerous in the neritic coastal waters of the Atlantic coast of North America than in the sargasso Sea. The abundance of plankton is generally higher in cold than in warm ocean waters correlated with the greater amount of phosphate present in colder water. Cold-water plankton tends to of be larger individuals size. There is generally in most taxonomic groups, however, a lower variety of species in cold than in warm waters. Annual productivity is also less in cold waters correlated with fewer generations per yaer. Productivity of zooplankton varies between 14 and 58 per cent of the net primary productivity.

Mollusks, fishes, birds, and mammals make up the nekton of the sea. Mollusks are represented by the squids; fish by the sharks, flying fish herrings, meackerels, as many others, including numerous varieties of small species; and mammals, by the seals, tortoises, and whales The distribution of fish is irregular, but in general they occur more abundantly in neritic waters than in the open ocean. Likewise, they are much more numerous in the epipelagic than in lower strata. Most pelagic fish, except sharks, possess a swimbladder useful for maintaining hydrostatic equilibrium at the depth where they occur; those fish that lack one are commonly bottom forms. In arctic waters fish are less abundant, and mammals relatively more important, than is the cause farther south. Birds, like many other marine animals, are more numerous in the neritic blochore than in the open ocean. In the ocean far from land occur only penguins, albatrosses, hearwaters, and petrels, and even these species become more common shoreward.

Other marine species in neritic water are tropicbirds pelicans, gannets, boobies, cormorants, frigate-birds ducks, gulls terns skimmers asks and murres. These marine birds may spend many days of weeks feeding and travelling over the water, but all must search out some shore cliff, or isolated islands on which to nest. Here they sometimes concentrate in enormous numbers during the nesting season because of the limiting number or suitable nesting locations available.

Benthos is of much greater variety in marine than in fresh water habitats. These animals are very abundant in the littoral zone and decrease in numbers with depth unit only scattered individuals are found in the deep ocean frenches. Benthos consists of sessile forms, the sponges barnacles, mussels, oysters, crinolds, corals, hydroids, bryozoans and some worms; creeping forms, such as carbs, lobsters, certain copepods, amphipods, other crustacoans, many protozoans snails, echinoderms, some bivalves, and some fishes; and burrowing forms, including must clams, worms, and some crustaceans. Sessile and creeping forms are often grouped as epifauna are burrowing forms as infauna. Epifauna in the littoral zone decreases in variety towards the poles since it is subjected composition of infauna remains about the same. In food habits, different species may be grouped as seston eaters, mostly sessile or semi-sessile forms that capture suspended food particles; sluggish motile forms collecting detritus or food particles from the bottom surface; sluggish forms that extract food particles from bottom material that they swalloos; carnivores, and scavengers.

Plankton and Nekton Biome is characterized by the predominance of organisms possessing life-forms adopted to keep them afloat. Plankton and nekton predominate, although the deep-sea benthos may be considered as belonging to this biome. Seasonal aspection may bring drastic changes in species composition, especially in plankton.

Dominance, in the sense used for terrestrial communities, probably does not exist, except possibly in the Sargasso Sea, where the floating vegetation establishes the habitat. The ecosystem is self-contained, however, since energy is derived from the sun and nutrient material continues to recirculate with little or no dependence on terrestrial resources. The sargassum community of the Atlantic Ocean is of special interest, on the floating sargassum alga accumulates and is held within a limited area by circular ocean currents. This plant belongs to the intertidal zone of the Caribean islands but in turn lose in large amounts along with attached animals during the hurricane season. It continues to grow thereafter, but does not reproduce. The fauna that it contains to a truly littoral one rather than pelagic, but because the algae to cold and ice erosion, but the species accumulates in fresh amounts as fast as old plants die, the animals reproduce and maintain a continued existence far from any shore.

As in fresh-water and terrestrial communities, bacteria in the sea are largely responsible for the final decomposition of excreta and dead bodies to make their essential nutrients available for reabsorption by the green phytoplankton. Nitrogen and phosphorus are least concentrated near the surface of the ocean, since this is the stratum in which they are most rapidly absorbed by the phytoplankton. Excreta and dead organisms sink during the process of decomposition, so nitrogen regeneration is most evident at depths of 500 to 1500 m. The total non-living organic matter, either dissolved or in the form of particulate matter, is generally much larger than the biomass of living organisms at any one time. Organic matter makes up less than one-third of the total particulate matter, and all of it sinks slowly through the water, requiring months or even years to reach the bottom. Much of the particulate organic matter is still undissolved and accumulates on the ocean bottom. Numerous species of invertebrates depend on it for food, especially on the bacteria that it contains. The deep-sea fishes feed on these invertebrates or are carnivorous on other fish. Many of them have very wide mouths, distensible stomachs, and formidable teeth.

In addition to these food corrections it is also likely that many deep-sea fish and larger invertebrates undergo vertical migrations, so that they obtain food by preying on living organisms at more moderate depths. Much that is known about the life histories of these deep benthic species has been summarized by Marshall. Especially fertile regions of the open ocean occur when there is deep mixing of waters by turbulence and upwelling. Vertical water currents bring nutrients up to the surface from intermediate depths where they had accumulated. Prominent regions of more or less permanent upwelling occur around the Antarctic continent, off the coasts of California, peru, and Somali, and off the west coasts of both north and south Africa. In many areas, very small phytoplankton and bacteria form the first link in the food chain, which goes next to the microzooplankton before reaching the carnivorous net zooplankton of copepods, euphasids, and other crustacean forms.

Most animals depending on small organisms and organic detritus for food have various filter-feeding mechanisms for straining the material out of the water. They do not actively search and catch individual items through directed actions. Invertebrate animals may also be able to absorb some essential salts and dissolved organic compounds to build their skeletal structures and for general metabolism, but there is considerable controversy on this point. The balcen or whalebone whales (Mysticeti) are toothless but possess large plates in their mouths that strain out the plankton (especially copepods, euphausiaceans, mysidaceans) that they use as food. Only occasionally are small fish as food. Only occasionally are small fish or other invertebrates ingested. Some whales reach tremendous proportions, and the differential in size between these animals and their food is one of the most remarkable in the animal kingdom.

Much more common is the feeding on plankton by squids, the young stages of most fishes, and such adult fishes as sardine, anchovy, menhaden, herring, and mackerel. The Menhaden is unique in having such fine-mesh gill-rakers that it can feed extensively on diatoms, which because of their smaller size cannot be readily secured by other large mariue animals.

Balanoid-Gastropod-Thallophyte Biome community extends form high-to below low tide levels on rocky shores. Benthic animals and attached algal plants are conspicuous and important, the benthos is mostly epifauna, as too hard to permit development of extensive infauna. When the tide is out the organisms are subjected to drying, the occasional inflow of fresh water, higher temperatures, and greater light intensities. Organisms to avoid desiccation when the tide is out by variously crawling under stones or thick algal growths, closing thick shells or operculae, retreating into crevices, or secreting a mucous seal.

Most organisms are also faced with the pounding action of waves, various holdfast or anchoring devices have developed, and many species protect their more delicate structures with a hard shell. The adaptations for life on the seashore are many and varied. The plankton and nekton associated with the benthon include many species not common to the oceanic biome.

Vertical zonation of species on rocky shores is usually conspicuous, although individual species may extend widely into adjacent areas. Beginning on the landward side there is a supralittoral zone mostly above the action of tides and inhabited as much by land as by marine animals. This is followed seaward by a supralittoral or Littorin firnge which is wetted by the highest tides and by the splashing of waves. Because of the presence of either Myxophyceae or lichens, this zone is often discovered; commonly, black. The fringe is especially characterized by large numbers of small snails and sometimes isopods. Next below this fringe is the midlittoral or balanoid zone.

It is strictly intertidal being covered and uncovered every day, and is occupied characterically by acorn barnncles. This zone is often divided into subzones with the brancles predominate in the upper portion, while, polychaets, colonial hydroids, or other forms are relatively more important in the lower part. The subzonation of algae as often also well marked. The lowest zone over exposed, and then only at extreme low tides, is called the infralittoral fringe. It is a transition area. The entire area between extreme high and low tides, including the mid-littoral fringes, when considered as a unit may be referred to as littoral, eulittoral, or tidal zone to distinguish it from the infralittoral or sublittoral zone that extends from the lowest of low tides to the edge of the continental shelf.

Brown algae from thick masses and give protection to those animals that find shelter in or under them. A fauna of copepods, ostracods, water mites, and young littorinids inhabit these seaweeds. In England, the numbers of individuals per 100 g of seaweed vary from about 44 on brown algae to over 13,000 on lichens. The animal life on rocky shores is varied and luxuriant. Several species of acorn barnacles, snails, marine limpets, marine mussles, goose barnacles, sea anemones, chitons, sponges, hydroids, bryozoans, flatworms, annelids, isopods, crabs, sea urchins, starfishes, tunicates, and insects are present. Total abundance of animals may run into tens of thousands of individuals per square meter.

Sublittoral Zone is not subjected to exposure by tides or to the pounding of surf but is affected considerably by wave action and the complete circulation of water. Animals move around somewhat more freely and there is less need for strong holdfast structures. Most organisms lack physiological tolerance for long exposure to the air and hence differ fundamentally in structure and more from the community described above. Laminarias or kelps are the largest of the brown algae and occur commonly in this community. They have root-like holdfasts attached to the bottom and their stalks, which are often several meters long, bear leaf-like branches that float at the surface in the larger species. A long list of animals find shelter and food in the kelp beds and especially in the protection of the holdfasts, polychaet worms are particularly abundant in these holdfasts. Filamentous red algae (Rhodophyceae) are also prominent. Abundant characteristic animals on the Pacific coast are sea urchins, sea cucumber, starfishes, snails, rock oyster, chitons, limpets, scallops, mussels, nudibranches, barhacles, crabs, hermit crabs, hydroids, tunicates, shrimps, and various fish. Distribution of fish species correlates strongly with the type of bottom or benthos that is present.

Seawater is often retained as depressions or pools in the littoral zone and hence organisms here are never completely exposed to the air. They are however, subject to high light intensity an increase in the temperature between tides. Tidal pools are usually rich in both plant and animal life, and some species are largely restricted to them. Red algae and kelps prefer the more shaded, cooler pools; the green algae and some of the smaller brown algae predominate in the well-isolated pools. Animals of both the sublittoral and littoral zones are found here.

Pelecypod Annelid Biome develops on depositing sand and mud bottoms in contrast to the biome just described that occurs on eroding-rocky shores. There is still a good deal of wave action over sandy botoms. Fine sand particles shift about almost continuously, and animals have difficulty in preventing their burrows from collapsing. In general, the water over muddy shores is shallower, quieter, and warmer. The mud forms a soft, compact bottom, but is also easily moved or shifted around by storms and wave action. Animal burrows in mud are more permanent. Species tend to segregate depending on the amount of organic matter present. Shores of high mud content may be low in oxygen because of decaying organic matter, so animal populations tend to be largest and most varied in a mixture of mud and sand. Tidal currents are weaker, and change in the level of water is less pronounced on sand and muddy shores than on rocky ones.

Important plants in this biome are the marine eelgrass, which is a seed plant and green algae, particularly the sealettuce, which grows in sheets either attached to the substratum or lying fragmented over large areas, and Enteromorpha, which grows in tufts or tangles. Occurring on eelagrass and sea-lettuce may be several kinds of epiphytic algae. These plans form extensive stands and are important to animals for attachment, shelter, and food.

Eelgrass was almost eliminated from the Atlantic coast in 1931-32, possibly because of a protozoan disease. This disturbance had a profoundly deleterious effect on the abundance of many animals, including the brant; a bird that depended on it almost exclusively for food, and on scallop and other coastal fisheries.

Twenty years later there was evidence that eelgrass was recovering much of its former abundance. Predominant animals are pelecypods, polychaete worms, particularly Arenicola and Nerels; starfishes, brittle-stars, sea cucumbers, crabs, amphipods, and snails. Populations may run to several thousands of individuals per square meter. A variety of small fish occur here. Birds include sandpipers, plovers and herons. The biome is worldwide in distribution, but the characteristic life-forms are represented by different species locally thus a number of secondary communities (Biociations) may be recognized.

Many of the animal constituents in this biome are burrowing forms. The sub-stratum of mud and sand holds considerable water and when the tide is out on exposed flats, pelecypods, worms and other animal constituents retract their fleshy organs into their burrows shells and remain in a water saturated environment. They are thus not exposed to the atmosphere with changes in the tide. Furthermore, most forms are generally tolerant of low oxygen and high carbon dioxide concentrations. In order to maintain respiration when retracted in their underground burrows these animals have long siphons, sometimes longer than their bodies, or long tubes or canals that extend to the surface. Through these they maintain a circulation of water, often by means of special pumping organs.

Coral reef are formed by the accumulation of the calcareous skeletons of myriads of organisms. They extend from the sea bottom at depths of 46 m or rarely 74m. to slightly above low tide level. The best formation of coral reefs is confined to warm waters above 10°C, although individual species may extend into colder regions. Predominant organisms involved are commonly the anthozoan stony corals and organ corals and the hydrozoan milliporids. Some reefs however are formed principally by forminifera and still others by calcareous algae. All massive coral structures employ calcareous algae as cement, these algae not only thrive in the pounding surf on the windward side of the reef, but by their growth are able to repair damage to the reef caused by storms. Most typical reef-building animals are colonial and of shapes varying from closely compact, globose, or encrusting, to loosely branched or dendritic, depending in part on their exposure to wave action. Each polyp in a colony secretes its own clacareous skeleton and when it dies the next generation builds on top of the old so that the accumulation of a lime structure is fairly rapid. The bright yellow or red colours or corals near enough to their water's surface for adequate light penetration are the result of algae, the zooxanthellae, which are either embedded in the body wall or free in the internal cavities.

In addition, there are bands of green filamentous algae growing to a depth of 2 or 3 cm in the pores or the insert coral skeleton that may have a biomass 16 times that of the zooxanthelate. In their photosynthesis these algae may absorb carbon dioxide and nutrients derived from animals of the coral reef and liberate oxygen of value to the animals. Perhaps because of this symbiotic relationship which requires solar radiation, living corals are largely confined to the upper, shallower waters. Coral animals actively ingest zooplankton, but apparently not phytoplankton, form the surrounding water. The three great biocycles-ocean, freshwater, and land-come into contact with each other around the margins of the seas. The change in the physical nature of the habitat from salt water to fresh water is a drastic one, but not more drastic than the change from salt water to land: The transition of animal and plant life is abrupt, and a zonation or physiographic succession of communities can be recognized. This transition from the ocean to fresh water and from the ocean to land as we see it today is of special interest since it parallels the probable evolution and dispersal of life in past ages.

Life is generally believed to have originated in the littoral region. Apparently no great group (phyla) of animals originated except in the ocean. The routes by which animals probably left the ocean and reached fresh-water and land have been various. Some animals probably migrated directly across sea branches; other probably ascended rivers, passed through marshes and swamps, or burrowed through soil.

Some animals were transferred from the ocean by land elevations which isolated them in bodies of water which gradually became fresh Immigration from the sea did not take place at one time. It has occurred many times in the past and is slowly progressing on many shores today. The most successful animal colnizers of the land have been: (1) the arthropods, which have in many cases developed booklungs or tracheae for breathing air; (2) The vertebrates, with lungs and dry skins; and (3) the snails, with slime and spirally coiled shells to prevent desiccation. There are at present many examples of animals which are in the midst of their transformation form marine to fresh-water animals, or from marine or fresh-water into land animals. Not only have plants and animals emigrated from sea to land, but there are countless instances when migrations have taken and are taking place in the opposite direction. Grasses, insects, reptiles, birds and mammals have left the land for the sea.. Fishes began in fresh water, but now range through the ocean at all depths.

2

Marine Ecology

Applied ecology

Although 71 per cent of the earth's surface is occupied by oceans and only 29 per cent by land, nearly all of the food and raw materials used by man is derived from the latter. This is in spite of the fact that agricultural soil is only a few inches thick and must be cultivated, protected from erosion, and fertilized, while the ocean with its chemical fertility, its photosynthetic production of basic plant food, and its great fisheries is an entirely natural resource ready to be harvested. However, fish harvesting in the ocean has definite limits determined by photoplankton primary productivity. It is estimated that maximum sustained yield to man is of the order of 100-150 million metric tons per year and in 1967, 6000,000 tons were being harvested. The ocean is relatively infertile, yet it covers most of the area; much more productive are the coastal areas, particularly the areas of upwelling but these are of comparatively small size. A large part of the production is taken by predators other than man and part of it must be left to maintain the breeding stock. The possibility of the ocean serving as an abundant future source of food for man is probably exaggerated. Seafood is important mostly as a supplementary source of protein. Man must look to other resource for his main energy requirements. The plankton of the sea represents a possible food supply for man. Its energy value is approximately 4 kcal/g dry weight, and it is more or less palatable.

However the expense involved in filtering and concentrating it is too great to be economical; poisonous species sometime occur, it is not easily digested and assimilated and consequently it has not as yet proved to be a feasible diet. The energy value of the plankton is used by man at the present time primarily as it is transferred into higher links of the food chain. Aside from the fishes, the chief marine organisms used as food are the oysters and other mollusks, shrimp, crabs, lobsters, and sea turtles. These are mostly animals of the continental shelf and estuaries.

There are a number of problems in the use and conservation of marine organisms. Natural beds of American oysters on the Atlantic coast have nearly all been exhausted through overfishing and pollution. Because of heavy erosion of the land, silt deposition has become excessive in most of the bays and estuaries and there is increasing difficulty for oyster spat to find clean hard surfaces on which to set.

Surfaces that are loose or covered with silt are not suitable since the spat is very small and easily smothered. A common practice is to return to suitable areas all shells of mollusks removed or to introduce other suitable hard objects to furnish the necessary substratum for oyster setting. Control of erosion over the watershed would greatly alleviate the problem. The trend is increasing to lease suitable areas of water and to farm oysters in the manner of an agricultural crop.

In spite of their position at or near the top of the food chain, the greatest utilizable food resource of the sea is its fishes. Ocean "farming" is largely limited to estuaries and salt mashes. Yiels in the Orient occasionally reach of even surpass 1000 kg/hectare-yr (880 Ib/acre-yr). Principal species are milkfish, greay mullets, eels, salmon, sea trout, tilapia, oysters, and shrimp. Conversion of marsh into ponds where water level, fertility, and cropping can be controlled has met with varying success in different parts of the world, but may be expected to expand as fish harvesting in the ocean itself approaches its yield limit.

Geographic distribution of marine organisms depends on their responses to current, temperature, and physical barriers; their local distribution is affected by waves and tides, type of bottom, salinity, and depth. Major division of the marine biocycle are pelagic (open water) and benthic (bottom). Major communities recognized are the oceanic plankton and nekton biome in the open sea, the balanoid-gastropod-thallophyte biome on rocky shores, the pelecypod-annelid biome on sand and mud bottoms, and the coral reef biome. Organisms making up the oceanic biome are widely distributed around the world but may be divided into warm-water, arctic, and antarctic faunas. Coral reefs are found only in the tropics. The two biomes on the continental shelf subdivide into warm-water, temperate, arctic, and antarctic faunas and into more restricted regions and subregions. The warm-water faunas are richest in species, especially in the Indo-Malayan and West Indian subregions.

Marine plankton include a greater variety of forms that does fresh-water plankton, although rotifers are nearly absent; cladocerans, less important. They possess various unique mechanisms for flotation. Although abundance varies greatly from place to place and from season to season, plankton is generally much more numerous in neritic coastal waters than in the open sea. Diel movements between the surface at night and greater depths during the day are pronounced.

Mollusks (squids), fishes, birds, and mammals constitute the nekton. The eaxonomic composition of the fish fauna varies with depth. Biolumines hence is exceptionally well developed among deep sea nekton and benthos. Benthos includes a great variety of sessile, creeping, and burrowing forms. It is very abundant in the littoral zone, and decreases in numbers with depth, although individuals are found in the deepest ocean trenches. There is considerable difference in the life-form and species composition of benthos occurring on rocky shores and on sand and muddy ones.

Zonation of species is more prominent on rocky than on depositing shores. Succession and dominance occurs in some situations, but is less important than in terrestrial communities. Coral reefs have many special features, but are now exposed in the Pacific and Indian Oceans to damage by a species of starfish. Food chains in the sea are similar to those in fresh water but the number of links and species composition varies in different communities. Productivity is especially high in regions where upwelling and turbulence bring nutrients from deeper levels up to the surface. The three great biocycles of ocean, fresh-water, and land come into contact around the margins of the seas. The succession from the ocean to land is abrupt and from the ocean to fresh water through estuaries only slightly less so.

Effective use of the ocean resources as food for man is largely limited to the continental shelf, regions of upwelling, estuaries, and coastal marshes. Plankton is abundant and has high productivity in these regions but is likely to be useful to man only as its nutrient material and energy are transferred with considerable loss into the higher food chain links of mollusks, larger arthropods, fishes, and other vertebrates. Costal regions need protection and management for good production and all waters kept clean from pollution of all sorts.

The three great water reservoirs of the earth-the seas, the continents and the atmosphere—are not in any sense self contained units but are in constant communication with one another, the relationships take the form of a circulation. Under the influence of solar radiation, water is constantly vaporized and emitted into the atmosphere in the form of water vapour. This process can occur in a great variety of ways.

On the one hand, water evaporates directly from the surface of seas, lakes and rivers, from glaciers and snowfields, or straight out of the ground. On the other hand, in the process of breathing, all living organisms, animals and plants alike, emit both carbon dioxide and water vapour in to the atmosphere. A third process is the emission of water vapour by the combustion of organic materials such as wood, coal and oil, which are to be found all over the earth. Easily the highest proportion of vaporized water emanates directly from the oceans, however. The water suspended in the atmosphere in the form of water vapour is of the greatest importance to the climatic conditions on earth. It conditions the composition of the air masses, exerts an influence on the energy conditions of the atmosphere, and substantially governs and sustains the water circulation.

The water content in the atmosphere is measured in terms of the relative humidity of the air: Whereas some portions of the vaporized water masses remain permanently suspended in the atmosphere in the form of moisture, others are condensed back by the cooling down of ascending airstreams and emerge in the form of clouds, fog, rain or dew. If the water cools still further, snow or hailstones may build up in the clouds. When the clouds get too heavy, precipitation begins and the moisture returns to the earth in the form of rain, snow or hail. If the precipitation goes straight into the sea or into lakes having no outlet, the water circulation will be complete. If it falls on land, some of it will accumulate by surface drainage in brooks, streams and rivers and so return to the ocean. Other forms of precipitation seep into the earth and replenish the groundwater, or if retained at an upper ground level as trap water will evaporate from there. The trap water is also available to sustain plant life, which absorbs it through its roots and returns it to the atmosphere as water vapour by respiration and transpiration.

This circulation, like all others on the earth, cannot occur in the absence of some motive force. The entire cycle is maintained by the regular inflow of solar energy. Of the total amount of energy absorbed by the earth, about one-third is utilized in maintaining the water circulation. The temperature, humidity and movement (wind) in the atmosphere together determine the level of evaporation.

Although the total volume of atmospheric moisture is very small in comparison with the total hydrosphere, owing to the circulation of the atmosphere an enormous amount of water movement takes place in the course of a year. To produce the annual precipitation on the earth of about 470,000 cubic kilometers, the water in the atmosphere about 12,300 cubic kilometers) must be replaced 35 to 40 times a year.

Sunlight penetrates the sea to a depth of about 1000 m (3000 ft). Animals living in this twilight zone consequently have very big eyes and exceptionally wide pupils. Like many nocturnal animals on dry land, deep-sea animals have all the sensory cells of their retinas protruding on rods. These rods, which serve to pick up what little light there is and convert it into nerve impulses, are unusually long and large. A nerve cell from the optic nerve is linked simultaneously to several rods. Under this arrangement an extremely high sensitivity to light is achieved.

At a depth of below 1000 m (3000 ft. or so, at which almost total darkness prevails, the fish have either no eyes at all or only very small eyes of limited capacity. It is now known that such deep sea fish find their way in the dark with the aid of sensory organs with which they are able to detect vibrations in the water. Many deep sea fish have very long organs of touch of a most remarkable kind: tentacles of great length with feeler-type floating ends and extensive tail ends. Many fish have long feelers furnished with claws and sharp points, which also serve to locate and trap their prey. Certain sea organisms are able to illumine their paths of their own accord or to radiate more or less intensive light (bioluminescence). In many cases a glow is cast by certain cells which are surrounded by reflecting cell groups.

Other animals can emit luminous substances into the surrounding water which provide light away from the animal concerned for some time and probably serve to camouflage its activities. In particular cases a symbiosis is established between luminous bacteria and fish whereby the luminous bacteria are in effect kept in a tissue culture by the larger animal.

Some varieties emit projector like light beams that probably help to locate the prey. Other deep sea fish have luminous bait at the end of long extensions, which take various forms and colours. In some varieties the luminous bait even hangs from an enormous jaw. In other cases light organs may help the male and female of a particular species to locate one another on the seabed for mating purposes. Many sea organisms can switch their light beams on and off, as it were, so as to confuse their opponents.

Many deep-sea fish have enormous teeth and jaws. And their jaws are often extremely flexible. This points to the fact that their nutriment may be found only at rare intervals, and it may then be very bulky and have to quell the animal's hunger for long periods. A number of aspects regarding deep-sea fish still remain to be clarified, however.

Like the mainland and inland waters, the oceans of the world are also subject to seasonal temperature variations. In the sea, however, these changes are more limited. This is due to the water circulation that takes place constantly within the oceans, coupled with the extremely high specific heat of salt water and the capacity that goes with it for storing energy. Except in the shallow shelf that surrounds the continents, the temperatures in the seas are consequently very uniform. In low geographical latitudes on each side of the equator, temperatures of up to 30°C (86°F) are recorded in the surface waters, while in shallow and enclosed waters they may rise in coastal regions to as high as 50°C (122°F).

Except in extreme cases the temperature variations between the coldest and warmest areas are in the 30°-35°C (54°-63°F) range. In polar regions and in equatorial waters the temperatures over the year remain remarkably uniform. As for deep-sea water, a constant water temperature can be assumed in all the oceans. The lowest temperatures are to be found in polar sea regions, where they can come close to the freezing point of seawater (-1.9°C, or 28°F).

Whereas in the lower latitudes seawater absorbs warmth from the atmosphere, at higher latitudes it emits warmth into it. The cooling of the water surface caused in this way leads to the formation of convection currents, which results in the intermingling of the water masses and the equalization of temperature between surface and deep water. This phenomenon arises from the fact that sea water (salt content 35%) attains its maximum density at –3.5°C, or 25.7°F (compared with 4°C, or 39°F, for pure water). In this respect sea water behaves quite differently from freshwater. It freezes on cooling before it reaches its maximum density.

From this it follows that no stable temperature stratification takes place in winter or in arctic regions, as in the case of freshwater, but that the intermingling in the sea is not interrupted. The heat accumulated in sea water is emitted into the atmosphere as the water cools, not as in freshwater where below a shallow surface layer the water maintains a constant temperature of 4°C (39°F). It is from this property that the sea acquires its importance in moderating the climate. Because of its lower specific gravity, at lower latitudes the warm surface water cannot promote convection currents. This gives rise to considerable drops in temperature between the surface and deep water levels and to the development of so called boundary surfaces between the two layers, which occur at depths of 100-500 meters (328-1640 feet).

In temperate latitudes a seasonal change takes place in the formation of convection currents and boundary surfaces. During the summer months, when the surface water is warmed by increased solar radiation, the boundary surfaces form at a depth of 15 – 40 meters (49 – 131 feet). In the autumn, when the water is gradually cooling off, the boundary surfaces disappear and convection currents build up.

Sea water is a complex solution of various salts, trace elements and gases. There is a measure of equilibrium between the input of soluble matter by the rivers, elutriation (or removal of suspended particles) from the atmosphere by rain, and the loss by precipitation and absorption of nutrients. The bulk of the soluble matter is washed into the sea through the weathering and erosion of rocks from the solid crust of the earth. Much of this matter is soon precipitated to form new rock deposits on the seabed, which become stratified over geological periods and can form new mountains again as a result of pressure movements in the earth's crust.

In shorter periods, variations can be caused in the composition of seawater by biological processes (occasioned by the temperature, for instance) and today in particular by the deposit of waste and toxic substances in the sea. In general, the quantity of inorganic material dissolved in sea water amounts to 35 grams per kilogram of water. This represents a solution of 3.5%.

To come down to details, sea water contains the following elements (average concentration):

Substance	*Concentration (milligrams per litre)*
Sodium	10,600
Chlorine	18,990
Magnesium	1,350
Sulfur	885
Calcium	400
Potassium	390
Carbon (As carbonates and Carbon dioxide)	23-28
Strontium	8.1
Bromine	65
Boron	4.6
Silicon	0.02 - 4
Fluorine	1.5
Nitrogen	0.02 - 0.8
Rubidium	0.12
Aluminium	0.01
Lithium	0.18
Barium	0.05

Iodine	0.05
Phosphorus	0.0001 - 0.1
Arsenic	0.003
Iron	0.002 - 0.02
Manganese	0.001 - 0.01
Copper	0.001 - 0.01
Zinc	0.005 -0.01
Lead	0.00003
Selenium	0.00009
Cesium	0.0004
Uranium	0.003
Silver	0.0003
Thorium	0.00005

Most of these elements are present in sea water in the form of salts, and a smaller portion in the form of dissolved gases. The most important of these are oxygen and carbon dioxide. The oxygen content fluctuates between 0 and 8.5 milliliters per liter. The high concentrations occur near the surface of the water, where the oxygen is in equilibrium with the oxygen in the atmosphere. A second source of the oxygen dissolved in the sea comes from the photosynthesis of phytoplankton, the drifting oceanic plant life.

At great depths it may happen that (owing to the intense activity of bacteria and animals that absorb oxygen) the oxygen content of the sea water falls to zero. In many places, however, owing to the downward trend of the convection currents, a large quantity of dissolved oxygen from the surface water is carried to considerable depths in the sea. An important part is played by carbon dioxide gas, which is present in considerable quantities in sea water. Since the basic ions of sodium, potassium and calcium are also present in large quantities in sea water, this facilitates the solution of relatively high percentage of carbon dioxide. Carbon dioxide is one of the basic substances for photosynthesis.

The plants living in the sea (especially plankton) take the carbon dioxide they need for photosynthesis directly out of the surrounding water. The second important effect of carbon dioxide in sea water is its function as a buffer (dissolved matter which keeps the pH value of the solution practically constant over wide areas). Normally the pH value of sea water lies between 7.5 and 8.4. As carbon dioxide and its associated marine chemicals are in equilibrium, the pH value of sea water is approximately constant as regards the input of both acids and bases.

The other gases from the atmosphere are dissolved in sea water in much lower concentrations than oxygen and carbon dioxide. The concentrations are as follows:

Substance	*Concentration (milligrams per liter)*
Nitrogen	between 8.4 and 15
Helium	0.000005
Neon	0.0001
Argon	0.06
Krypton	0.0003
Xenon	0.00005

A particular phenomenon is the enrichment of sea water by trace elements that occur in considerable concentrations in living organisms. An example is provided by the ascidian (a tunicate), a small, mostly clinging animal that increases the element vanadium in sea water up to 50,000 times its normal concentration. It is known today that many other trace elements such as iodine, arsenic, nickel, zinc, titanium, chromium and strontium are also very much increased in the water by decaying organisms.

Certain fish are known to contribute chromium, nickel, silver, tin and zinc. Similarly, some of the substances produced by humans get into the sea as waste substances. As such a build up of substances in the food web takes some time, the damage caused by them is often not noted until too late. The increase of chlorinated hydrocarbons, for instance (especially pesticides such as DDT), reaches its maximum concentration in fish only after a period of 11 years from its production.

Also of great importance in its effects on life in the sea is the content of ammonium compounds, nitrates and phosphates. As these are absorbed by plants to build up their bodies, their content in sea water varies considerably according to the presence of plant life. The following concentrations in sea water have been established:

Substance	*Concentration (milligrams per liter)*
Ammonia	0.4-5.0
Nitrate	1-600
Nitrous oxide (particularly NO_2)	0-15
Organically combined nitrogen	30 - 200
Phosphates	1-100
Organically combined phosphorus	1-30

Sea and the seabed

The oceans cover nearly 71% of the earth's surface, or about 361 million square kilometers. This enormous volume of water is not spread evenly over the earth's surface, but varies sharply in area and depth. Three extensive oceans separate the main land masses of the American, Eurasian and African continents from one another. With an area of 180 million square kilometers the Pacific Ocean accounts for nearly half the total sea surface of the world. It is followed in size by the Atlantic Ocean with a surface area of 106 million square kilometers, and the Indian Ocean with 75 square kilometers. The other seas (Mediterranean, Black sea, North sea, Baltic sea, etc.) are included in the Atlantic area.

There are also substantial differences in the matter of sea depths. The greatest known sea depths are in the Pacific Ocean, where they extend at some points to over 10,000 meters (6.2 miles), whereas the average sea depth is no greater than some 3700 meters (2.3 miles).

Near the coast the sea is generally quite shallow, and the seabed declines gently to an average depth of 200 meters (656 feet). The shallow coastal ledge surrounds almost all the coasts of the continents like a girdle. This girdle of shallow seabeds is known as the continental shelf. The sediment that is carried down into the sea by the rivers all the year round is deposited primarily in this area. The continental shelf is bordered by the continental margin, from which the continental slope drops away. From this point the sea bed falls sharply to greater depths. This often provides gradients of 1 : 15 and angles of gradient of over 45°. Occasionally a vertical face is found in this region.

At about 3000 to 6000 meters (1.8 to 3.7 miles) from shore the continental slopes give way gradually to the deep sea bed. The decline to the deep-sea bed seldom occurs in the continental slope in a uniform manner, however: it is often punctuated by hollows and ravines. The deep sea bed proper is uniform and even over wide areas. But in certain sectors the sea bed is intersected by still deeper troughs, the deep-sea trenches. At these points it may drop to a depth of 7000 meters (4.3 miles) or more.

Most of these deep-sea trenches are to be found on the fringe of the Pacific adjoining Asia. In order sea regions, on the other hand, the seabed rises to form big plateaus, which cover wide areas of the oceans. These plateaus, or submarine ridges, can be likened to the mountains on the continents, though they are much more sharply delineated. The biggest known sea obstacle is the Mid-Atlantic Ridge, which stretches in the shape of on S from north to south midway across the Atlantic Ocean and roughly follows the coastline of the American continent. Such submarine ridges and plateaus play a very important part in setting the pattern of ocean currents and the exchange of waters between the individuals regions of the sea.

Sea currents

The water masses in the oceans are not dormant bodies but are in constant motion. If the movements of the water are on established lines they are referred to as marine currents. The causes of these currents are very different. The most important factors affecting marine currents are wind, density variations within the water masses, and differences in the heat flow between water and atmosphere. When these factors occur in combination they may serve to reinforce one another as well as to neutralize one another.

For the most part of the direction of individual ocean currents is determined by the earth's rotation the shape of the continents, submarine ridges, and tidal currents. Owing to the multiplicity of determining factors, any estimate of the direction of the resulting marine current is extraordinarily complicated. The velocity of the ocean currents compared with those in rivers is substantially lower. If the wind sets the surface water in motion, the direction of the current does not necessarily follow that of the wind.

Owing to the rotation of the earth and the Coriolis forces generated thereby, the currents in a particular sector are linked to the direction of the wind. In the northern hemisphere all the currents are deflected clock wise to the right, and in the southern hemisphere to the left. Since at the same time the prevailing winds are deflected likewise, the deflecting forces receive additional reinforcement. The deflection of the water currents is thus all the stronger the deeper the water columns are below the surface.

Basically, two types of marine currents are distinguished: surface currents and underwater currents. The most important surface currents are found in the equator belt between the northern and southern tropic zones. The northest and southest trade winds provide the motive force for these big equatorial currents. Between the individual continents these currents are diverted in their directions and deflected to the north and south. Since the Coriolis forces are intensified as the geographical latitude increases, the original current direction is gradually reversed. Consequently a powerful flow of surface currents develops. In the middle of the cycle, zones are encountered with relatively modest surface movements (for example, the Sargasso Sea in the North Atlantic).

The pattern of surface currents is roughly the same in all the oceans. The water masses that flow north and south from the equator toward the poles cool down gradually on the way, more and more rapidly as the geographical latitude increases. Their density rises in the process, so that water masses sink to a lower level as they go and eventually return to the equator as cold seabed currents. In all cases in which the wind carries off big masses of water, these must be replaced by a return flow. This happens as a result of either an influx of surface water or an influx of water from a lower level. Water masses flowing toward the poles and so becoming cooler set off the deep water currents. Regions in which surface currents combine to produce deep water currents are known as convergence areas.

Under the influence of surface, deep water and sea bed currents, a constant exchange of water masses develops in the course of time in all the big oceans.

Energy from the sea

If it were possible to utilize a mere 0.5% of the head stored in the form of temperature differentials in the oceans of the world, man's energy problems would all be solved. This concept, however, utopian it may sound, is not in fact utterly realistic. Sea-heat power plants fall within the field of technical possibility. The idea of utilizing the energy stored in the ocean is not new. It was first suggested in 1881 by the French physicist Jacques d'Arsonval. His fellow countryman George Claude erected the first sea heat power plant in Cuba in 1929. Its power output then amounted to 22 kilowatts. Its performance was satisfactory, but it was uneconomical, as Claude's technical resources were inadequate. American environmental engineers have now developed the idea. Design work has begun at the University of Massachusetts for a sea heat power plant to be erected in the gulf stream of the coast of south Florida.

The theory of a sea heat power plant is as follows: between various water depths there is normally a temperature differential which can be utilized for energy production. In the tropics, that is between the celestial spheres of Cancer and Capricorn, the surface waters of the oceans have an almost unvarying temperature of 25°C (77°F) over the whole year. At a depth of 1000 meters (3200 feet) or so, on the other hand, the prevailing temperature is only 5°C (41°F). This temperature differential can be utilized as in conventional power plants by letting the liquid on the "warm side" evaporate or simmer. The steam drives a turbine and is condensed on the "cold side." As the heat differentials are in a narrow range, water is not suitable as a medium. First calculations indicate that propane gas would be a very suitable gas for circulation in sea water power plants. It boils at temperatures of under 25°C, and can return to liquid form at 5°C. The power plant could be installed on a floating island in the open sea.

Power plants of this kind could provide a realistic technical solution for the utilization of solar energy, for the water is heated by the sun, and the oceans serve as energy stores. The temperature differentials arise as a result of circulation between the poles and the tropics. Sea heat power plants could also acquire much greater importance. The cold water pumped up from the depths of the sea could serve to do more than jut cool the turbines. It still remains cool enough to condense water vapour drawn off from seawater into a vacuum chamber. In this way the power plant can extract drinking water from the sea. It is estimated that a plant with an output of 100 MW of electric power could provide some 200 million liters of drinking water a day. In contrast to the development of nuclear energy, especially by fast breeder reactors, no serious new technical problems are posed by this form of utilization of solar energy.

The periodic alternation of ebb and flow on the sea coast is caused by forces that, in addition to wind and the earth's rotation, are exerted by the influence of sun and moon on the water masses of the oceans. The flow of the tides is highly complicated, and varies from place to place. Since the days of Isaac Newton the attraction forces of the sun and moon have been recognized as the cause of the movement of the tides. Their influence is vastly different in strength, however, and the stronger effect must be attributed to the moon. Two separate lunar forces have to be distinguished; the attraction power of the moon and the centrifugal force arising from the rotation of the moon and the earth (at the same point of concentration). Whereas the centrifugal force remains constant at each point of the earth's surface, the attraction force of the moon changes in inverse ratio to the square of its distance from the earth. This means that the attraction force of the moon on the side of the earth facing away from the moon is less than that on the side of the earth facing it. The result of this is a horizontal force that tends to concentrate the water masses of the earth at two specific points, of which one is directly facing the moon and the other is on the precisely opposite side of the earth. At these two points tidal crests are thus produced. In consequence of the earth's rotation and of lunation (the approximately 29 day period between two successive new moons) in an ideal situation, these would travel round the earth in a period exactly corresponding to the length of a lunar day (24 hours 50 minutes).

The sun two exerts tidal forces on the earth. The sun's mass is, of course, substantially greater than that of the moon, but it is also at a very much greater distance from the earth. Because of this, the tidal forces of the sun amount to only 46% of those of the moon. The change of tidal forces in the course of a month emerges from the interplay of the forces of the sun and moon. Thus, the pull from the sun and the moon reach their peak at times of full and new moon and combine to produce spring tides. In the first and last quarters of the moon the orthogonal directions of their forces are directly opposed to one another, and so lead to a reduction of the tidal forces and result in the occurrence of neap tides.

Spring tides and neap tides occur twice in the course of a lunar month. The position of the continents prevents the tides from registering ideal periodic changes and so produces many irregularities. As the vast water masses, once they are in motion, record a natural period of oscillation, the periodic changes in the tides and the natural motion of the water can overlap and so produce very complicated tidal phenomena. On occasion this can result in resonances, which will produce a maximum expansion of the tidal range (upto 14 meters), as can some times happen on the coast of Brittany. In tidal power plants an attempt is made to use this energy for human needs.

Apart from the tidal forces, wind and air pressure have considerable influence on the extent of the tidal variations. Thus constant wind pressures are capable of producing independent tidal ranges of about 1 meter. Storm conditions sometimes give rise to extreme anomalies which manifest themselves as storm tides.

Tidal power plants

Tidal power plants are a particularly attractive way of utilizing the regenerative forces of nature for purposes of power production. Solar energy and lunar energy can be converted into electric power by this means in the same way as in a water works. The process extends over a period of 12 hours and 24 minutes, that is, half the period it takes the moon to circle the earth. As the moon is the nearest of all the heavenly bodies to the earth, the force of gravity exerted by the moon has a measurable influence on the earth. In the big water zones of the earth (the oceans) the result is that where the moon is directly overhead, owing to its attractive power, the water level is raised somewhat (flood tide), whereas in other regions it will be below the norm (ebb tide). These two phases are particularly sharply delineated on the coastlines of seas and oceans.

At specially favourable points on the coast, tidal differences can be distinguished of 10 meters (32 feet) and more. If at such a point on the coast, a bay or a river mouth is shut off by a sluice of floodgate, energy can be obtained with the aid of turbines driven by water currents set up by the alternate filling and emptying of the bay. The maximum power produced by a tidal power plant is determined by the potential energy of the water mass stored in a basin during the flood tide and by the tidal period. The coefficient of efficiency of this energy utilization lies between 20% and 25%. The pioneer in the erection of tidal power plants was West Germany. In the First World War a small tidal power station was in operation in Husum, using the flow and ebb of the current, in a former oyster-culture basin, in order to supply houses in the neighbourhood with electricity. The first big tidal power station came in to operation in 1966 at the mouth of the river Rance in France.

Today its output amount to 240 megawatts, and should be raised eventually to 320 MW. Altogether, 10 turbines are set in a dam 750 meters long, and they work in both directions, using both the incoming and outgoing tides. The tidal range (the difference between high and low tide) averages about 10 meters, with a maximum of 13 meters. In 1968 a small plant of 400 kilowatts was started up in the USSR at the mouth of the Kislaya, 80 km northeast of Murmansk. A larger plant of 320 MW is projected for the Lombowska River on the northeast coast of the Kola Peninsula.

The following table shows part of the power available on the earth from tidal energy. Possible performance in the various locations ranges from 2 to 20,000 MW. The total potential performance for all these locations amounts, according to preliminary estimates, to 64,000 MW (compared with the output of a present day nuclear power plant of 1200 MW).

Glacier power plants

After many years research work in Arctic stations, where he was conversant with the structure and dynamics of the Greenland ice sheet, a Swiss hydrobiologist came up a short time ago with an unusual project for energy production. Enormous quantities of ice melt in Greenland every summer and run down into the sea from land 2000-3000 m (6500-9800 feet) lakh.

If normal power stations were built on the coast in Greenland, enormous quantities of electric power could be produced by this means. The technology of the necessary hydraulic power stations would be standard, but the construction material for the dams and the supply and pressure, ducts would be something quite new, namely rock hard glacier ice. As the biggest island in the world, Greenland has a surface area of about 2 million sq. km. (760,000 sq.m.). On a conservative estimate something like 500,000 sq. km. (190,000 sq. mi) would be available for the installation of storage basins. With the sun shining for about 2000 hours per annum, some 8 kwh of energy could be produced each year from 1 sq. m. of storage lake area. From the estimated 500,000 sq. km of storage lake area, about 4000 billion kwh of useful energy should be obtainable each year.

This represents an electric power output of about 200,000 MW, approximating the output of 200 large atomic power stations. During the summer an extensive canal system, corresponding to a network of streams, would have to be built inside Greenland. The ice melted by the suns heat would run along these canals into big storage lakes. In the course of the flow of the melted ice water, which would be warm compared with the ice it came into contact with the streams would expand of their own accord, so that relatively little technical energy would be required for the construction of the canal system. Owing to the differences in elevation from 2000 to 3000 m, the melted ice water would shoot through ducts from the storage lake down to normal, big hydraulic power stations installed on the coast. The storage lakes are required mainly to ensure that energy production will be available also in winter. In the winter a layer of ice 1 to 2meters thick forms on the surface of the storage lakes and protect the water below from further freezing. The water below the layer of surface ice could thus be drawn off for energy production as required.

The necessary barrages, and the supply and pressure ducts, can be modelled by suitable techniques with the aid of the ice. Tested procedures already exist for the construction of ice channels in glaciers. By means of a circular cutting guide (a steel tube with an interfacing rotating saw tooth rim), cylinders, can be cut out of the glacier ice having a diameter of about 10 m (33 feet). With a subsidiary circular saw appliance the ice cylinder cut out lengthways can be split up into semicircular portions and lifted out on to the canal bank by means of a rotating table turned at an angle of 180°. These segments can be stacked together quite easily to form dams, whereupon they rapidly freeze up again.

By means of such glacier power plants, cheap energy could be produced in large quantities without causing any pollution of the environment and without the consumption of law materials. For transmission of the energy there are two possibilities:

(1) The electric current produced can be conveyed directly by submarine cable to North-America and Europe: or

(2) This is probably the better solution, with the aid of the electric energy produced in the hydraulic power station the water can be split up into hydrogen and oxygen, and the hydrogen can be liquefied and conveyed by tanker to the country of consumption. It could then be used for heating, the driving advanced motor vehicles, or in fuel cells for electricity production.

Petroleum and natural gas

Petroleum and natural gas are the most important sources of energy and are the raw materials most in demand by the chemical industry today. For the most part, petroleum comprises a mixture of several hundred or even thousand hydrocarbon constituents. In many cases these are the only constituents, while in others a large number of other organic compounds are present, such as oleic acid, asphaltene, gums and a variety of sulfur and nitrogen compounds.

The vast proliferation of hydrocarbons stems from the tetravalenc of carbon and its many possible compounds in the form of chains of different lengths with single, double and triple bonds, of rings of different bond types and sizes and of the most varied bonding with one another: and it also allows the formation of side chains. Gums and asphaltenes are high molecular weight organic compounds, which give to the oils their dark colour and increase their viscosity. The sulfur and nitrogen compounds are in the form of chains or rings, in which carbon atoms are replaced by sulfur or nitrogen atoms.

The explanation of how petroleum is formed is one of the most difficult problems encountered in geological research. Almost all the facts point to its organic development from decomposition products of plant and animal organisms that were deposited in the mud beds of waterways, were preserved there from immediate putrefaction by the lack of oxygen, and then formed rock bitumen. One problem regarding this explanation of the origin is that organisms are composed to a large extent of oxidized compounds whereas petroleum consists of reduced (oxygen-free) compounds.

Reduction is conceivable, however, only as a result of energy input. In the first phase of transformation at least, the necessary energy could not have been derived from the heat of the earth, as the petroleum would then still contain elements from the chlorophyll and blood pigment, which will not sustain a higher temperature than 200C° (424°F) and will persist only in an oxygen free environment.

One possible reaction, which also occurs in lower temperatures and is anaerobic (without free oxygen) is biological reduction by bacteria. In the sediment in water and in oil a whole series of anaerobic bacteria can be recognized that are able to reduce organic substances and to transform them into fatty acids, methane, and ethane, and also into other hydrocarbons. The hydrocarbons in question do not form petroleum, however.

The further transformation of the long chain compounds (fatty acids) into petroleum with its light paraffins (5-7 carbon atoms) can occur only as lower temperatures and in the absence of active clays as catalyzers or at great depths under high pressures by thermal decomposition. Under this thermal decomposition or fission, long chain hydrocarbons will be split up into methane and other light gaseous hydrocarbons.

Natural gas is produced in the same way, but contains carbon dioxide, nitrogen, hydrogen sulfide, and mixtures of rare gases in addition to hydrocarbons. A distinction is made here between dry gases, which consist almost exclusively of methane, wet gases (ethane, propane, butane, etc.), and acid gases with mixtures of hydrogen sulfide. The formation of petroleum and natural gas thus possibly represents a process that embraces some very different reactions (bacterial and thermal decomposition or fission) and extends over long periods. The formation of the most recent petroleum fields dates back roughly one million years.

Salt deposits

In the weathering of volcanic rocks the compounds dissolved are mainly those of the alkaline earth metals calcium and magnesium, together with those of the alkali metals sodium and potassium, whereas the oxides of silicon are in effect insoluble. Part of the potassium is removed from the weathering solution by clay minerals, in which the potassium is incorporated. The potassium, calcium and sodium, along with magnesium, dissolved carbon dioxide, and sulfur compounds, are carried down the rivers into the oceans, where they eventually form salts.

In open sea water the salt concentration is too low for the salts to be deposited. Owing to evaporation of the water, however, the concentration can be raised to the limit, which results in the deposit of the precipitated salt. This presupposes the delimitation of sea basins, in which certain conditions must be present. The loss by evaporation must exceed the inflow of water. And the shores of the inland lake or of the sea bay must be so flat that no more material is fed into the basin from the land.

The first substances to settle are the least soluble carbonates and sulfates. This can also occur in very small concentrations biogenetically in the case of marine organisms which by their metabolism absorb the lime as a stroma supporting tissue substance in their scales. Some 40% of the sea bed is covered with what is known as foraminiferal ooze, formed from the shells of dead protozoa and from clay substances. In the further process of deposit and sedimentation, rock salt is produced, and finally the most easily soluble potash salt.

The sinking of the bed of the basin, a rise in its shoreline and an inflow of new water masses will mean that the water formation process is repeated. The salt formation thus occurs only during a static phase in part of the earth crust. In many regions several such cycles can occur in succession. The clays washed into the basin at times of increased erosion of the surrounding land surfaces protect the salt deposits from being washed away.

Salt formation is possible both in inland waters and in the sea. The salts differ from one another, however, in their chemical composition, which is more astonishing in that not only the inland waters but also the seas receive their mineral constituents from the land surface. This involves the supposition that the oceans have an original supply of salt which is only slightly modified by the fresh supplies washed in from the land.

As the various salts are deposited one after the other, they tend to remains in layers one upon another. Clay and carboniferous rocks are deposited first from the shore of the basin into the middle; sulfates and chlorides are deposited in the basin's interior. In this way salt basins are formed with their typical salt distributions. From salt deposits, which are overlaid by sediment, salt masses can form. This depends on the fact that salt begins to flow even when there is very little difference in tension in the sediment.

3

Management of Marine Environment

Up to this time we have been primarily concerned with the technical aspects of pollution. Space has been devoted to discussion of what pollution is, where it comes from, and where it goes in the marine environment. Now we must consider how to control this pollution so that the problems resulting from it are kept to a minimum. The previous sentence has a number of words in it which should probably be defined very carefully, but probably never will be. For example, the statement that pollution should be controlled so that the resulting problems be kept to a minimum may be interpreted in many different people since a problem for one group is not necessarily a problem for clear-cut. Just as one man's trash is another man's treasure, one man's pollution is another man's enrichment, and this is not the only dichotomy that faces a conscientious marine manager. There are problems of jurisdiction involved in whether the responsibility for running the operation lies with the federal government, a local government, or some regulatory commission, and always there is the application of priorities supposedly set by society as a whole. The basic tool the manager has to work with is the law, however, and this is where we begin.

The Legal background

The legal background for pollution control goes back to the Rivers and Harbuors Act of 1899, recently interpreted so as to be used as a pollution control measure. This act set up responsibilities for protecting navigational and environmental aspects of all navigable waters to the U.S. Army Corps of Engineers. The Corps therefore has the responsibility not only of protecting navigable waters so they remain navigable but also protecting them against their loss as a viable vehicle for various other uses that society considers desirable.

An interesting aspect of this law and one reason it has become such a powerful tool in the hands of the environmental protectors is the redefinition of navigable waters. It turns out that the modern definition includes just about every stream going into a large river in the United States. Thus the Army Corps of Engineers was given the responsibility for protecting the environment 1899 and to all intents and purposes still retains this primary responsibility as far as brackish and salt water is concerned.

In 1934 the Fish and Wildlife Coordination Act was passed. This has since been amended many times, but essentially it involves the fact the U.S. Fish and Wildlife Service and The National Marine Fishers Services have the responsibility for determining the effect of any proposed project on fish and wildlife resources. They then report to the crops of Engineers which makes the final decision as to whether or not the proposed project is allowed.

In 1948 the Federal Water Pollution Control Act was passed and this also has been emended periodically. It requires the Corps of Engineers to apply environmental standards and criteria in approving the disposal of spoil in navigable waters. The most recent amendment of this act was the Federal Pollution Water Control Act of 1972. This a complete rewrite of the 1948 law and it set out four basic requirements. In the first place, a national goal for the elimination of all pollution from America's waters by 1985 was proclaimed. This is the famous zero discharge goal. Note that this is not a mandate to have zero discharge by 1985, but as a national goal it is something to aim at and it is to be hoped that we will come as close as possible. Second, the Act of 1972 set as another goal the addition of secondary treatment to all municipal sewage treatment plants by 1977. This goal has not been met but there has been a strong effort in that direction. Third was the effort to encourage the use of new, more advanced treatment and disposal methods by 1983 so that some of the problems will be resolved by the use of advanced technology rather than by simply improving on present methods. And last, the act established an industrial cleanup program with restrictions becoming tighter with the passage of time. Each year the requirements involving effluent standards will be tightened so that these will be continuing cleanup of the nation's waters. This particular aspect of the bill was backed by stiff penalties including both fines and imprisonments.

This 1972 Act is the basic law under which most antipollution suits are brought. The Water Pollution Control Act of 1948 encouraged the creation of uniform laws to control pollution, supported research, or firms to cease practices leading to pollution, and established the Federal Water Pollution Control Advisory Board. This has been succeeded in recent years by the Council Environmental Quality.

The year 1965 saw the passage of the Water Quality Act. In this act states were given an opportunity to adopt and enforce federal water quality standards for interstate waters. The Clean Water Restoration Act of 1966 authorized massive federal participation in the construction of sewage treatment plants. About 3.5 billion dollars were allocated to be spent between 1967 and 1971.

The National Environmental Policy Act of 1969 provided preparation of environmental impact statements when the U.S. Army Corps of Engineers determined it to be necessary. The Act also declared it to be national policy to encourage the production of enjoyable harmony between man and his environment.

The Water Quality Act of 1970 addressed oil pollution from vessels and offshore facilities, federal permits, sewage pollution from vessels and hazardous substance discharged into the nation's waters.

Also in 1970 recognisation plan No. 3 was submitted to the Congress by the Chief Executive. This reorganization plan established the Environmental Protection Agency, setting up the organization and transferring responsibility for various activities from other agencies. Unfortunately, the executive order does not address the problems of the objective or the purpose of the Environmental Protection Agency (EPA) and this objective or purpose has been left to the Agency Administrator to interpret for himself. This omission has resulted in a general grey area with EPA being as strong or as weak as the Administrator and Congress want it to be.

In 1972, in addition to the amendment to the Water Pollution Control Act, two other act of some import to the protection of the marine environment were passed. The first of these was the ocean Dumping Act of 1972. This act requires the Army Corps of Engineers to apply Environmental Protection Agency standards and criteria in approving ocean disposal of dredge spoil materials where transport passes through

United States territorial waters. This is an interesting law because it controls the material that originates in United States ports and not that material which is dumped in United States water. Consequently no matter where the material is dumped, as long as it originates in a United States port, the Corps of Engineers has some control over it.

The other act passed in 1972 having important ramifications to the marine community was the Coastal Zone Management Act. This act gave the individual states primary responsibility for determining land and water uses to more effectively balance environmental protection and economic development objectives in the coastal zone. It delineated the coastal zone as including all navigable waters and defined them as all waters up to the mean high tide line, including lands wholly or partially covered at high tide, whether privately or publicly owned. Under this act large amounts of money have been given to participating states, and all coastal and Great Lake states have so far indicated a desire to participate. Funds are initially for planning purposes aimed at developing a general zoning plan for the use of the coastal zone. Later funds will be available for the implementation of these plans.

In an attempt to get at specific causes of pollution, the Ports and Waterways Safety Act was passed in 1972 which addressed the problem of pollution from ships. This act allowed for ship design and construction regulation with respect to possible environmental damage and it applied to all United States flag vessel as well as all foreign vessel entering United States waters carrying either oil or hazardous liquid cargo in bulk. Vessel design and operational standards for all these vessel in United States waters were finally formulated on 23 January 1977. In this manner the United States government is attempting to prevent as many large catastrophies involving vessel carrying oil or hazardous materials as it possibly can by simply not allowing marginal vessel to navigate within the territorial limits of the United States.

Another fact of marine pollution having a source outside the continental area is involved with driving for oil and gas offshore. The Outer Continental Shelf Lands Act gave the responsibility of Granting leases for continental shelf drilling to the Department Interior. These leases require the leases to reimburse the federal government for any oil spill cleanup cost and in addition they require the installation of blowout prevent equipment on the wells themselves.

International Covenants

The foregoing is a brief list of the basic framework of federal laws which govern the discharge of waste products into our terristorial waters. In addition there are a few international covenants under which the United States operates. The Intergovernmental Maritime Consultative Organization (IMCO) has sponsored three conventions resulting in a number of regulations. The first of these was the 1954 Oil pollution convention which was amended in 1962 and 1969. This convention places limitations on the rate of discharge, the oil content, and the distance from land for oily ballast discharge water from ships. The enforcement of this convention is left up to the flat state, that is the country where the ship is registered.

The second convention was the 1971 amendment to the oil pollution Convention which branched out in different direction by addressing vessel design. Unfortunately this part of this amendment has not been rectified by any maritime nation.

In 1973 a ship pollution convention was sponsored by IMCO, and this convention resulted in a set of regulations establishing standards for ship board sewage treatment equipment and also specified the requirement for segregate ballast tanks for new ships of specified sizes. It also specified methods for storing dirty oil ballast residue, oil discharge monitoring systems, and oily water oil extraction systems. Unfortunately this convention also has not been ratified by any maritime nation. Consequently, behaviour on the high seas is left strictly to the conscience of the individual ship's master.

At this time there are also no international agreements on ocean dumping or the environmental effects of seabed resource exploitation. There have been many attempts to draw up an International Law of the Sea agreement but as of this writing none has been successful.

Jurisdictional Responsibility

One of the problems facing a marine resource manger is the problem of jurisdictional dispute. Who does have responsibility? In the four general areas the responsibility is somewhat dispersed. The first of these areas is water drainage, capture, or use which is exclusively on a local level. Since this is primarily a problem of private rights which is usually involved with state of private ownership. This area does sometimes get involved as a pollution source so it is of concern to us. The third area of interest includes the bays and coastal waters which are controlled by a combination of state and federal regulations. Generally speaking, the state has control over resources and the federal government has control over navigational and environmental considerations, but there are many exceptions.

Most state laws are not quite as stringent as the federal environmental requirements so that the federal requirements must be obeyed. However, there are some state laws more strict than the federal and when this is the case, the state laws take precedence. The last areas is the region beyond the coastal region wherein the responsibility is somewhat loose. We have seen that there are no viable international agreements for the deep ocean, but in many cases the United States has acted unilaterally to protect its continuous waters. With the passage of the Ports and Waterways Safety Act and the Outer Continental Self Lands Act attempts have been made to protect against the effects of oil and hazardous material, cargo ships and offshore oil-wells.

Political Processes

Once the problem of jurisdiction is settled, there then appears the problem of political processes. The political process is such that technical standards will almost always yield to such things as hardship cases, emergency situations, or strong public sentiments. Consequently, any decision to be made where the environment is involved must have a public input or else the decision will probably not be effective. The manager must not only face an often emotional public, but also individual agencies, both state and federal, working at cross purposes. For example, the Environmental Protection Agency is primarily concerned with water quality, the U.S. Fish and Wildlife Service is primarily concerned with fish habitat improvement, while the Army Corps of Engineers has a primary concern in the areas of navigation improvement. These concerns must be balanced against common public needs such as high employment, protection of science environments, and housing demands, very often these conflict very strongly so that at least one of the many groups must eventually compromise. This compromise, in the long run, must be based on some sort of a set of societal objectives. Society must somehow or other determine the most important things it wants from its marine resources.

The activities range from aesthetic enjoyment of the area to commercial shipping and waste disposal. Obviously waste disposal is not exactly the type of activity to enhance aesthetic enjoyment, nor is utilizing the coastal zone for military maneuvers encouraging to the maintenance of a reguge or a sanctuary. Some of the uses of the marine coastal area must be sacrificed in certain cases for other uses which society deems more important.

Somehow or other society must set priorities so, that the areas can be managed to obtain the ends that society wants from them. This is a very important point and one that is often completely ignored. In very few cases has society overtly set down priorities for the use of marine areas, and until priorities are specifically stated, marine area managers will be forced into making bad decisions. It is to be hoped that some of the planning being done under the Coastal Zone Management Act will involve priority setting, especially regarding the use of particular areas. If this is the only outcome of the coastal zone management act, it will indeed be a valuable contribution to the management of the activities of society in the marine coastal zone.

Costs, Risks, and Benefits

In order to set priorities in a rational manner, managers must by one means or another determine benefits, costs, and risks associated with any and all activities. Once these three parameters have been quantified, then cost/benefited rations may be determined and priorities may be set on the basis of these ratios. However, this is much easier said than done. All three of these parameters are usually quite qualitative and very difficult to quantity. Benefits, for example, are often what people perceive them to be and therefore are essentially a political evaluation rather than an exact calculation.

Costs can often be determined accurately in terms of the actual physical nature of the activity. Buildings, machinery, and labour can be quantified in terms of their cost. However, very often an attempt to control pollution or the effect of pollution on society results in costs that simply cannot easily be quantified.

Risks also are difficult to evaluate. How much is a life worth? Does it make a difference if it is yours or someone else? Thus we find that we must be satisfied with some approximation to these three parameters. Some methods for obtaining approximations to values for costs, risks, and benefits will be discussed below.

The cost versus pollution control curve, is an exponential curve wherein the initial costs of controlling pollution are relatively inexpensive, but the final 5 or 10% of pollution control may cost as much as the initial 90 to 95%. The benefit pollution control curve, on the other hand, is parabolic in shape. Here the benefits in the initial cleanup phase are quite large while the benefits acquired from the final stages are quite small. We might consider then some sort of a cost/benefit ratio, knowing these two functions.

The optimum cost benefit ration is determined on the basis of the incremental cost per incremental benefit. If, example, an additional dollar of environmental control will produce more than a dollar's worth of benefits, then it is more effective to spend additional money on control. If, however, additional control results in fewer dollars worth of benefit, then it appears that the control process has been carried too far. The optimal level of pollution control is not at point A where the cost of pollution control and benefits are the same, but is at point B, where the rate of increase of cost per unit pollution control is equal to the rate of increase of benefit per unit pollution control.

From a cost benefit analysis then it appears that it is not desirable to completely clean up the environment since the benefits accrued would not be worth the expenditure required. However, this is not the complete story. It is obvious that in certain cases even a small amount of pollutant is not acceptable because of the danger to health. Thus the risk too much be considered.

Each activity and each pollutant has an associated risk, some of these to the environment and some to man. It is difficult to quantify these but one method commonly used is to determine the number of fatalities per million hours of exposure for each person involved in the activity considered. This is expressed as a statistical probability. Table 1 is a listing of risks expressed in this manner for various common activities.

Table 1: Risk Table

Risk	*Death rate per million hours of exposure*
Voluntary	40.0
Rock climbing	6.6
Motorcycle	2.4
Scheduled airline	2.4
Smoking cigarettes	1.2
Death by disease	—
Including old age	1.0
Private auto	0.95
Sking	0.71
Railroad and bus	0.08
Involuntary	—
Electric power	0.002

Notice that the activities are divided into two groups, voluntary and involuntary activities. The voluntary activities are those which the individual can decide for himself whether or not he wishes to do. Notice that many of these activities have a probability very close to that of death by disease, including old age. Others, however, such as rock climbing, have an extremely high risk associated with them and therefore are only for the adventuresome.

Interestingly enough, the risk associated with the one involuntary activity listed, electric power, is less by about three orders of magnitude than most of the risks in the voluntary portion of the table. Apparently then we are loath to let others do in to us what we happily do to ourselves. Pollution, of course, falls within this area of involuntary activities since any pollutant discharged to the marine environment is not directly controllable by any individual. Consequently we would expect that the risks associated with pollutants would be down in the area of that of electric power rather than up with that of railroad and bus travel.

In order to quantify priorities, it if necessary then to develop some sort of risk benefit ratio, which, in turn, requires quantification of benefits. One possibility of quantifying benefits is to simply assume that in the case of voluntary activities the amount of money spent on the activity by the average involved individual was proportional to its benefit, while in the case of involuntary activities, the contribution of the activity to the individual's annual income as proportional to its benefit. Here risk is plotted relative to the benefit for various kinds of voluntary and involuntary exposure.

From these graphs and some other works that has been done, a number of conclusions can be drawn. First, the public is apparently willing to accept voluntary risks roughly a thousand times greater than those involved with involuntary exposure. Second, the statistical risk of death from disease and old age appears to be a psychological yardstick for establishing the level of acceptability of other risks. Third, the acceptability of risks appear to be crudely proportional to the third power of the benefits, whether they be real or imagined. Fourth, the social acceptance of risks appears to be directly influenced by public awareness of the benefits of an activity as determined perhaps by advertising or the number of enhanced by increased public awareness.

A determination of the level of optimum pollution control and general management schemes involved with addressing the total pollution problem is not as easy one. We find that everything costs something. There is no such thing as a free lunch. For every cleanup process involved there is a cost. Sometimes this cost is minimal but other times the cost is extremely high. For example, it has been estimated that in order to meet the 1983 goals of the Federal Water Pollution Act or 1972 it would cost 350 billion dollars just to trust municipal sewage in an adequate manner. This includes the cost of controlling nonpoint sources along with sewage treatment plant updating. Whether or not the America public is willing to spend this much on this sort of program is at this time unclear, but the American public must be media ware of the necessity of costs and trades of any cleanup program. If we are going to spend this amount of money for pollution cleanup then there will not be as much money available for other activities, and once again we must decide which to these activities, and once again we must decide which to these activities is more important to us. But the decision can only be made if we have as much data as possible in hand to allow as accurate as possible a determination of benefits, costs, and risk involved with each process.

The Future of the Marine Environment

In the previous pages we have seen that the oceanic volume is extremely large, while at the same time, that portion of the oceanic volume available for pollutant discharge is relatively small. Consequently, we hope to have demonstrated a need for some kind of marine pollution management since there is a very real problem associated with dumping wastes in the ocean.

It has also been shown that an ever increasing population, distributed primarily around coastal areas, will inevitably increase the total amount of waste discharged to the oceans. This is coupled with the fact that technology is continually growing and its growth will be associated with an increasing amount of pollution per capita with the passage of time. It all boils down to the realization that the total volume of water available for waste dilution will remain relatively constant while the total amount of waste will probably increase as far into the future as can be foreseen at this time.

Management Requirements

Fortunately, however, in those nations which have reached a relatively high level of technology, there is an increasing awareness of the problem and a public requirement that planning and management proceed in order to utilize the marine resource in the best manner possible. In order to do this a number of requirements must be met.

In the first place the effects and pathways of all pollutants dumped into the ocean must be known. This is an extremely difficult task. Many of the pathways are known but the effects are not. For other pollutants the effects are well known but the pathways back to man are still mysterious. This obviously will require a great deal of research, and even then there is no guarantee that all effects and pathways for all pollutant materials will ever be known.

Second, the average residence time for all materials discharged into the marine environment should be known. Here again we are faced with an almost impossible problem due to the tremendous amounts and number of different materials discharged into the oceanic environment.

There should also be a continuing monitoring of the environment if only to determine gross changes so some action may be taken before the situation gets out of hand.

Lastly, we must continually determine and redetermine what people consider to be important. The more and folk ways of society constantly change, altering values and priorities.

Setting Priorities

At this time managers have no clear understanding as to what people's priorities are, nor is there any real indication that the people themselves have any great insight into their needs and desires. We do not know, for example, whether the major portion of the populace considers sport fishing or ocean dumping to be higher in priority with respect to usage of the marine environment. We do know what the small special interest groups have to say about this situation, but in terms of jobs lost or consumer goods price increases which would result from the discontinuance of ocean dumping, there is very little information. In order to determine society's needs and desires the people must first be educated as to the costs, benefits, and risks associated with any environmental protection solution being considered. Obviously a much better choice of alternatives can be made if the advantages and disadvantages may very well be a utopian dream, but it certainly should be the goal of each manager to come as close to this as possible.

At the present time choice are made on the basis of limited knowledge since not all of the costs, risks, and benefits are available to the manager making a decision, even those that are available to the manager are usually not available to the public at large so that the manager's decision can be evaluated. This situation must change if utter choice is to be avoided.

Once our cards are on the table where they may be seen by all interested parties, we may proceed by setting goals that are both popular and attainable. A goal such as "zero discharge by 1985" is not an attainable one and when such a goal is set and not met, very often the result is a certain cynicism regarding all future goals.

Goals, Guidelines, and Standards

At this point it may be desirable to define some words commonly used in the management of the marine environment. In particular there are four words needing clarification: goal, guideline, criterion, and standard. Although the definitions which follow may not necessarily agree with those in a standard dictionary, they follow the usage of most people involved in marine area management, standard: A plan established by governmental authority as a program for water pollution prevention and abatement.

Criterion: A scientific requirement on which a decision or judgement may be based concerning the suitability of water quality to support a designated use.

Guideline: An acceptable methodology for achieving any given standard.

Goal : The ultimate standard which all current standards may eventually approach.

Involving the Public

Thus goals must be set with two criteria in mind. One is the scientific requirement defined above, but there is also a personal requirement on the part of the public based on its sense of priority. The public will not support a particular criterion, even with substantiating scientific data, if it interferes markedly with the present lifestyle. Until the citizenry can be educated to the risks involved is not accepting scientifically based criteria, looser criteria must surface. But it is the duty of the manager not only to choose the acceptable criteria but also to attempt to educate so that more logical criteria may receive public support.

Along with the choice of particular goals, standards, criteria, and guidelines for a particular time, it must be assumed that these are not permanent but may very well change with the passage of time. Both the environment and public attitudes must be constantly monitored to effectively meet the needs of a changing society. With a proper monitoring system, not only may the standards, criteria, and guidelines be change but also the goals may be update. In this manner the public is made a working part of the management process adding support to the process and consequently making it more effective. The Castal Zone Management Act was designed along these line and it has been in operation long enough for a major portion of coastal states to have prepared detailed plans on the optimum use of coastal areas. These plans are undergoing extensive public hearings and it is to be hoped that when they are finally adopted the public will actively support them. If this is indeed the case, it can be hoped that the effect will, at the very least, be to stop the increase in marine pollution and may be even reverse the trend by decreasing pollution. In any event, however, regulations set down to protect the environmental quality of the marine environment will be enforced with popular support.

Impacts Associated with Cleanup Techniques

Cleanup Effects on Marshes

The equipment used for several cleanup techniques considered here has no impact on the marsh itself. For example, mechanical and weir skimmer are deployed in tidal channels, and pools, not in the marsh proper. Vacuum skimming in itself produce no impact on the marsh, but it is frequently accompanied by substantial foot traffic. Food and equipment traffic and considered secondary impacts and may, in themselves, produce substantial adverse effects. The following sections are modified from Maicro *et al.*

Effects of Traffic

The most obvious type of disturbance caused by traffic in a marsh is physical breakage of plants. In both grass-dominated and succulent-dominated marshal, physical damage effectively reduces the amount of photosynthetic tissue and may expose the interior of the plants to toxic fractions of the oil. Plants are likely to recover from one such event, but recurrent trampling may clear a part that will persist for years. If the soil is soft, as it is in many marshes, roots and rhizomes may be broken and thereby accelerate erosive processes.

Foot traffic potentially accelerates erosion even where the substratum is firm and the rhizome may remains essentially intact. Shorelines that consist of steep escapements are particularly vulnerable. Cleanup activities that entail foot traffic should be used in such regions only after other methodologies have been considered and rejected.

Sometimes it is necessary to transport heavy equipment to remote portions of marsh. The impacts of foot traffic described above apply even more strongly to vehicular traffic. Traffic on soft marsh soil may bury plant stems and leaves and reduce their productivity until they resprout or grow back above the soil surface. Further, traffic under these conditions is likely to bury oil. In the anaerobic soils that characterized mangroves and marshes, residual oil may persist for years. If the buried oil is toxic, it may inhibit the growth of anything in the contaminated zone until it eventually dissipates.

Flushing

Low pressure flushing with sea water (from a nearby source and thus likely to be of a salinity to which the marsh is accustomed) may be beneficial if used with caution. Where vegetation cover is continuous and sediments relatively stable, low pressure flushing may be effective in removing substantial amounts of oil from vegetation. Drawbacks of the method are:

— All oil is not removed from leaves and a sufficient amount may adhere to the waxy plant cuticles to cause damage. This is especially true when the oil is fresh in which case it adsorbs onto leaves very strongly an penetrates them.

— Foot traffic required to deploy the flushing equipment may cause damage.

— Oil flushed to creeks, etc., will be available to re-oil the marsh or other areas unless properly collected or otherwise removed.

Where vegetation cover is incomplete where much bare mud is in evident, or where sediments are sort and muddy, sediment disturbance or erosion may produce additional damage to that of the oil. Wherever possible, sediment disturbance should be avoided.

High pressure flushing may cause some erosion, local rearrangement of the substrate, and physical damage to the plants. These forms of damage may be less severe than similar impacts caused by foot traffic, but this depends upon mode of deployment. High pressure flushing may cause oil to be driven into the substrate. If steam or heated water is used, marsh animals and plants in the spray pattern may be killed or stressed by thermal stock.

Sorbents: Sorbent pads, oil snares, and similar cleanup aids have two major drawbacks:

— They are usually used by a large group of personnel who heavily traffic the marsh and

— They must be recovered. Additionally, if cleanup teams are not trained in the use of these material, there is chance that oil may be missed with a shallow layer of the substrate in the course of recovery.

Because complete recovery of sorbent materials is seldom possible in a field cleanup exercise, remanants of sorbents may persist. Most remanants are merely unsightly, although some may ensure birds and animals. Large concentrations of undergraduate materials could block the light from an appreciable portion of the marsh surface and consequently reduce marsh productivity in that region. Biodegradable sorbents avoid many of these problems.

Oil sorbent materials (synthetic and biodegradable) should always be recovered from the marsh, those that are not collected are a potential source of recontamination and a hazard to marsh animals.

Cutting

Cutting of oiled plants is a cleanup technique that entails direct physical destruction of plant tissues. As such, it severely reduces the amount of photosynthetic tissue and may expose the interior of the plant to toxic substances in the oil. Moreover, cutting operations are likely to require a great deal of foot traffic and the attendant adverse effects.

Cutting is probably most beneficial with certain species of grasses and rushes that have been heavily contaminated with viscous oil and are not subject to natural cleaning. If the entire aerial portion of the plant is coated, the roots are likely to suffocate unless some passage way is opened to the interior of the plant. Cutting accomplishes this, provided that free oil that might replug the cut stem has been removed from the surrounding marsh. However, if oiled marsh plants are not thoroughly coated with oil air can still diffuse down the stem to the foots, so that cutting is unnecessary unless other threats are present.

Spartina marshes are very tolerant of occasional cutting, especially late in the growing season. Saltwort marshes are less tolerant. Burning is sometimes an effective method of removing oil and contaminated vegetation from a marsh without encouraging injurious foot traffic. Spartina marshes can with stand occasional burning. In fall and winter, they die back to a state of dormancy. During this period, the plants are dry and may support burning. In fact, fall burning of marshes used for agriculture is a commonly applied management tool. During the dieback period, burning can be achieved in spartina marshed without damaging the buried portions of the plants and can stimulate their regrowth. In all other seasons, however, not only in Spartina difficult to burn, but the growing portions, shoots, and buds are injured by burning. However, this damage does not necessarily permanently harm the marsh since the underground portions of the buried plants are likely to sprout and replace the destroyed portions soon after the burning. Saltwort marshed do not die back seasonally and the plants do not have large, protected underground systems; thus, burning is injurious at any time.

Soil Removal

Removal of soil entails elimination of marsh plant habitat and should be avoided. Nonetheless, if the substrate is heavily saturated with toxic oil and no predicted to recover naturally, this may be the only available cleanup technique. On soft areas of fine mud, it may not be feasible at all.

Dispersant Chemicals

Dispersant chemicals have been applied to oil in salt marshes following spills and in a number of experimental situations. In many cases, these have caused additional damage to the oil alone, and in some cases can be demonstrated to enhance the penetration of oil into intertidal sediments. Recent evidence suggests that new generations of dispersant may cause little additional geological effects to oil along when used at appropriate concentrations. However, the value of using them in most cases if unclear particularly on extensive marshes where, following application, dispersed oil may enter creeks to affect other part of the marsh or intertidal systems. They may be of value in cleaning small and stable fringing marshed in combination with low pressure flushing, but, in general, dispersant use is not recommended for salt marshes. It should be borne in mind that spraying of near dispersants onto vegetation produces damage and correct dilution to manufacturer recommendations is vital.

Marsh cleaning methods do not appear to decrease damage done by oil and often increase in. The need for cleanup should be carefully reviewed before any action is taken.

Cleanup Effects on Mangroves

Few publications are available that deal directly with the effects of oil spill cleanup on mangroves. The several observations of the effects cleanup on mangroves at the Florida Keys oil spill of 1975. So many authors summarize effects of cleanup of marine wetlands and include numerous general statements concerning mangroves.

The following summary is based on the publications and the personal observations several scientists made during cleanup operations within oiled mangroves.

Recovery of Marshes from Oil Damage

Although a definition of recovery has been attempted, mainly to distinguish the process from that of restoration, the definition includes the terms structure and function. The majority of scientific literature on the effects of oil deal with changes in the structure of marshes relatively few deal with the function of marshes let alone the part oil damage may play. Hence, we may be able to determine the time at which a marsh returns to something approaching its original structure, but not necessary. Alternatively, a similar marsh function could be achieved with a different structure. This is a line of investigation that deserves further attention, but at present we can do little but recommend that marsh structure be used in the assessment of recovery.

In an earlier section, the rate of recovery of salt marshes has been shown to be considerably influenced by a large number of factors. Their precise action and interactions are often poorly known, which means that in practice each spill must be treated as unique and assessment of damage must be dealt with in each case on its own merits little more than generalization is possible from the scientific literature.

Recovery processes begin when oil toxicity is reduced or removed. In most cases, recovery starts irrespective of the activities of man, although cleanup or other action may influence the rate. Where oil damage is relatively light and little of the toxic material remains in the system recovery can be rapid, either by regrowth from rootstock or from seeds. Baker reports that single oilings in field experiment, although toxic to many salt marsh species, may produce effects detectable only for one to three growing seasons. Where oiling is repeated or where damage is severe and toxic materials are retained in sediments, recovery may take much longer, and the effects of the spill may be detectable over decades. Where erosion of sediments takes place, recovery may not occur.

Oil Spill Prevention and Cleanup in the Vicinity of Coral Reefs

Prespill Mapping

Prespill contingency planning is now an accepted part of preparation for, and response to, oil spills. Vulnerability mapping has been used by several authors to identify those area of shoreline that may be particularly sensitive to oil spill damage and to help ensure that damage due to the use of inappropriate cleanup procedures is minimized. One frequently used vulnerability index was devised by using the assumption that coastal geomorphology frequently determines the types of ecological communities found there. Information about points of access to a spill site is essential in the event that men and equipment must be deployed at shore notice. Therefore, accessibility mapping is an important adjoint to vulnerability mapping.

Coral reef vulnerability to oil spill damage will vary with reef type, zonation patterns, and tidal actions. For example, in a fringing reef, the seward facing reef creast is generally exposed to high wave stress; here oil will probably have a short residence time before being dispersed naturally. In contrast, wave action is a lot less severe in the shallow reef flat that frequently supports seagrass beds. Here, a long oil residence time with a correspondingly high risk of oil damage is likely. Similarly, oil that strands on reefs with a limited tidal range will likely tend to persist for longer periods than that in areas with large tidal ranges.

Although vulnerability and accessibility mapping techniques are now well established, little evidence suggests that such techniques are being applied to reef ecosystems. Some reef areas are well mapped and information is readily available on the location of refineries, tanker terminals, oil platforms, and major tanker routes. e.g., International Union for Conservation of Nature and Natural Resources. This information can be used to produce maps that help locate areas of high potential risk. Newly developed techniques for mapping large areas of coastline, such as low altitude video overflights seem particularly suitable for use in reef areas but have yet to be applied.

Cleanup and Treatment of Spilled Oil

The sensitivity of reef ecosystems and the likelihood of their being impacted by oil will depend upon a variety of factors, including the quantity and type of oil and the degree of weathering. The likelihood of ecological impact will also vary according to whether the reef is an emergent, shallow submergent, or a deep water type. The field and laboratory studies reviews indicate that the likelihood of damage is increased if the oil is incorporated into the water column of if it comes into direct contact with the coral surface. This, therefore, places the mergent or shallow submergent section of a reef as areas of high potential sensitivity. It also indicates that any cleanup of treatment attempt should endeavour not to enhance the transport of oil into the water column or into the permanently submerged sections of a reef.

Careful consideration should be given to the treatment of oil in the vicinity of a reef as situation may develop where the cleanup or recovery attempt may be more damaging then the oil alone. Baker has pointed out that merely the shipping activity associated with the cleanup attempt may be damaging due to sediment resuspension by propellers and anchor drag breaking up corals.

Although practical experience of oil cleanup in the vicinity of coral reefs are lacking, mechanized techniques for containment and recovery of oil using booms and skimmers are acceptable as they do not cause oil to sink or become incorporated into the water column. Any restriction on use of these techniques in coral areas is likely to be brought about not by the risk of ecological damage but by other environmental considerations such as high current speed, severe wave action, or shallow water depth that make their deployment impossible.

At present, only few data are available on the impact of dispersants and dispersed oil on corals. Most information that is available has been derived from laboratory studies. Laboratory studies have also been carried out on biota associated with reefs. Both categories of study noted damage by dispersed oil, but the applicability of these in vitro data to a field situation is questionable. Similarly, these studies used early generation dispersants which of themselves, where toxic to the corals. Using dispersants currently available, indicated that concentrations of 20 to 50 ppm dispersed oil in a 24-hour exposure produced temporary stress reaction in corals. Few deleterious effects from 24-hour exposures at 1 to 5 ppm were observed.

An oil removal technique that cannot be recommended for use in coral areas is the application of particulate sinking agents. These materials absorb oil and because they have a density higher than that of sea water, sink with the oil attached. Deleterious effects could be expected from the sunken oil coming into direct contact with the corals.

Several methods currently in the developmental stage appear to be potentially suitable for use in coral areas and other marine environments likely to be sensitive to oil. Among these are agents that have been developed that, when added to oil, gel in a semisolid form that can then be recovered. Research is also being carried out to develop nutrients that accelerate the bacterial biodegradation of oil.

Several studies have shown that corals are seemingly uneffected by a layer of oil floating on the water surface. Therefore, where unsuitable hydrographic conditions or problems of access preclude the use of mechanical containment and recovery techniques, it is probably best, given our present knowledge, to leave the oil alone to weather naturally.

Measures of Damage at the Species Level

Structural changes occur on a reef when a species or combination of species that are dominant components of a system are replaced by other species are eliminated from the system. If the replacement of elimination of a species is significant, then community, or functional level changes can become evident.

Changes in species richness, coral cover, and species diversity are potential criteria for the assessment of catastrophic structural damage to corals and any subsequent recover. Loya has modified the Shannon-Weaver diversity measure for use with corals as well as any encrusting assemblage. Grigg and Maragos used these parameters to describe recolonization by hermatypes on lava flows, as did Sheppard when assessing the impact of harbour construction on corals. Porter *et al.* used species richness, coral cover, and relative abundance to assess structural recovery of hermatypic corals following hurricane damage.

In a recent paper, pearson argued that measures of diversity, percentage cover, and similarity taken individually do not provide useful measures of either damage or recovery. He suggested that measures of damage and recovery should totally incorporate measures of percentage cover, mean colony-height, surface-index, species diversity, and similarity indices. In addition, because reefs are dynamic systems that can undergo change due to numerous environmental factors, any observed structural changes should be evaluated in terms of the structural characteristics of neighbouring reef systems.

Measures of Damage at the Community Level

The structural diversity of reef ecosystems is paralleled by their function a complexity. When attempting to assess damage and recovery of coral reefs in functional terms, a useful line of investigation may be the development of indices that provide a measure of total reef functions or malfunction.

One major functional characteristic of reef ecosystems is their high rate of primary production that may be 10 to 100 times greater than that of the phytoplankton in surrounding waters. Much of this reef primary production is attributable to benthic algae. A principal determinant of this high rate of productivity in nutrient poor areas is the retention and recycling of nutrients within the reef. This feature may be a useful means of determining the status of total reef function. For example, Pilson and Betzer found that, although concentrations of phosphates in water passing over a reaf were low, there was no difference in the upstrem and downstream levels, thereby indicating that a reef recycling mechanism was present. Evidence of phosphate recycling has been found by Pomeroy *et al.* There is also evidence of ammonium and nitrate recycling mechanisms. An increase in nutrient loss suggestive of a breakdown in nutrient recycling mechanisms may be a potential indicator of a total reef malfunction. Further evidence for the steady state nature of a reef ecosystem is provided by the ratio of gross production to community respiration (P/R) that frequently approaches unity.

Again, any large be change in P/R ratio could be indicative of reef malfunction.

Coral Reef Recovery

Our ability to measure recovery in a coral reef system hinges on the success of a program to define or measure than is damage. Endean said that complete recovery "involves the return of those species typically associated with corals and forming part of the coral reef community in the particular geographical region concerned and the re-establishment of the complex relationships normally existing among the species". While this definition is theoretically correct, from a practical sense in terms of measuring recovery, it is probably too broad. Coral reefs are among the most complex marine ecosystems in terms of communities of structure and ecological function. Monitoring all aspects of reef biology in an attempt to confirm a recovery or to define a stage of recovery is not feasible. There are, however, aspects of reef structure and function that could logically be used as indicators of a level of recovery. Specifically, a coral reef has patterns of species composition, abundance, dominance, reproduction, recruitment, growth, and mortality among the hormatypic organisms. A gauge of recovery may be generated by comparing qualitative observations and quantitative measurements of these patterns on the recovering reef with those presumed to be characteristic of the chosen model of a fully recovered reef at the site in question. This methodology, however, requires the assumption that recovery of the coral organisms will eventually result in the recovery of the entire reef community.

Few reefs in the world have been subjected to quantitative ecological assessments. The means that it is unlikely that any site-specific information will be available for comparative purposes. However, reef morphology and biotic community structure are typically similar over a definable range of variation within the area or region. Therefore, there is likely to be a basis upon which to roughly estimate the former structure and condition of nearby unimpacted reefs existing under similar conditions of natural environment, along with the remains of the impacted reef. If it is possible to infer pre-impacted structure from regional patterns, there is at least a structural and functional model for a recovered reef at the locality in question.

The measurement of recovery is complicated by the fact that recovery on coral reefs tends to be a long-term process. Endean found that the recovery period is correlated with the extent of the damages inflicted on the hard coral cover. Small scale localized destruction from natural events generally requires less than 10 years for recovery provided that major sectors of the community remain virtually intact and the area is conductive to coral growth. Heavy destruction requires 10 to 20 years for full recovery, while especially severe impacts may require several decades for complete recovery. If a chronic source of pollution is present in the area of the damaged reef, recovery may be further prolonged or may not occur at all e.g. see Rinkevich and Loya.

Cleanup

What cleanup measures are appropriate and what are their relative effectiveness are critical questions regarding oil spills in Tundra and Taiga. Whenever possible, hydrocarbon spills should be avoided or their effects mitigated. Several measures can be employed to help accomplish this. All above ground fuel storage containers should be contained within a pit or depression lined with a hydrocarbons in previous layer. Oil pipelines should be designed to withstand weathering, corrosion, and limited displacements such as those due to earthquakes. Finally, whenever possible, oil pipelines should be routed to avoid sensitive ecological stress such as populations of endangered species. Unfortunately, containment or avoidance is not always possible, so cleanup measures for the various soil and vegetation types must be considered.

Once a spill has occurred, the choice of celanup strategies will depend upon the type of oil soiled, the nature of the spill the amount of oil, the season of the spill, and the location of the spill. Site aspect, vegetation, and soil types are critically important factors. In addition, the presence of permafrost in most areas of tundra and much of the taiga will preclude the use of many cleanup methods routinely used in warmer climates or nonpermfrost areas.

For example, in permafrost areas with a high ice content, any surface disturbance, such as removal of the oil-soaked organic soil surface horizon, tillage, or vehicle movement will induce thermal degradation of the permafrost and subsidence (thermokarast), which will increase rather than decrease total environmental damage of the site. Under such conditions, passive (or no active) cleanup should be considered. Passive measures may also be the best means of facilitating natural recovery in cases of small spills of crude oil or contained or limited spills of industrial oils with high proportions of light fractions, much of which will be readily lost by volatilization. However, recent work by Linkins and Fetcher has shown that residual oil in the Oe-OI horizon of Tussock Tundra soils may alter reproductive and biomass allocation patterns of *Betula nana* and *Eriphorium vaginatum* such that their successful reestablishment in oil-contaminated soils is questionable.

When active cleanup measures are necessary, there is heavy reliance on site access for transporting equipment and manpower to the spill. In remove locations, this can involve considerable cost as well as the environmentally damaging unless it can be accomplished with the appropriate equipment, especially during the persnow or thawed soil times of the year or snow presses on. Generally, the choice of which active celanup techniques are used depends upon the time of year when cleanup must occur. In winter periods when the ground is frozen or snow covered both access and cleanup are facilitated. The dormant stage of the plants and low winter temperatures that aid in cooling and congealing crude oil so that its spread is limited both contribute to minimizing damage. Snow also acts as an absorbent and cushion protecting surrounding vegetation from oil exposure as well as vehicle damage. Generally the oil-contaminated snow can be mechanically scraped off the site, removed, and placed in properly contained areas such as was done at the February 1978 Steele Creek spill along TAPS.

Burning the spilled hydrocarbon may also be used as a cleanup measure either before or after mechanical removal. Combustion may be difficult to initiate and generally will be incomplete. However, burning can help to remove the more toxic light fractions of the oil if done soon after the spill occurs. Small spills may be difficult to ignite if not immediately burned, but large spills seem to burn readily even several months later. This may be due to a large proportion of the light fractions being rapped within the soil in large spills as surface weathering produces as extensive asphalitic cover. Burning is relatively inexpensive, but may leave a tarry residue on the surface that can inhibit microbial decomposition of the oil and vegetative recovery.

Finally, following any winter cleanup procedure, appropriate measures should be taken to ensure against, remobilization of the oil during snow melt. Such measures as absorbent booms, straw, or in nonpermafrost and thaw stable permafrost areas, containment ditches or dikes may be used. The hydrocarbon will then be intercepted or contained to facilitate removal.

The choice of active cleanup measures during the summer or snowfree period will depend upon the phenological stage of the plant, the soil moisture content, depth of the soil water table, and ice content of the permafrost as previously discussed. Mechanical removal of oil contaminated soil should be considered only at times when potential damage to plants is great from prolonged extensive contact with the hydrocarbon, the ice content of the permafrost if low, and there is relatively easy access to the spill site. Also, the volume of the spill should be such that natural recovery is unlikely and there is high potential for extensive contamination of adjacent areas through contained movement or later remobilization.

If removal of the contaminated soil is not possible, burial can be considered. However, burial should be done only in thermally stable, frozen material since subterranean remobilization can occur and cause contamination of adjacent areas.

Oil may also be removed by floating the oil and vacuuming it off the surface of the water. This was used successfully at the TAPS value 7 spill in July 1977, ready access to the site as well as availability of a large volume of water, a wet site, and feasibility of containment. However, in some cases, oil may continue to appear on the surface of the water for a year of more after the spill as it is displaced from the surface organic horizon.

Finally, manual cleanup with minimal soil disturbance should be considered in permafrost areas. Absorbents such as straw or commercial materials can remove much of the oil present on the ground surface. Although costly and very time consuming, this method will minimize any physical disturbance and decrease the chance of thermal degradation of the spill and adjacent sites.

The extensive reliance on reseeding with non-native species and long-term fertilization, whereas a relatively easy but expensive means of revegetation, does not guarantee optimal long-term revegetation or restoration. Observations of natural restoration on a 1949 disturbance and on a 1970 disturbance at Barrow, Alaska suggest that it may be preferable to let some hydrocarbon disturbances recover naturally through reinvasion by native plants in lies of reseeding with exotic plants. Recent work discussed by Shaver *et al.* that shows that the shallow organic soil horizons can serve as a major seed bank for revegetation suggests that preservation of the upper organic soil horizons may also be preferable if possible to maximize potential for native plant reestablishment. Their discussion also points out the possible deterrents of fertilization on delaying restoration of the natural vegetation.

Penetration of the hydrocarbons into the soil plant rooting zone as previously discussed will influence the choice of revegetation/restoration techniques. On wet sites where there is limited penetration of the hydrocarbon into the soil rooting zone, natural recovery by the native vegetation may be sufficient if cleanup activities adequately remove the surface hydrocarbon contamination. On drier sites, however, where the hydrocarbon will rapidly penetrate the soil rooting zones, killing the majority of the vegetation, it may be necessary to institute extensive soil cleanup, rapid revegetation efforts. This will be especially true if site stability (othermokarst, slope erosion, etc.) is a problem. Regardless of the cleanup, revegetation/restoration activities it should be reiterated that care should be taken to preserve of site integrity. Slower spill site revegetation/restoration should always be preferable to risking both on and off site degradation.

Hydrocarbons spills in the Arctic and subarctic cause both short-and long-term effects on the soils microbial populations, vegetation, and wildlife. Although a number of descriptive studies on the effects of hydrocarbon spills have been conducted, these have generally focused on short-term effects. Furthermore, there has been very limited development in our understanding of the important mechanisms of the direct toxic effects of oil and the effects of altered soil characteristics on organisms. When our ignorance in these areas is compounded by our limited knowledge of the in site rates and nature of hydrocarbon degradation in cold soils, it makes it very difficult to estimate effectively the duration of the influence of hydrocarbon in the soil. Likewise, it is very difficult to predict which cleanup, revegetation techniques will be most successful in alleviating hydrocarbons related deterrents to microbial population and vegetation growth.

Development of better methods for restoring Arctic and subarctic hydrocarbon spills requires a commitment to long-term research efforts focusing on integrated cleanup, revegetation/ restoration research. Research should focus on the development of integrated postspill functionally based ecosystem efforts to determine and evaluate the relative importance of factors limiting site restoration. These studies should be connected on new sites that have been thoroughly described and on existing spills sites where adequate documentation exists as to the specific cleanup and revegetation activities that were employed. Efforts should also focus on natural hydrocarbon seep areas and long-term unaided spill sites where native vegetation exists. Integrated research efforts directed toward these goals as well as toward associated off site cleanup and revegetation disturbances should then begin to provide the information necessary to formulate effective revegetation/restoration programs in Arctic and subarctic areas. Unfortunately, until research is initiated, there will be limited advancement in more effective, less costly revegetation/restoration practices.

4

Marine Resources

By 1992, India could start commercial production of nearly 3 million tonnes of dry nodules a year to replace and reduce its import of nickel, copper, cobalt and manganese. Besides, India has world's one fifth marine area with rich fauna. However till now the major fishing area is confined to an offshore belt of 1 sq. km. only, and the rest of the Exclusive Economic Zonel (EEZ) is untouched, which abounds in fishes of large variety. Also, the 1981 estimate of India's offshore oil reserves were around 1100 million tonnes and the gas reserves being 12,000 $\times$ 10^9 cubic feet. But even then she is notable to meet her 50% of domestic requirement.

Lack of coherent maritime policy, unplanned ocean management system, inherent technological backwardness, in addition to her comparatively new awakening towards ocean resources and maritime trade, are perhaps the main causes for her being underdeveloped in this field. A brief survey of the EEZ resources of India can be categorized under two categories namely living

(1) nonliving,

(2) living.

Nonliving resources of India's EEZ: A General Account Growing attention towards exploration of oil and gas, particularly after 1973 world oil crisis, mostly in the continental shelf region, and a distinct shift towards mineral exploration and exploitation in whole of the EEZ after the final declaration of UNCLOS III in 1982, other than regular search for non-conventional sources of energy within the said region represent the overall marine activities taking place in the fields of scientific and economic development taking place in respective EEZ. The main reason behind the enhancing research programs by both developing and developed nation is the increasing demand of mineral requirements by modern societies, in an almost undefined and unpredictable volume, supplemented with the fact that land resources are either on the verge of depletion level or otherwise their vital importance has been realized as a reserve in near future.

Found mostly beyond EEZ, manganese nodules and polymetallic sulphides are of special value, as they consist of strategic metals, viz., cobalt, platinum, chromium etc., in a concentrated form. Classification of nonliving resources have been made on various basis. In the continental margin area unconsolidated sedimentary deposits include sand and gravel, calcium shells, placers, beaded phosphorites, metalliferous or brine rich sediments, while barities and phosphorites form the major modular and crust deposits.

Selective sorting of mineral grains occurs by mechanical winnowing of wind, waves and currents, and by gravity setting and concentration. Among the selected production figures for sand and gravel from marine environment, UK and Japan top the list by producing more then 165,000,000 tons, having value more than $330,000,000 (USD) and 84,700,000 tons having value $170,000,000 (USD) respectively, mostly from a depth ranging between 35m-50m.

Calcareous sands, shells and coral sands are of course renewable biological resources, but they need special care while exploited at a commercial scale, because of their direct effects on the coastal marine environment. Even offshore bank exploitation may have an impact on the beach amenities. Found in nearshore zones, placer deposits are mechanically concentrated heavy detrital materials which originate from eroded offshore rocks, often discharged by river work in considerable amount, in the form of black or dark stringers and lenses on modern beaches.

Past sea level changes, recurrent wave actions and dominant tidal currents have however produced major locational changes, including their nature and depth of occurrence. While buried placers are little known, cassiterite exploration in Southeast Asian tin belts undoubtedly will reveal several examples, although this still remains a fact that general placers are richer on modern beaches than on submerged ones. Further wider shelves have greater number of placer deposits. A comprehensive account of the United States' EEZ placer deposits was recently given by Beauchamp and Cruickshank including its comprehensive economic futurology. In India, National Institute of Oceanography has taken the sole responsibility of mapping, exploring and exploiting these huge deposits, mostly available on the western coast of India, in the form of tin placers, complex heavy minerals, precious metal placers and rare diamond accumulations.

Besides biotite, biotite-muscovite, and cassiterite, the tin placer deposits contain pyrite, ilmenite, zircon, tourmaline and monazite, commonly found in India, Burma, Thailand, Malaysia, Indonesia, Cornwall (UK) etc. Among the complex heavy mineral sands containing principally ilmenite, rutile, zircon, monazite, garnet, and magnetite, the iron-titaniferous sands have been identified at commercially exploitable level at

Southern Japan, East and West Australia, California, Oregon, Alaska, New Zealand, India, Bangladesh and Sri Lanka mainly, besides USSR, Poland, Mozambique, Italy, Philippines, Argentina, Mexico and Brazil. As regards monazite, mineral placers were identified especially offshore India and Sri Lanka. Precious metal placers containing gold, platinum and related metals have been mainly found concentrated in Alaska, Oregon, California, Nova Scotia, Lapter Sea (USSR), Southeast Australia, Bering Sea etc. Diamond accumulations containing mainly kimberlite, epidote, ilmenite, magnetite, and pyrite has its only known commercially exploitable deposit at Hottentot Bay near Orange River in Namibia.

Beaded phosphorite minerals mainly in the form of carbonate fluorapatite are found in the upwelling areas like Peru-Chile slope, North and Southwest Africa, Western Australia, and in the continental shelf areas of Congo, Baja California. Metalliferous and brine-rich sediments, known in sufficient concentration in Red Sea Spreading Center, contains mineral assemblages like clays, hydrous oxides, carbonate and sulphides. However the most important brine deposits are found in the Atlantis II Deep, where economic estimates suggest about 3×10^6 tons of metals, excluding iron which forms almost 29% of the deposits. Nodule and crust deposits have been reported present, although in less exploitable quantity off southern India and in the East Indies region. Phosphorite nodules and crusts, generally present on submerged marine plateaus and continental rises viz. Blake Plateau, the California Banks, Agulhas Bank, the Chatham Rise, and in some scattered seamounts.

Known manganese nodules deposits of both mononucleate and polynucleate types are most abundant in deep seas of Pacific (in Equatorial North Pacific nodule belt, Southwestern Pacific Basin, Peru

Basin, Chile Basin, South Tasman Basin and Northern Tahiti Basin), Indian Ocean (South Equatorial basin, Crozet Basin, Central Indian Basin and Western Australian Basin) and in Atlantic Ocean (in Western Atlantic Basin, Drake Passage, Western South Atlantic and Blake Plateau). Much interest is presently focused on occurrences of cobalt rich ferromanganese crusts on seamounts and oceanic crusts, some of which have already been discovered within the EEZ of USA. Massive deposits of polymetallic sulphides have attracted recent attention. They are generally found at mid-oceanic rideges viz. stratiform sulphide bodies at Atlantis II Deep, Red Sea, sulphide mounds surmounted by chimneys at Eastern Pacific deposits and coalesced mounds surmounted by chimneys at Galapagos Spreading Center with much concentrated quantities of zinc (Zn.), copper (Cu), and gold (Au) besides some traces of arsenic and cadmium.

Although exploration in Pacific have yielded much regarding their location and quantity, the possible existence in Indian Ocean, that too in considerably exploitable amount, is yet to be tested and quantified in economic terms. In India, much emphasis has been there during the Sixth and the Seventh Five Year Plan regarding the surveys to locate and map the availability of living and nonliving resources of the Exclusive Economic Zone and that of the continental shelf. Different governmental agencies viz. Department of Ocean Development (DOD), National Institute of Oceanography (NIO), Oil and Natural Gas Commission (ONGC), Oil India Limited (OIL) etc., with their maximum emphasis on fisheries and hydrocarbon resources, are burdened with solving the problem of energy requirement of this world's second most populated country. Further, the northern Indian Ocean is one of the few oceanic regions of the world which comes under the influence of the monsoon. The uniqueness of this region, therefore, lies in the seasonal and interannual variation that it exhibits. Little is known about the nature of this variability and lesser still, about the causes behind it. Rigorous efforts are being made by sophisticated research vessels like ORV Sagar Kanya and FORV Sagar Sampada. Their utilization for some years has been going up to 82.6%. Besides, other individual and collective efforts by scientists all over the country is directed in a multidisciplinary format. The survey of the entire EEZ, according to DOD, is expected to continue for a decade or so. Intensive surveys are being undertaken to map out the nonliving resources especially minerals and hydrocarbons. Estimation of potential fisheries resources and its maximum sustainable yield is being made.

The important considerations which need immediate attention from different governmental and nongovernmental agencies regarding India's EEZ are:

1. Clarification of the level up to which present EEZ utilization is going on;
2. Demarcation of optimum limit of EEZ utilization both in terms of exploration and exploitation;
3. Projected need of marine substances both living and nonliving from the EEZ by 2000 A.D., by a realistic evaluation of both protein requirements and energy substitution in different sectors;
4. Technological requirement for the fullest exploitation of EEZ resources and extent of foreign collaboration or technology transfer to be required by 2000 A.d. for its sustainable exploitation;
5. Fixation of priority level, to be given to the frontier areas of ocean development in India and share of EEZ management in that, particularly in the fields of food (protein), minerals,

transportation, recreation and energy, all aiming at improving India's socio-economic conditions;

6. Planning of offshore construction and required operational structure in total and the investment to be incurred.

Nonliving resources

(a) *Freshwater from sea* : The desalination technologies under consideration by the concerned governmental agencies are (1) by solar stills, (2) by flash distillation, (3) electrodialysis, (4) reverse osmosis, the last being most widely used, generating capacity of plant generally varying anything between 10,000 to 15,000 litres per day, most useful for the dry coastal areas of Indian Peninsula, presently drinking brackish water with salinity ranging from 5 to 20% in most of its rural areas. Central Salt and Marine Chemicals Research Institute, Bhavnagar has already done necessary research and development work and has made available the technology of "reverse osmosis" to BHEL, for setting up desalinization plants. One such pilot plant has been recently installed at Puthagram, near Madras. Work on the second plant with same capacity of 50,000 liters potable water per day is continuing and is expected to be installed in the East Godavari district. In addition of salt, the system also remove harmful matters, like bacteria from brackish water. Besides it saves much energy as compared to the conventional thermal desalination system, thus being economically viable alternative.

Although a serious threat to future large scale desalination program at global level, particularly for the vast desert areas along the oceans, is from the comparatively cheaper huge icebergs to be fetched from southern oceans, although it awaits further technological advancement and a major breakthrough in the understanding of the mysterious characteristics of icebergs, particularly the dangers to be encountered by its cleavage in any phase of its displacements. However, for localized use in coastal areas, desalination process is still economical and rather indispensable.

(b) *Drugs from the sea:* Although this utilization of marine resource is of much recent origin, by now at least 100 plants and small marine organisms have been recognized for the manufacture of important lifesaving drugs in India. More than forty are of special value, some of them containing remarkable antifertility properties, viz. Glacilaria species, with sufficient prostaglandins. At present a great need is there in India to set separate shell for studying and culturing these marine microorganisms, both of floral and faunal nature, and to help successfully in deriving and synthesizing the bioactive substances which are useful in curing many incurable diseases.

Studies in India clearly suggest that all the species of marine algae, those exhibit antifertility properties may also contain prostaglandins. Their multiple use and suitability to human health is being further researched, but the most important aspect still lies with the fact that their potential presence either in the form of deposition or dissolution is still not economically beneficial for large scale economic exploitation with the existing state of technology, understanding of distribution pattern and density.

(c) *Marine chemicals:* Lesser quantitative concentration and difficult extraction methods are the major hurdles in deriving most of the chemicals economically, about 60, from the seawater. Commercial exploitation as yet has been successfully managed only for six chemicals viz. sodium, chlorine, magnesium, bromine, calcium and sulphur.

Greater possibility is also there in future for deriving potassium, iodine, uranium and gold from seawater. However, optimistic proposals supported by major research findings in this field leaves us with the only hope that by 2000 A.D.

India will be able to make use of its EEZ waters, mainly coastal, in deriving at least the rare chemicals which are dissolved in seawater and the same time are not easily available on land, provided concerted effort is being made to develop sufficient technological capability to meet the requirements of the complex stages involved in this process. Besides some marine organisms concentrate trace elements in their bodies by a factor of 10,000 to 1,000,000. Cultivation and harvest of such organisms could perhaps provide a way of concentrating trace metals dissolved in seawater so that they can be commercially recoverable by biochemical means.

Seventy-one per cent of the total solar energy i.e. about 106 watts reaching the earth is absorbed by oceans, thus blessing the later with the huge/energy potential. Apart from being renewable and continues the added attraction of ocean energy forms lies in their being pollution free, resulting in remarkable minimization of health hazards, and the great competence for fulfilling the local energy requirements particularly offshore. The leading countries in this field of research are USA, Japan, France, UK and the Netherlands, implementing mostly the total systems approach, successfully overcoming the attached disadvantages.

Costal inlets are best for tidal energy resources. Technology for the utilization of tidal powers in all possible physical situations is already being developed. La Rance, since 1967, has been successfully supplying 240 MW of power to the French electric grid. In the same way, nearshore tropical and subtropical oceans are best for vertical temperature gradient, thus for Ocean Thermal Energy Conversion (OTEC). Areas of strong persistent currents, such as most of the western coastal boundaries of the world oceans are almost suitable for extraction of energy from ocean currents. River outlets are most suitable for extraction of -the salinity gradient energy. Similarly coastal areas with large persistent waves can contribute maximum wave energy while wind turbines located in artificial or natural islands, near the shore, can generate maximum wind energy.

In India, research and development activities are going on a large scale regarding the derivation of above mentioned forms of ocean energy. However the forms of energy which has already been derived or could , be derived in the very near future with sufficient technological feasibility are OTEC, wave energy, and tidal energy only.

(d) *OTEC:* OTEC utilizes the temperature difference which exists between the surface seawater (28-30°C) and the water occurring at a depth of 800- 1000 metres (5-7°C) : to generate power through the medium of a suitable fluid which vaporizes at high temperature and condenses at low temperature and in this process turns a special type of turbine.

According to feasibility studies OTEC power is economically competitive with fossil and nuclear powers. Directives establish a US national goal of 10,000 MW on line by 1999, from OTEC facilities only. Some of the best potential sites are located near the islands of Lakshwadweep and Andaman and Nicobar Islands groups. Only two islands, namely Kavaratti and Minicoy were found to offer possibilities for installing on OTEC plant, preferably each of I MW potential.

From the available bathymetry and temperature profiles around the islands, it has been found that a depth of 1000 metres will be available within the distance of about 3 kin from the islands and a temperature difference of 20°C between the surface and 1000 in depth throughout the year. Therefore, it has been considered that a shore based plant is ideally suited for these island sites, which also have big lagoons on western side. These islands are of a coral origin and detailed studies for placing the cold water pipeline on the sea-shope are necessary. Kavaratti was found relatively more uniform.

Besides, in the technological field, procurement of metal components viz. plate heat exchangers, cold water pipes, turbogenerators, pumps, etc. are most vital for successful exploitation of OTEC potentials. Technology to fight corrosion and bio-fouling, for longer life of installed offshore machines, is also of vital relevance.

The law of the sea is silent on the rights and obligations derived from energy extraction from the high seas and on disputes arising from such extraction, for instance, by a grazer, within a country's EEZ, upstream from another nation's EEZ, and on the issue discharging its return water above the thermocline, thereby degrading the downstream resources.

While the worldwide OTEC potential is expected to be around 10 million MW, the same around the Indian coast has been estimated to be 50,000 MW (i.e., 0.2%) only. Around 3000 kin along the Indian coast down from Bombay on the west coast up to Visakhapatnam on the east coast, a temperature difference of 20°C throughout the year is a available. Thus India has more than 3 lakh sq. km of tropical waters in her EEZ where sufficient temperature gradient exists throughout the year.

Thus while estimated global OTEC potential is approximately 10 times the total world electric power production today, in India, the OTEC potential is about 15% of our total installed power generating capacity, hence necessitating the indigenous technological development and rapid scientific transformation relevant to this field. According to one estimate by Kurachi, approximately 1 million tons of cold water must be pumped up per hour to produce 100,000 KW of electricity from OTEC plant 13, i.e. power needed for pumping operations alone is as much as 10% of the generated power.

Even then, OTEC seems to be a useful addition to energy arsenal of the present world, if anyhow brought to the level of larger cost effectiveness. But it is too early in the development process to make any kind of economic assessment of the potential role of OTEC plants in the national and international energy picture. For what they are worth, cost estimates for very small plants seem very high even at experimental level.

But what this means in terms of a possible full 400-500 14 megawatt plant, is simply impossible to determine at the moment. The history of technology transfer from government to prime industry and from pilot plant to operating levels is not one that would generate optimism. The USA with ultimate plan of 400 MW plants at and around isolated islands near Hawaii, Japan with 10 MW floating plants and 20 MW land based plants on the island of Nauru, France with 5 MW land based plant on the island of Tahiti, the Netherlands for islands of Ball, Sweden with proposals for the islands of Jamaica, UK with 10 MW floating plants and with plans of commercially profitable 40 MW plants, have either started functioning or are scheduled for the same in near future. The sums of money are very large, may be around US$60 million for a 10 MW floating plant.

However in the Indian situation, as elsewhere, this baseload OTEC resource, by both of open and hybrid close cycles, seems to be of practical value favourably to southward situated islands where modest contribution to small and medium scale intraregional energy needs could be met successfully.

(e) *Wave energy:* Global wave energy potential is of the order of 45 $\times$ 10^{18} Watt. Variation of annual average value can be, for example, from 3 KW/m of coastline in the Mediterranean to 90 KW/m in the North Atlantic. The seasonal variation is remarkable i.e. in winter 6 times greater than the summer one. The principal recent studies have been made in UK, Japan, but interest has also been shown by France, Norway, Sweden, India, and the USA.

Inventors have proposed many devices for large-scale wave energy collection and transmission to land, including, oscillating water columns, floats, moving pistons, rockers or paddles, and deformable bodies of both mechanical and pneumatic types. However on a small scale, wave energy already provides the modest power needs of remote navigation buoys, including a large one, Kamei, in the Sea of Japan.

In general, a 100m dome with 11 in diameter and 20 in high dome could generate 4000 KW from 2 meter high waves, a system known as dam-atoll system, made firstly by Lockheed Corporation. In simultaneously acts as a breakwater also which in turn, would have effects on the littoral movement and disposition of sediments.

Thus, apart from small impediment to navigation and commercial fishing, the major problem of wave-power recovery has been from the very hostile marine environments viz. strong storms and winds. Besides, it may also be feasible to combine power dissipation with power extraction in future breakwater construction.

The use of wave power by navigation buoys will continue and should expand because it is a good example of on-site energy use, particularly at islands. However, at this primary stage of scientific achievement in this area, estimates of capital costs are highly speculative and subject to greater uncertainty, particularly when taking into account the likely future increase in the costs of energy derived from nonrenewable and depleting fossil fuels. In India, available informations based on visual observations indicate that annual average wave height along the Indian coast is of the order of 1.5 in with the wave period of about 6 seconds. But scientific data collected off Kalpakkam and near Kakinada on east coast, using wave rider buoys, indicate wave heights of more than 2.5 to 3 m, even during non-monsoon period.

This suggests that the annual average wave power potential along the Indian coast may lie anywhere between 5 KW/m and 15 KW/m. For total Indian coast, the wave energy potential is around 6,000 MW. Multipurpose Wave Regulatory Systems (WRS) are being employed and fixed near the appropriate sites off the Indian coast, so that further designing of wave energy devices could be done after taking into account the collection of climatic data, prospects of coastal protection from wave erosion and about other uses of coastal waters viz. aquaculture, transport, harbour developments, etc.

Indian wave regulatory systems have been proposed to be set off the Madras coast at approximate water depth of about 10 meters and a distance of about 500 meters from the shore. Thus in India, a wave energy system exclusively for generation of electricity, does not seem to be economic.

A multifunctional system is being employed after incorporating the modifications to the oscillating water column reported in 1984 in Norway (i.e. The Harbour

Concept). One twin turbine motor of 150 mm diameter has been successfully fabricated for demonstration, besides completion of studies on variation of wave energy at different depths, thus finding the optimum water depth, wave refraction studies in different lengths, completion of demonstration model on wave energy including a wave maker for a 1.2m wide flume and an oscillating water column to absorb the waves with a matching turbine proven in the 4 m wave flumes and generator to produce electricity.

(F) *Tidal energy.* Today France, the USSR, the UK and China are in the forefront of tidal energy development while the USA, Canada, the Republic of Korea, India and Argentina having made serious efforts towards its advancement, both in single and multiple type basins as well as single tide or double tide type.

The peak efficiency of tidal power plants can reach 80%-90%, but for the simplest systems, the baseload is nil. Of the tidal power schemes now operating, only one is commercial in scale since 1967 with an output of 240 MW at LaRance in France (with coast approximately US $120 million and produces electricity at a cost of 3.5 cents/kWh.

The second one is an experimental one at Kislaya Cuba on Russia's Kola Peninsula in Barents Sea with some 400 kW capacity. In China large number of small plants in function is reported, while two sites of extreme potential are being developed by Canada and UK in Bay of Fundy and in Severn Estuary respectively, the later with estimated supply of 10% of the total England's annual demand for electricity.

An alternative location across the Bristol Channel, west of Minehead, would even yield twice this amount. A recent review of the economics of the proposed tidal energy schemes in the bay of Fundy concluded that they were equivalent to the nuclear plants and markedly superior to the coal fired thermal plants. The total tidal resource of world oceans has been estimated at 3 x 101 megawatts. Only 2% of these, at relatively 30 sites around the world, is suitable for harnessing at economically feasible level. Even then, it is significant because it represents 5% of the 1980 worldwide power generation from all sources.

In other words, it is estimated that tidal power could displace between 5% and 10% of other energy sources in the area. Further, the plants have high reliability and a long life of around 75-100 years and appear to increase four times in numbers in coming 50 years. India's Gulf to Kutch is one of the most suitable location. Work has been in full swing to complete the feasibility report by March 1987. The other possible sites, according to 1966 survey, are the Gulf of Cambay and the Sunderbans, having annual average tidal range of 6 m and 3.5 m respectively. The maximum tidal range found, yet in India, is in the Gujarat offshore areas i.e. around 11 m.

According to Prof. E.M. Wilson, installed tidal capacities in the Gulf of Cambay, the Gulf of Kutch, and the Sunderbans are about 7300 MW, 100 MW, and 15 MW with estimated cost of around Rs. 1925 crores, Rs. 600 crores, and Rs. 15 crores respectively. The *7300* MW plant at Gulf of Cambay, if installed, will be able to contribute as much as 20% of India's total installed power capacity today. Realizing the potential, Gujarat State Electricity Board and Department of Energy, Government of India have jointly taken up a detailed project study in collaboration with Electricity de France, along with 9 other interested government agencies.

The project envisages construction of three main dams over the Hansthal Creek, the Sara Creek and the Phang Creek, having 3.1, 0.7 and 0.5 km. of length respectively. The three dams will be connected with each other by a 30 km. long dyke carrying a road on its top, however the only proposed powerhouse will be over the Hansthal Creek, functioning for 12 hours a day, 6 hours in each tidal cycle, producing 600 MW of electricity. The CWPRS has already prepared a physical model of the tidal power project at Khadagwasla with a revised estimate of 5.3 crore, controlled by Kandla Port Trust. If the present siltation problem across here is solved anyhow, then this project will at least save Rs. 2-4 crores per year.

(g) *Currents:* Important currents, prevailing mostly in western parts of world oceans, include the Gulf Stream and the Guinea, the Brazil, the Mozambique, Japan (the Kuroshio) and the Australian currents. Both linear and rotary systems are being employed with large ocean coriollis turbines to derive this very diffuse energy source. For example, the Gulf Stream has the highest velocity (more than 2 m/s) and the power of its core with an average width of 50 km and depth of 120 in has been estimated at 24 GW.

Assuming utilization of 20% at an efficiency of 40%, the resulting 2 GW of electric power would not amount to a significant fraction of world's energy supply. Besides the efficiency amounts to little more than 50%. However, if suitable submerged generators could be designed, they might be placed in gaps between atolls, where currents are often violent.

Particularly if they are relatively close to the shore, these might be able to satisfy the limited energy needs of small neighbouring populations. Further, the navigational use of an ocean current can significantly reduce the transit time of ships travelling in its direction, which is a useful way of capitalizing on this energy source. The prospects of current energy on western coast of India is quite considerable, although not much development or technological breakthrough has yet taken in this field.

(h) *Offshore Wind Energy:* Placing wind turbines in offshore areas is environmentally advantageous. It reduces frictional losses. Although the net profit is only about *22%.* Prospective site selection for installation of these turbines in India's EEZ, after surveying the different physical parameters in detail, is yet to be finalized. However, an imported wind generator has been installed for the first time in India to operate a lighthouse at Kanai Creek, Gujarat, with a power output of around *300* watts. The UK~ the USA, Denmark and Sweden are leading in this field of utilization of wind energy.

Offshore wind generator systems would have to be relatively large in order to defray the high cost of power connection to the shore. In real terms, a successful wind power system is the sail driven vessel. If only a small fraction of the world's commercial transport fleet could be replaced by wind assisted ships, a significant amount of oil could be saved, seemingly of much importance for Indian foreign exchange savings.

(i) *Salinity Gradient:* Extraction of 240 mb of existing equivalent pressure by use of semi-permeable membranes on a very large scale has the potential to provide an overall substantial amount of energy. Its development might capitalize firstly on its abundance and secondly on possible low efficiency small plant. Further the power density of salt domes and brines, which is much larger than normal seawater, might make it a favoured application for salinity gradient density.

World's major salinity gradient resource areas include coastal regions just offshore of major river basins such as Yangtze, Amazon, Congo, the Ganges an Mississippi rivers. In India, the Sunderbans and other large deltaic and estuarine points are potential places for generation of energy from salinity gradient.

Further i India, the total freshwater discharge from rivers an streams flowing into the sea amount to about 23 x 101 in sec., which could provide a power potential of about 54.8 101 MW. The energy density of this source is equivalent to about 250 in waterhead for a salinity difference of 35 ppt. However only a little work has been done on the technique of extraction of power from salinity gradient.

Although still at an experimental level, countries with larger EEZ have indeed possibility of extracting the following resources.

(j) *Magnetic ocean energy* production by magneto hydrodynamic generator (MHD) uses geotrophic currents and long strip that is wound with a flatwire, thus the flowing current produces electric current of 5 mho/m.

(k) *Marine biomass energy* in the form of CH^4 and CO^2 can be obtained mainly from Macrocystic and Giacilaria species. Current global estimates claim that marine biomass power could be competitive with conventional energy production. The prices would run about $18 per 100 m^3 with ayield of 112 tons/hectare/year. Major technological breakthrough is still awaited.

(l) *Marine chemosynthetic energy is* mostly associated with the vents near the seafloor great rifts, and from unusual marine faunas like worms, mussels, and clams found at depths around 2550 in and below using economically worthless H^2S for the purpose would be cheap and will also reduce pollution and eliminate a water product, helping indeed in alleviating cost of the source material.

(m) *Geothermal energy* associated with rift zones and areas of intense volcanic activity are possible marine economic sources, particularly those who are coastal and insular in nature lying within the EEZ limit.

(n) *Heavy water viz.* deuterium and tritium, abundantly dissolved in oceanic water when fused at great temperatures releases great amount of heat, easily usable to generate electricity. Japan is seriously doing the pioneering work in its EEZ related to heavy water energy.

(o) *Radioactive energy* from marine sources is being developed. Japan Metal Mining Agency has started constructing experimental factories for the retrieval of uranium dissolved in seawater. Currently the Siemens Corporation of the USA is also attempting to use marine redioactive chemicals and radioactive wastes being dumped in oceans as energy sources. Current models are producing around 1.50 watts at a cost of $5 a watt and needs attention for possible economic viability after 5 years.

In a nutshell, we may comment in the field of other marine energy resources discussed just above, economic viability through capital investment and technological attainment, are the main points to be stressed upon in near future for any commercial level exploitation of these infinite renewable energy sources present in the ocean. The Indian situation in all these areas are yet at experimental exploratory level. Production, however, may be feasible within 15 years from now.

From the available geological and geophysical data, it has been estimated that the continental shelf around India up to a depth of 200 in, with an area of around 452,000 km^2, can have a potential oil reserve of 1 billion tonnes and natural gas around 271 bcm approximately. Recent offshore hydrocarbon discoveries indicate that the potential oil and natural gas reserve is very promising and we can look towards this in the coming 21st century with considerable optimism. Most of the contemporary drilling activities in offshore area is carried out at depths of 200 in or so generally.

Further, the Indian offshore oil reserves are of period Mioceane, Oligocene and Eocene.

Proven offshore reserves represent a quarter of the world total reserves. About 90% of these reserves are estimated to be under the continental shelves, mostly under the respective coastal states jurisdiction. The overall strategy for the commercial development of offshore hydrocarbons depends on a careful appraisal of the potential for oil and gas and on technological and economic factors. Further much of the world's offshore oil and gas, mostly under EEZ, areas will be discovered and produced only if the relevant governments adopt a regulatory or fiscal policy appropriate to the realities involved.

Even the present reserve is considered to be maximum of 345×10^9 MT, feasible to be produced, it would not sustain consumption at current levels beyond the year 20 10. New findings of sufficient magnitude, able to sustain demand beyond the year 2000, would have to be made at twice the present discovery rate, but it can be visualized that even this optimistic scenario could only maintain A-situation in which oil and gas could be consumed as fast as it could be produced.

In India most of the known petroleum resources are confined to the narrow belt of tertiary strata which constitute the outer margin of the extra-peninsular mountains along their whole line of contact with the peninsular block of Deccan viz. the Rann of Kutch, the Cambay Gulf off Piram Island (dome), Bombay High and the Andaman and Nicobar Islands. The number of wells drilled in the offshore areas, by ONGC, was 36 in 1980 with a hole depth of 77,167 in against a total of 109 wells and 193,734 m of depth 32. According to the 1983-84 estimates, the ratio between production and consumption of oil in India is 1:1.3 approximately.

New discoveries have added to the attainment of self-sufficiency. Reduction in production as well as in consumption and efforts to supplement the fossil fuels by nonconventional and renewable sources of energy can only take us well within the 21st century, probably up to 2020 to 2025 A.D. Impressive achievement in last 15 years can be visualized with the fact that, in 1970, ONGC started offshore drilling, firstly near Aliabet in Gulf of Cambay. In early 1974, the Sagar Samrat drilling platform at Bombay High, acquired from Japan, started functioning, reaching production of more than 230.95 million tonnes in 1980, thus fully realizing the contribution of offshore oil reserve in national economy. In the field of natural gas, world proven reserve reached 90,325 billion cubic metres as per January 1, 1984.

World commercial production of gas in 1983 reached 1584 bcm. In India, the total reserve of natural gas according to 1980 estimates was 351.91 bcm, the offshore share being 270,96 bcm. 1982 total production was around 24.12 bcm with respective states contributions viz. Gujarat (48%), Assam (31%) and Bombay (21%). The 1980 and 1981 productions were respectively 19.25 and 19.97 bem. Location wise, natural gas (chiefly marsh gas with some other gaseous hydrocarbons) usually accompanies the petroleum accumulations, thus supplying the propulsive force which carries the oil from the oil-sands into the wells and if the pressure is sufficient, brings the oil up to the surface.

Since gas is both essential for the production of the oil and is also valuable as source of fuel on the oilfields, care is being taken now to prevent the huge waste of gas which was formerly so common. The country is fortunate to have discovered natural gas offshore the Andaman and Nicobar Islands, west coast of the Gulf of Cambay and Kutch and in basins of Brahmaputra, Godawari and Cauvery Basin. Principal present offshore supply being the Bombay High, producing 270.96 bcm. But Gujarat coast was on top in production of natural gas utilized between 1976-1980 i.e. 6.95 bcm, the others in series being Assam and Bombay High with value 4.55 bcm and 3.12 bcm respectively, making a total Indian production of 14.62 bem. However, the national objective, to be satisfied, is in need of compact and accurate programs with more developments in seismic surveys and interpretation capability, development of suitable shallow water indigenous mobile drilling platforms, much advancement in capability for design, fabrication and installation of fixed production platform, the same in the case of submarine pipelines, marine equipments, instruments, and sophisticated research vessels for further study, research, and resource development.

Seafloor deposits, within the EEZ jurisdiction of India, fit for present commercial production, comprise only of sands, gravels, corals, lime, shells and relatively small quantities of tin, titanium and iron. However potential seafloor mineral resources are, immense and includes both oozes and clays, phosphorites and manganese nodules, the rich muds and brines (found in oceanic rift areas) and the newly discovered polymetallic sulphides and cobalt crusts (in relatively deeper oceans). Sulphur is also being exploited but on a minor scale. Continental shelf rocks contain a variety of hard minerals, from coal and iron to tin, but only small quantities are being extracted commercially. For all this, ocean mining has to cope with availability, accessibility, advisability, and legality, among other factors.

Although Asia remains the continent with overall greatest promise of deposits of these valuable minerals, the superficial mineral deposits of Indian Ocean includes a wide variety of terrigenous, biogenous and authigenic mineral deposits.

The beach and offshore place deposits of the Indian Ocean may be some of the largest in the world. The biogenous deposits comprise of the corals on shallow banks and on the continental shelves and the oozes in the deep sea. The authigenic deposits consists of the phosphorites, found both along continental margins (S. Africa and western India), and around seamounts in eastern and western Indian Ocean. The continental margins of S. Africa, east Africa, southern Arabia, western India and the Andamans are marked by strong upwelling and provide nondepositional environments which are conducive to the formation of phosphorites. The polymetallic nodules found mostly in Central Indian Ocean Basin, beyond the national EEZ limit, cover an area of 10-15 × 106 km^2 and the resources are estimated to be about 1.5×10^{11} tonnes.

In recent past, the exploration and exploitation of mineral resources of India's EEZ have attracted considerable attention. Until the 1960's, the Indian Ocean was the least studied of the world oceans. It was mainly the International Indian Ocean Expedition of 1960-65, organized by UNESCO and ICSU, which considerably enhanced our knowledge of the ocean and mineral resources of this hitherto unexplored region.

Recent exploration of mineral resources of lesser value, in shallow offshore areas, has actively started, seeing its growing importance. The prospects of offshore mining in India's EEZ were studied in detail in 1977. By now, survey of her total EEZ is supposed to be complete with maximum required oceanographic informations, later helpful in exploitation activity.

Tertigenous deposits: Occurrences of heavy mineral concentrates usually known as "black sands" are reported from many localities of Indian coast, which contain ilmenite, rutile, zircon, magnetite, monazite, garnet, kyanite, and tin in significant proportions. The offshore extensions of some of these placer deposits have been explored. But only offshore tin placers are being exploited at present. Most of the terrigenous deposits occur along the coast of Kerala between Quilon and Cape Comorin. The deposit is reported to contain 17 m tonnes of ilmenite, 1 m tonnes of rutile, 1.2 m tonnes of zircon, and 0.2 m monazite tonnes of. Ratnagiri coast (Maharashtra), Tinnaveli, Ramnad, Tanjore (Tamil Nadu), Visakhapatnam, Yarada, Waltair, Bhimunipatnam (Andhra Pradesh) and the coastal areas off Orissa.

Although the 25 km stretch along the coast from Neendakar to kayamkulam of Kerala state is supposed to have the richest deposit of offshore heavy minerals. Ilmenite concentration ranges from 17 to 79% in the area of Ratnagiri coast, forming an estimated reserve of 4 × 10^6 tonnes.

Further exploration of offshore placers will be guided by the proximity to onshore placers and examination of the relict sands on the middle and outer shelves. The present data indicate that along much of the western shelf, from the Gulf of Kutch i.e. Vengurla to the vicinity of Mangalore, the relict sands consist of oolites and biogenous materials. The extensive zone of potentially rich sands continues east to the Gulf of Mannar. However, it needs careful examination before starting the extensive exploitation.

Worldwide offshore mining of sand and gravels currently exceed the offshore productions of all nonfuel minerals in both value and volume. But in the Indian case it has to compete with onshore deposits, mostly near coastal urban centres viz. Cochin, Madras, Visakhapatnam and Calcutta. But at the same time, the growing deepening of the sea near the land, is likely to increase coastal erosion.

Biogenous deposits : Besides shell deposits of Crassostrea madrasensis, C. cucullata, Villorits cyprenoides, Modiolus sps. and Metritrix sps., the other major biogenous deposits are the corals and the deep see pelagic oozes. The best known deposits are in the Gulf of Kutch and in the Vambanad lake (back waters) of Kerala. Production from both these days being more than 1 million tonnes. Lagoons of the Laccadive Islands, the Andaman Islands shelf area and in the Gulf of Mannar and the Palk Strait appear to be promising. In general, an examination of the bottom sediment map within EEZ of the seas bordering India shows relict oolite and biogenous sands on the middle and outer shelves in the western coast continuously from the Gulf of Kutch to the vicinity of Mangalore and in patches along the eastern coast.

Biogenous residues and the calcareous sands, amounting to 1135 m tonnes around Laccadive Islands can be economically attractive when exploited. Regarding ornamental and semiprecious stones, India is becoming increasingly important as a supplier of marine ornamental shells and the exports have risen from 20 tonnes in 1969 to 466 tonnes in 1979. Further, India is yet not reached exploitation up to the optimum level, thus the way is still open for more exploitation and exports.

Authigenic (Chemogenous) deposits: The chemogenous deposits, formed due to rapid chemical reactions on the ocean floor in the vicinity of the Indian coasts, are found in the form of barium nodules off the west Andaman and the Laccadive Island coasts, phosphorite nodules off the north Andaman, and polymetallic nodules in the Central Indian Basin, of course beyond EEZ area under exploitable jurisdiction because of India being a pioneer investor.

In the area of production and reserves of phosphate rock, India is holding 13th position in the world, with her 1980 production measuring 0.6 million tonnes out of an estimated reserve of 108 million tonnes. This phosphate deposit is marked with vital presence of valuable uranium, 100 to 200 parts per million. Algal and oolitic limestones, are also present off Saurashtra through Goa to Kerala coast. Further India's agro-dominated economy needs phosphorous as major fertilizer, thus making offshore exploration for phosphate deposits unavoidable in near future. Gypsum crustals are found in the inner shelf off the Maharashtra coast between Vengurla and Bombay in the form of silty clay or clayey silt.

In general, a partial survey of EEZ of India has established that the offshore extension of heavy mineral placers on the western shelf are much larger than those available on land territory of India and coastal areas of other neighbouring countries.

Further large areas of the seabed in the India's EEZ, both deep and shallow, are covered by biogenic sediments, but their economic viability is still in doubt. But for islands like the Andaman and the Nicobar and the Laccadive, whose economies are becoming increasingly dependent on tourism, restraint would have to be exercised on the ruthless extraction of available mineral resource deposits. Systematic exploration and exploitation of Indian coasts for the phosphorite deposit is going to be indeed important in near future for purpose of self-sufficiency in fertilizers. Exploration of India's EEZ is nearing completion now.

Much emphasis should be placed on analysis and interpretation for greater understanding of the nature of deposits and technology needed for its proper exploitation. Besides exact location of valuable mining sites and detailed worldwide study of market position of these derived minerals, both in terms of physical availability and economic valuation, is must before undertaking any major capital intensive mining business in hand.

In fisheries, India occupies the 8th position in the world in terms of total annual catch, however the amount is the least in the world when calculated per fisherman engaged in this activity.

Regarding the need, based on futuristic studies, the projected fish requirements of India's population by the year 2000 A.D. is estimated to be 11.4 million tonnes. Her EEZ is still half-heartedly utilized as proved by the fact that 50.6% of total annual catch of over 4.47 million tonnes from the Indian Ocean is harvested from the narrow coastal zone only, i.e., area lying between the shore and 28 meters depth range. The zone lying between 50 meters and 200 meters depth line contains 38.3% of total marine potential, while only 11. 1% of the total potential is there in the depth beyond 200 meters, i.e., 11.6% and 79.4% of area of total EEZ respectively. In other words 9% of the inshore zone of EEZ produces more than 50% of the fisheries.

Further the fisheries potential of the Indian Ocean is estimated at 14.4 million tonnes, of which the demersal fishes account for 7.4 million tonnes, the shoaling pelagic fishes for 6.0 million tonnes, the large pelagic fishes for 0.7 million tonnes, and the crustaceans and squids for 0.25 million tonnes. Prawns are found mostly within 50 meter depth area of EEZ, the only known exceptions being off the south western coast in depths of 275 to 700 meters. Similarly a large trawling ground of deep water lobsters, discovered beyond the 50 meters depth, was located between Quilon and Cochin. Tuna, having a wide migratory range, has been traditionally harvested from India's EEZ around the Minicoy and Laccadive Islands, although at lower levels.. Approximately 60% to 70% of the high priced tuna species of the Indian Ocean were taken by three non-Indian Ocean States namely Japan, Taiwan and South Korea. In 1976 India caught approximately 7-10% of the tuna and tuna-like fishes in the Indian Ocean. Yellowfin and skipjack are the two major species of tuna found within and close to the Indian EEZ. Being the only underutilized tuna variety, skipjack, is in commercially exploitable potential in the Indian Ocean. India's catch of skipjack from Minicoy and Andamans through live bait method has gone up since 1973.

Besides tuna fishing requires highly specialized and technologically sophisticated operations in which India has little experience. Joint ventures and increased transfer of technology in the field of tuna fisheries is the need of the time. Production through aquaculture has been increasing rapidly in recent past which can be evidenced with the fact that in 1980 its production was estimated to be 12.1% of the world's nominal catch, while in 1975 it was only 8.6%. India also leads in fin fish production in the world with an annual production reaching approximately 830,201 tonnes in 1981. But the fact remains that still 65% of the total Indian marine fisheries comes through traditional methods of fisheries only.

A comparative study shows that marine fisheries production in India has increased from 0.55 million metric tonnes in 1951 to over 1.6 million metric tonnes in 1980. On the economic front it contributes only about 0.5% of the GNP and 2% of the total export earning per year which, while considering its vast EEZ area, seems to be a very meager amount.

Of the total annual catch of around 2.5 million metric tonnes in 1980, 1.6 million metric tonnes were marine products; the aquacultures have been 850,000 metric tonnes, i.e., around 50% of the total marine products. However, by the year 2000 A.D. India could be producing 7 million metric tonnes through aquaculture. In the case of field prawn production in 1982, about 30,000 hectares of brackish water have been demarcated. Under government sponsored plan it is proposed that at least around 5,000 hectares should be added annually for prawn culture in marine water. Thus in the field of mariculture an estimated 1.7 million hectares of estuarine or brackish water areas and 8.9 million hectares of inshore waters are to be utilized along the Indian coast within its EEZ limit.

Finally for the successful resource management in Indian EEZ, the Indian government has recognized the main thrust areas for the optimization of investment at present, mainly high priority areas, manpower development has been sought at higher skilled levels which would successfully result in improving socio-economic condition of the vast population living mainly on the sea cost of the country. Steps to start political and legal shells to understand the application of various process of UNCLOS III, mandatory transfer of technology and other associated complex issues like conservation, boundarly demarcation, pollution and protection of nation's interests in the EEZ are being sincerely undertaken. Comparative cost analysis in exploitation of these living and non-living resources is being seriously studied and their strategic importance being realized.

Energy from the Sea

The water masses in the oceans are not dormant bodies but are in constant motion. If the movements of the water are on established lines they are referred to as marine currents. The causes of these currents are very different. The most important factors affecting marine currents are wind, density variations within the water masses, and differences in the heat flow between water and atmosphere.

When these factors occur in combination they may serve to reinforce one another as well as to neutralize one another. For the most part of the direction of individual ocean currents is determined by the earth's rotation the shape of the continents, submarine ridges, and tidal currents. Owing to the multiplicity of determining factors, any estimate of the direction of the resulting marine current is extraordinarily complicated. The velocity of the ocean currents compared with those in rivers is substantially lower. If the wind sets the surface water in motion, the direction of the current does not necessarily follow that of the wind.

Owing to the rotation of the earth and the Coriolis forces generated thereby, the currents in a particular sector are linked to the direction of the wind. In the northern hemisphere all the currents are deflected clock wise to the right, and in the southern hemisphere to the left. Since at the same time the prevailing winds are deflected likewise, the deflecting forces receive additional reinforcement. The deflection of the water currents is thus all the stronger the deeper the water columns are below the surface. Basically, two types of marine currents are distinguished: surface currents and underwater currents. The most important surface currents are found in the equator belt between the northern and southern tropic zones The northest and southest trade winds provide the motive force for these big equatorial currents. Between the individual continents these currents are diverted in their directions and deflected to the north and south. Since the Coriolis forces are intensified as the geographical latitude increases, the original current direction is gradually reversed.

Consequently a powerful flow of surface currents develops. In the middle of the cycle, zones are encountered with relatively modest surface movements (for example, the Sargasso Sea in the North Atlantic). The pattern of surface currents is roughly the same in all the oceans. The water masses that flow north and south from the equator toward the poles cool down gradually on the way, more and more rapidly as the geographical latitude increases. Their density rises in the process, so that water masses sink to a lower level as they go and eventually return to the equator as cold seabed currents. In all cases in which the wind carries off big masses of water, these must be replaced by a return flow. This happens as a result of either an influx of surface water or an influx of water from a lower level.

Water masses flowing toward the poles and so becoming cooler set off the deep water currents. Regions in which surface currents combine to produce deep water currents are known as convergence areas. Under the influence of surface, deep water and sea bed currents, a constant exchange of water masses develops in the course of time in all the big oceans. If it were possible to utilize a mere 0.5% of the head stored in the form of temperature differentials in the oceans of the world, man's energy problems would all be solved. This concept, however, utopian it may sound, is not in fact utterly realistic.

Sea-heat power plants fall within the field of technical possibility. The idea of utilizing the energy stored in the ocean is not new. It was first suggested in 1881 by the French physicist Jacques d'Arsonval. His fellow countryman George Claude erected the first sea heat power plant in Cuba in 1929. Its power output then amounted to 22 kilowatts. Its performance was satisfactory, but it was uneconomical, as Claude's technical resources were inadequate. American environmental engineers have now developed the idea. Design work has begun at the University of Massachusetts for a sea heat power plant to be erected in the gulf stream of the coast of south Florida. The theory of a sea heat power plant is as follows: between various water depths there is normally a temperature differential which can be utilized for energy production.

In the tropics, that is between the celestial spheres of Cancer and Capricorn, the surface waters of the oceans have an almost unvarying temperature of 25°C (77°F) over the whole year. At a depth of 1000 meters (3200 feet) or so, on the other hand, the prevailing temperature is only 5°C (41°F). This temperature differential can be utilized as in conventional power plants by letting the liquid on the "warm side" evaporate or simmer. The steam drives a turbine and is condensed on the "cold side." As the heat differentials are in a narrow range, water is not suitable as a medium. First calculations indicate that propane gas would be a very suitable gas for circulation in sea water power plants. It boils at temperatures of under 25°C, and can return to liquid form at 5°C. The power plant could be installed on a floating island in the open sea.

Power plants of this kind could provide a realistic technical solution for the utilization of solar energy, for the water is heated by the sun, and the oceans serve as energy stores. The temperature differentials arise as a result of circulation between the poles and the tropics. Sea heat power plants could also acquire much greater importance.

The cold water pumped up from the depths of the sea could serve to do more than jut cool the turbines. It still remains cool enough to condense water vapour drawn off from seawater into a vacuum chamber. In this way the power plant can extract drinking water from the sea. It is estimated that a plant with an output of 100 MW of electric power could provide some 200 million liters of drinking water a day.

In contrast to the development of nuclear energy, especially by fast breeder reactors, no serious new technical problems are posed by this form of utilization of solar energy. The periodic alternation of ebb and flow on the sea coast is caused by forces that, in addition to wind and the earth's rotation, are exerted by the influence of sun and moon on the water masses of the oceans. The flow of the tides is highly complicated, and varies from place to place.

Tidal Power Plants

Tidal power plants are a particularly attractive way of utilizing the regenerative forces of nature for purposes of power production. Solar energy and lunar energy can be converted into electric power by this means in the same way as in a water works. The process extends over a period of 12 hours and 24 minutes, that is, half the period it takes the moon to circle the earth.

As the moon is the nearest of all the heavenly bodies to the earth, the force of gravity exerted by the moon has a measurable influence on the earth. In the big water zones of the earth (the oceans) the result is that where the moon is directly overhead, owing to its attractive power, the water level is raised somewhat (flood tide), whereas in other regions it will be below the norm (ebb tide). These two phases are particularly sharply delineated on the coastlines of seas and oceans. At specially favourable points on the coast, tidal differences can be distinguished of 10 meters (32 feet) and more. If at such a point on the coast, a bay or a river mouth is shut off by a sluice of floodgate, energy can be obtained with the aid of turbines driven by water currents set up by the alternate filling and emptying of the bay.

The maximum power produced by a tidal power plant is determined by the potential energy of the water mass stored in a basin during the flood tide and by the tidal period. The coefficient of efficiency of this energy utilization lies between 20% and 25%. The pioneer in the erection of tidal power plants was West Germany. In the First World War a small tidal power station was in operation in Husum, using the flow and ebb of the current, in a former oyster-culture basin, in order to supply houses in the neighbourhood with electricity.

The first big tidal power station came in to operation in 1966 at the mouth of the river Rance in France. Today its output amount to 240 megawatts, and should be raised eventually to 320 MW. Altogether, 10 turbines are set in a dam 750 meters long, and they work in both directions, using both the incoming and outgoing tides. The tidal range (the difference between high and low tide) averages about 10 meters, with a maximum of 13 meters. In 1968 a small plant of 400 kilowatts was started up in the USSR at the mouth of the Kislaya, 80 km northeast of Murmansk. A larger plant of 320 MW is projected for the Lombowska River on the northeast coast of the Kola Peninsula. The following table shows part of the power available on the earth from tidal energy. Possible performance in the various locations ranges from 2 to 20,000 MW.

Glacier Power Plants

After many years research work in Arctic stations, where he was conversant with the structure and dynamics of the Greenland ice sheet, a Swiss hydrobiologist came up a short time ago with an unusual project for energy production. Enormous quantities of ice melt in Greenland every summer and run down into the sea from land 2000-3000 m (6500-9800 feet) lakh. If normal power stations were built on the coast in Greenland, enormous quantities of electric power could be produced by this means. The technology of the necessary hydraulic power stations would be standard, but the construction material for the dams and the supply and pressure, ducts would be something quite new, namely rock hard glacier ice. As the biggest island in the world, Greenland has a surface area of about 2 million sq. km. (760,000 sq.m.). On a conservative estimate something like 500,000 sq. km.

(190,000 sq. mi) would be available for the installation of storage basins. With the sun shining for about 2000 hours per annum, some 8 kwh of energy could be produced each year from 1 sq. m. of storage lake area. From the estimated 500,000 sq. km of storage lake area, about 4000 billion kwh of useful energy should be obtainable each year. This represents an electric power output of about 200,000 MW, approximating the output of 200 large atomic power stations.

During the summer an extensive canal system, corresponding to a network of streams, would have to be built inside Greenland. The ice melted by the suns heat would run along these canals into big storage lakes. In the course of the flow of the melted ice water, which would be warm compared with the ice it came into contact with the streams would expand of their own accord, so that relatively little technical energy would be required for the construction of the canal system. Owing to the differences in elevation from 2000 to 3000 m, the melted ice water would shoot through ducts from the storage lake down to normal, big hydraulic power stations installed on the coast.

The storage lakes are required mainly to ensure that energy production will be available also in winter. In the winter a layer of ice 1 to 2meters thick forms on the surface of the storage lakes and protect the water below from further freezing. The water below the layer of surface ice could thus be drawn off for energy production as required. The necessary barrages, and the supply and pressure ducts, can be modelled by suitable techniques with the aid of the ice. Tested procedures already exist for the construction of ice channels in glaciers.

By means of a circular cutting guide (a steel tube with an interfacing rotating saw tooth rim), cylinders, can be cut out of the glacier ice having a diameter of about 10 m (33 feet). With a subsidiary circular saw appliance the ice cylinder cut out lengthways can be split up into semicircular portions and lifted out on to the canal bank by means of a rotating table turned at an angle of 180°. These segments can be stacked together quite easily to form dams, whereupon they rapidly freeze up again.

By means of such glacier power plants, cheap energy could be produced in large quantities without causing any pollution of the environment and without the consumption of law materials. For transmission of the energy there are two possibilities:

(1) The electric current produced can be conveyed directly by submarine cable to North-America and Europe; or

(2) This is probably the better solution, with the aid of the electric energy produced in the hydraulic power station the water can be split up into hydrogen and oxygen, and the hydrogen can be liquefied and conveyed by tanker to the country of consumption. It could then be used for heating, the driving advanced motor vehicles, or in fuel cells for electricity production.

Petroleum and natural gas are the most important sources of energy and are the raw materials most in demand by the chemical industry today. For the most part, petroleum comprises a mixture of several hundred or even thousand hydrocarbon constituents. In many cases these are the only constituents, while in others a large number of other organic compounds are present, such as oleic acid, asphaltene, gums and a variety of sulfur and nitrogen compounds.

The vast proliferation of hydrocarbons stems from the tetravalenc of carbon and its many possible compounds in the form of chains of different lengths with single, double and triple bonds, of rings of different bond types and sizes and of the most varied bonding with one another: and it also allows the formation of side chains.

Gums and asphaltenes are high molecular weight organic compounds, which give to the oils their dark colour and increase their viscosity. The sulfur and nitrogen compounds are in the form of chains or rings, in which carbon atoms are replaced by sulfur or nitrogen atoms. The explanation of how petroleum is formed is one of the most difficult problems encountered in geological research. Almost all the facts point to its organic development from decomposition products of plant and animal organisms that were deposited in the mud beds of waterways, were preserved there from immediate putrefaction by the lack of oxygen, and then formed rock bitumen.

One problem regarding this explanation of the origin is that organisms are composed to a large extent of oxidized compounds whereas petroleum consists of reduced (oxygen-free) compounds. Reduction is conceivable, however, only as a result of energy input. In the first phase of transformation at least, the necessary energy could not have been derived from the heat of the earth, as the petroleum would then still contain elements from the chlorophyll and blood pigment, which will not sustain a higher temperature than 200C° (424°F) and will persist only in an oxygen free environment. One possible reaction, which also occurs in lower temperatures and is anaerobic (without free oxygen) is biological reduction by bacteria. In the sediment in water and in oil a whole series of anaerobic bacteria can be recognized that are able to reduce organic substances and to transform them into fatty acids, methane, and ethane, and also into other hydrocarbons. The hydrocarbons in question do not form petroleum, however. The further transformation of the long chain compounds (fatty acids) into petroleum with its light paraffins (5-7 carbon atoms) can occur only as lower temperatures and in the absence of active clays as catalyzers or at great depths under high pressures by thermal decomposition. Under this thermal decomposition or fission, long chain hydrocarbons will be split up into methane and other light gaseous hydrocarbons. Natural gas is produced in the same way, but contains carbon dioxide, nitrogen, hydrogen sulfide, and mixtures of rare gases in addition to hydrocarbons. A distinction is made here between dry gases, which consist almost exclusively of methane, wet gases (ethane, propane, butane, etc.), and acid gases with mixtures of hydrogen sulfide. The formation of petroleum and natural gas thus possibly represents a process that embraces some very different reactions (bacterial and thermal decomposition or fission) and extends over long periods. The formation of the most recent petroleum fields dates back roughly one million years.

Salt Deposits

In the weathering of volcanic rocks the compounds dissolved are mainly those of the alkaline earth metals calcium and magnesium, together with those of the alkali metals sodium and potassium, whereas the oxides of silicon are in effect insoluble. Part of the potassium is removed from the weathering solution by clay minerals, in which the potassium is incorporated. The potassium, calcium and sodium, along with magnesium, dissolved carbon dioxide, and sulfur compounds, are carried down the rivers into the oceans, where they eventually form salts.

In open sea water the salt concentration is too low for the salts to be deposited. Owing to evaporation of the water, however, the concentration can be raised to the limit, which results in the deposit of the precipitated salt. This presupposes the delimitation of sea basins, in which certain conditions must be present. The loss by evaporation must exceed the inflow of water. And the shores of the inland lake or of the sea bay must be so flat that no more material is fed into the basin from the land.

The first substances to settle are the least soluble carbonates and sulfates. This can also occur in very small concentrations biogenetically in the case of marine organisms which by their metabolism absorb the lime as a stroma supporting tissue substance in their scales.

Some 40% of the sea bed is covered with what is known as foraminiferal ooze, formed from the shells of dead protozoa and from clay substances. In the further process of deposit and sedimentation, rock salt is produced, and finally the most easily soluble potash salt.

The sinking of the bed of the basin, a rise in its shoreline and an inflow of new water masses will mean that the water formation process is repeated. The salt formation thus occurs only during a static phase in part of the earth crust. In many regions several such cycles can occur in succession. The clays washed into the basin at times of increased erosion of the surrounding land surfaces protect the salt deposits from being washed away. Salt formation is possible both in inland waters and in the sea. The salts differ from one another, however, in their chemical composition, which is more astonishing in that not only the inland waters but also the seas receive their mineral constituents from the land surface. This involves the supposition that the oceans have an original supply of salt which is only slightly modified by the fresh supplies washed in from the land. As the various salts are deposited one after the other, they tend to remains in layers one upon another. Clay and carboniferous rocks are deposited first from the shore of the basin into the middle; sulfates and chlorides are deposited in the basin's interior. In this way salt basins are formed with their typical salt distributions. From salt deposits, which are overlaid by sediment, salt masses can form. This depends on the fact that salt begins to flow even when there is very little difference in tension in the sediment. Differences in tension are produced, for instance, by movements in the earth's crust or differences in erosion levels in the overlying rocks.

5

Acquatic Environment

A large number of different substances, with varying biological effects enter the aquatic environment from a large number of sources on land and at sea; the result sometimes being the potential occurrence of many unforeseen ecological catastrophes. Some substances, once believed to be harmless, have subsequently proved to cause large scale and unforeseeable damage to aquatic organisms. The state of aquatic environment, acting as the ultimate sinks of pollution, in many respects mirrors environmental degradation that follows various human activities. Many big drainage basins and rivers around the world are being devastated by intensive human activities. Developed countries, with generally stricker water quality legislation, are experiencing some success in reducing pollution from municipal and industrial sources. However, too many lakes still suffer from excess pollutant loads from diffuse sources such as atmospheric deposition, agricultural runoff, urban stormwater, road deicing salts. etc. In particular, lakes are becoming eutrophic, and numerous large lakes around the world are chocked with algae and aquatic plants which impair water quality and put a strain on valuable water resources. Pollution of the seas has been regarded as only a local environmental threat. However, pollution distributed around coastlines of most continents is now beginning to threaten also the open seas. It is evident that enclosed and isolated seas are the most vulnerable.

The most well-known examples include the Aral Sea, the Mediterranean, the Black sea and the Baltic. Looking at the sea as a pollutant recipient, it receives polluting inputs from atmospheric fallout, land-based discharges, ship dumping of industrial and municipal waste and sludge and from offshore gas and oil production. All these sources contribute almost all types of known pollutants and an increasing number of reports serve as warning of the gradual deterioration of the oceans. The geographical distribution of the various water related problems throughout the world indicates some important difference with regards to the character of the environmental stress and extent of preventive efforts.

Developed countries of 25 years ago were characterized by localized areas with intense water pollution problems due to industrial or municipal sources. Today measure have been taken to reduce omissions from industrial and municipal sources. However, the gradual introduction of a large number of new chemical compounds and technologies has resulted in much higher number of contaminants today. The original situation, which local intense pollution from a limited number of well defined sources has been transferred into a situation with widespread contamination by a large variety of compounds from a multitude of sources.

In *Eastern Europe*, the situation 25 years ago was not much different from developed countries with intense localized pollution. The desire to catch up with the developed countries contributed to a philosophy wherein environmental matters had an even lower priority in the East. The failure to economically make environment a priority issue led to the lack of measures for controlling sources of industrial and municipal pollution. Today, the intense local pollution has exhausted many natural buffering systems and has become regionalised intense pollution. In addition is the effect of new chemicals and new technologies. It is not clear as to whether some of the most environmentally degraded countries will manage to bring the situation under control by themselves.

Developing countries were only affected to a very limited extent by chemical and industrial pollution 25 years ago. Today, this picture is changing. "Industrial-free zones" and other concentrations of heavy industries in developing countries have replaced the Ruhr, Osaka and Pittsburg as industrial pollution "hot spots". As the desire to industrialize and improve material living conditions and balance of payments is very strong in many developing countries there are clear risks that the mistakes made in Eastern Europe and some developed countries may be repeated.

With regard to global concerns, the environmental affects of redistributing the world's production of toxic chemicals banned in many developed countries to the developing countries have been much discussed in recent years. The problems are related to large scale social issues which would required major efforts to turn around and to long term development processes which many be too late to correct if environmental degradation goes any further.

There are two major sources of pollutants to aquatic ecosystems: point sources and nonpoint sources. In most developed countries, environmental regulations, as well as the changing structure of industry have led to greatly reduced omissions from point sources. There has been much less focus on reducing pollutant loads from diffuse sources such as urban and agricultural runoff, even though these sources are becoming increasingly important. In terms of remedial measures, efforts to reduce point-sources omissions, especially in less developed countries, should continue. Also to the extent possible, products that release high levels of toxic materials during their use and disposal should be banned, or recycled extensively. Such efforts will help to reduce the leadings of toxic materials to aquatic ecosystems. However they will not solve all the problems. Much more concern must be given to environmental impacts from various land use practices.

Basically, environmental problems are caused by ignored or poorly understood natural laws. A fundamental fact is the rain falling onto land eventually finds its way to rivers, lakes and finally to coastal areas. The underground part of this water movement is slow, so that it may take considerable time to reach a river. The fact that the mobile water combines a unique dissolving capacity with high chemical reactivity explains how pollutants can be transported along aquatic pathways from fresh to marine waters. These effects are accelerated when rainwater is acidified from being polluted by atmospheric contact with acidifying air pollutants. Water is also a life sustaining liquid. Indeed, the lives of plants, animals, and human beings are based on the complex patterns of water flows.

Consequently, all land based activities tend to cause disturbances to life cycles if they involve soluble hazardous substances reaching toxic concentrations in the water supplied to plants, animals or humans. However, because of the time each water unit needs for its transportation along the various pathways, the quality response in aquifers, rivers and coastal waters will appear only after a certain time delay. This time delay introduces a political dilemma, in view of the low awareness among most groups in society of these basic principles of the hydrologic cycle. The dilemma is further strengthened by the societal tendency to react only when problems have become visible and evident, not when they are first predicted by application of the fundamental natural laws controlling the natural environment. Today media attention, intellectual, manpower, financial, etc. tend to focus more on retrospective effect analysis than on prospective regulation of activities predicted to cause future damage. Politicians need to adapt their water-related pollution control activities to the principles of the water cycle, and give higher priority to preventive measures. Sometimes it is too late or too expensive to remedy water pollution problems once they are discovered at a river mouth. Water should not be treated as a victim of pollution or as a technical issue necessary to provide a public water supply. It is therefore important to consider:

— the introduction of integrated land and water management methods;

— the evaluation of land use impacts on water including maps of sensitive groundwater areas;

— the use of river basins as the basis of planning activities, due to their value as special units for the management of water-related environmental problems;

— the introduction of administrative bodies with the ability to use a river basin perspectives; and,

— the proper education in terms of broad understanding of the water cycle among planners and policy-makers.

Many people still believe that a characteristic feature of a forested area is the purity of the water in its streams and lakes. New insights into modern forestry operations call for a re-examination of this belief. Afforestation is often considered an appropriate management operation for drainage basins reserved for urban use. Recent studies have demonstrated that total water runoff may be decreased by a forest cover-a disadvantage believed to be more than compensated for by the even runoff from forests, and particularly by the better quality of the water from the forested land. It is also generally believed that the afforestation helps to control erosion, thereby preventing silting of streams and reservoirs. Forestry operations such as clear-cutting and ploughing, fertilization, ditching and draining swamps can lead to increased leaching of humic materials, plant nutrients and sediments. It also increases the water flow.

One of the most debatable environmental effect in increased nitrate concentrations after clear-cutting and fertilization with ammonium nitrate. Phosphorus, a key element in all plant production, is also lost in increasing quantities from ditching and draining peatlands, Losses of other elements have also been reported in connection with peatland drainage with or without fertilization. Increased washout of nitrogen and phosphorus from forested areas can trigger the eutrophication process in streams, lakes, rivers and coastal areas. Peak values of inorganic nitrogen in forest streams close to sites receiving fertilizers may be toxic to aquatic organisms. Nitrate values close to or even exceeding, world-wide accepted health limits have been reported on numerous occasions. Therefore, one of the greatest concerns is the health risks associated with increased concentrations of nitrate, causing transformation of blood haemoglobin to methaemoglobin, and/or by formation of carcinogenic nitrosomines.

The major environmental impacts of tomorrow will depend primarily on two types of pollutant emissions. One results from different production processes, including the transportation of goods and individuals, while the other results from the products themselves. While emissions from industrial production processes have been recognized for a long period and the emissions from the transportation sector are being highlighted at present, the emissions from "consumption" processes have not yet been considered to any great extent. It is being more often argued that the accumulation of hazardous p pollutants in goods and products within society should be more widely accepted in the future. A case study, from a research project on chromium in Sweden, shows how the substance is accumulating in the environment. A major portion of the chromium is found in products themselves. From these products, chromium can disintegrate into the environment. Calculations of total chromium emissions to the environment were based on emission coefficients, which are the fractions of the materials or products released into the environment in mobile forms within a specific time period—a decade in this example.

The main conclusion from the project was that the yearly "consumption emissions" are presently higher than the "production emissions". Thus, the environmental load of chromium seems to be more related to consumer patterns than to production patterns. The calculated proportions of chromium is sediments in different parts of the study area indicated that emissions from different industries have resulted locally in large quantities of chromium since the beginning of this century. Tannery discharges dominated chromium emission to water during the period 1920-1950.

After 1950, chromium emissions to water become increasingly related to emissions from the expanding steel industry. Today, the chromium originates from the more diffuse "consumption emissions" which are a function of the population distribution, with the large city areas dominating. Therefore, an important challenge for the future is to integrate both past and present knowledge of the use of toxic materials in society, when defining future strategies for water management. This will encourage increased awareness and discussion of the importance of the use of materials and "consumer" behaviour.

It should also have the effect of accelerating the production of environmentally viable substitutes and minimization of losses. Riverbeds and sediments in lakes and pasta; areas act as the ultimate sink of pollutants, i.e. where they are finally deposited. Therefore, element distributions in sediments reflect the load patterns over time within separate sub-drainage basins. More emphasis must be given to studying total flows of elements in the technosphere and their consequences as reflected in the aquatic environment.

Eutrophication of waters

During the last 20 years, the word "eutrophication" has been used more and more to denote the artificial and undesirable addition of plant nutrients, mainly nitrogen and phosphorous, to waterbodies. In some situations, this view can be misleading, since what is an undesirable addition to one waterbody, manifested by an intense proliferation of algae and higher aquatic plants, and their accumulation in the waterbody in excessive quantities, leading to fish kills and odour problems. These accumulations can result in detrimental changes in the water quality and in the living organisms, of waterbodies, which can interfere significantly with human use of the water resource - problems that are well-known all over the world and that are regarded as one of the most pervasive threats to aquatic ecosystems. Eutrophication, in the original sense, represents the natural aging process of a waterbody. A waterbody receives inflows of water from its surrounding drainage basin, along with materials carried in the water from the land surface, for example, following ran storm or from irrigation drainage. Materials associated with rain, snow and aerosols, as well as with groundwater inflows, can also directly enter a waterbody. The observed water quality and biological communities therefore, reflect the cumulative impacts of all the water and material inflows into the waterbody. Over time, a waterbody will be slowly filled in which soil particles and other materials carried by inflowing water, gradually enriching these sediments with nutrients and organic debris.

The organic material input, in turn, promotes plant growth which traps even more sediment until the depth of the waterbody decreases markedly and it eventually becomes a marsh, and, ultimately, a terrestrial system. This process usually takes many hundreds of thousands of years to occur, and is largely irreversible. Waterbodies undergoing such natural eutrophication generally have a good water quality and exhibit a diverse biological community throughout much of their existence. In an early phase of human settlement in a drainage basin, the growth of algae and other aquatic plants in a waterbody in the drainage basin is usually minimal, and generally in balance with the input of plant nutrients.

However, densely populated human settlement of a drainage basin, and the associated clearing of forests, development of farms and cities increased use of fertilizers and detergents, etc., usually changes the natural eutrophication process in a dramatic way, accelerating it. The runoff of most materials from the land surface to a waterbody, and ultimately to the sea, is greatly enhanced as the soil surface is covered and its permeability decreases. An increased input of plant nutrients can stimulate algae and aquatic plant growths which, in turn, can stimulate the growth of fish and other higher trophic level organisms in the aquatic food chain. This latter phenomenon is often termed cultural eutrophication to distinguish it from the natural process.

During the aging process of a waterbody, part of the imported nutrients, especially phosphorous, are accumulated and absorbed into the sediments at the bottom of the waterbody. Under natural conditions, only a small part of the sediment phosphorus pool is released back into the water column, so-called "internal loading". In overload waterbodies this nutrient regeneration increases and can play an important role in defining the trophic status of freshwaters. It was earlier believed that phosphorus release from the sediments occurred only in anaerobic bottom waters because of chemical reduction of iron (III) to iron (II)-compounds. Such conditions frequently occur in the hypolimnetic waters of deep lakes during the thermally-stratificated period—a processes easily demonstrated in laboratory experiments and field studies.

Recent sediment research, however, has shown phosphorus release from the sediments to be a much more complicated process, involving interactions of physical, chemical and biological mechanisms. The process includes mineralization of organic matter, desorption, dissolution of salts, ligand exchange equilibria, etc.

The main factors regulating the internal loading rates are redox conditions, nitrate concentrations, mineralization, effervescence, bioturbation, different sediment characteristics, high pH-values, diffusion, wind-induced turbulence and effects of phytoplankton and macrophytes growth. Substantial amounts of phosphorus can also be released into the water column the from sediments in shallow, well-mixed waterbodies. The dynamics and magnitude of phosphorus release from sediments in these types of waterbodies are affected primarily by physical factors, such as seasonal variations in water temperature and year-to-year differences in the water flushing rate. These factors, in turn, moderate chemical and microbiological processes which regulate the exchange of substances between sediments and water. Recovery of eutrophic waterbodies is delayed in many cases because of internal loading of phosphorus, which is able to maintain excessive levels of nutrients in the waterbodies. After the vegetation growth period, the major part of in-lake phosphorus is again deposited into the sediments, thereby allowing it to once again enrich the water column during the next growth season. This recycling process can go for a long period of time, jeopardizing the success of many eutrophication control programmes. Knowledge of the different mechanics regulating phosphorus release from sediments is a prerequisite for development of sound water management practices for eutrophic waterbodies.

In waters receiving excess quantities of nutrients, there is usually an increase in primary production: i.e., the production of planktonic algae and other aquatic vegetation. A moderate increase in the degree of eutrophication in nutrient-poor and slightly nutrient-rich waters can have some positive benefits with regard to increased fish production and yields.

Many people favour optimization of the reuse of aquatic plant nutrients; e.g., for aquaculture, the production of fish and other aquatic food organisms, as well as for irrigation and fertilization purposes. However, increased inputs of nutrients leads to several negative impacts, with vast direct or indirect effects on oxygen conditions, sediments, benthic vegetation types and fauna. Available evidence suggests that the symptoms of eutrophication of waters are basically similar in arctic, temperate and tropical/subtropical regions. The differences that do exist are related primarily to deviations in magnitude and/or timing. The typical characteristics of eutrophication are:

— a shift in algal community from diatoms to a dominance of green and blue green algae, causing so-called algal blooms, resulting in turbid waters with low transparencies and odour problems;

— expansion of macrophyte growth; and,

— oxygen depletion of bottom waters, causing widespread elimination of benthic fauna and fish-kills.

A specific noticeable eutrophication problem is the appearance of *toxic algae*. The more degraded as ecosystem becomes the more readily a few specialized species can dominate the biocommunity, causing impoverishment of species diversity. Algae, capable of excreting toxic substances, can dominate the plankton community during periods when the in-lake conditions are specifically favourable to them.

The existence of toxic algae has been known since long time, i.e. in connection with suspected cases of poisoning of livestock. Since then, research activities have been focused to identify the active toxins and their chemical and toxicological characteristics. Some of the toxins have been identified as saxitoxins and microcystins and have been found to be associated with heavy blooms species of the algal genera Anabaena, Microcystis and Aphanisomenon. However, other types of algae can also excretetoxic substances. The gradual eutrophication of many coastal waters increase the risk of the appearance of toxic algae.

A well known example during recent years is the sudden blooms of dinoflagellates such as those of Chrysochromulina polylepsis in the costal areas of Skagerak and Kattegatt, close to the North Sea, which caused great harm to the aquaculture industry raising fish and mussels for consumption. Blue-green algae occasionally have proven to be a potential health risk to human beings.

In numerous cases, people have been reported to become ill after swimming in waterbodies with algal blooms, the symptoms being allergies fever, vomiting and diarrhoea. In cattle numerous deaths occur annually due to the strychnine like action of these toxins in ingested at eutrophic watering points, especially in warmer climates. For a long time the sea was considered as an almost infinite resource. However, the natural enrichment with nutrients and the resultant enhanced algal growth along coastlines due to up welling by currents, known as "red tides", indicate that the same type of eutrophication processes also occur in the marine environment. The ongoing excessive nutrient loads to coastal waters in many developed countries have increased during recent years, causing a growing number of eutrophication problems.

In many coastal waters near towns and industrial plants, eutrophication and oxygen depletion were tangible problems long before they began to be noticed further out at sea. They became particularly serious where pollutants were discharged in locations with limited water exchange, such as inlets, estuaries and coastal archipelagos. Harbours with heavy traffic have proven especially vulnerable to environmental degradation. Serious oxygen depletion, elimination of benthic fauna and fish and mussel kills caused by blooms of toxic algae have now been reported from an increasing number of sites along coastal areas in many countries. These waters mainly receive nutrients via rivers of from the open sea.

Contrary to deteriorating freshwater conditions associated with excessive phosphorus inputs, nitrogen is commonly regarded as the major growth limiting nutrient in coastal waters. Elevated concentrations of nitrogen in riven waters have often been observed close to agricultural areas, where highly mechanized "industrial" agriculture has been targeted for the development of sound land-use practices whereby nutrient emissions to water can be kept at a minimum. A waterbody undergoing cultural eutrophication can be treated so that it will again exhibit an "aging" rate more characteristic of natural eutrophication. However, for waterbodies undergoing extensive and difficult to administer. Nevertheless, past scientific studies have provide ample evidence that technically effective control of eutrophication of lakes and reservoirs is possible. Whether or not effective control also is economically feasible, however, depends on the dominant factors in a specific situation.

During the last several decades, a number of studies focusing on the eutrophication problem and the relationship between nutrient load and responses in waterbodies of different character have been undertaken. Many types of eutrophication relationships and mathematical models, both simple and complex, eutrophication study have been presented in the scientific literature.

In a world-wide eutrophication study during the 1970's carried out under the auspicious of the OECD, a number of the empirical models were tested and evaluated. Many of these models proved to be practical tools for managerial efforts to control eutrophication and have found a wide application. The effective control of eutrophication of lakes and reservoirs is strongly linked to control of the basic causative factor, namely the input of excessive quantities of aquatic plant nutrients.

Based on the limiting nutrient concept, practical experience suggests that an effective, long term eutrophication control measure for fresh waters is to reduce the phosphorus load to the waterbody. Since the beginning of the 1970's, world-wide efforts to control eutrophication have been focused on treating pointsource municipal and industrial sewage in treatment plants, using chemical precipitation agents to eliminate phosphorus.

Other remedial actions have been nutrient diversion or modified land-use practices to reduce nonpoint source pollution from rural and urban areas, as well as in-lake control measures primarily aimed at reducing internal loading. The gradual eutrophication of many waterbodies close to densely populated areas in several developed countries has been slowed down. In some cases, eutrophication process has been reversed and water quality improved. However, eutrophication of waters still ranks as one of the most pervasive water problems on Earth. If has not been possible to stop the increase in nutrient loads to waterbodies from nonpoint sources. Lakes and reservoirs in many agricultural areas are still threatened by excessive nutrient enrichments. For costal areas, ways have to be found to reduce also the nitrogen input, Increased efforts are being devoted to supply the existing waste water treatment plants with facilities for nitrogen removal. However, a considerable part of the nitrogen input originates from nonpoint sources, mainly as a consequence of intense farming activities. However, atmospheric inputs make up a considerable part of the total nitrogen input to a waterbody. Effective means to control nitrogen inputs to waters comprise several types of activities for reducing the pollutant load mainly from the agricultural, transportation and energy production sectors. For some decades, Scandinavian countries, Canada and the northeastern parts of United States have suffered from increasing inputs of acidic airborne compounds originating from sulpher and nitrogen emissions in Europe and North America and their long range atmospheric transportation.

It was the alarming conditions in lakes become suspiciously clear, and their beds were being gradually covered by ever thicker growths of white moss. Since the connection between fish kills and acidification was first observed in the mid 1960's, it has been proven beyond any doubt that acid precipitation in drainage basins with frantic rock types, can lead to drastic changes in the animal and plant communities in lakes. Several ten thousands of lake in the Scandinavian countries, Canada and the northeastern parts of the United States are presently so acidic that vulnerable and important plant and animal species have become extinct.

In the field of paleolimnology, research workers have been able to illustrate the dramatic, and almost instant, decrease in pH that started only some decades ago. Sediment cores, being "fingerprints of the past", bear clear evidence of the acidification process with the occurrence of so called "indicator organisms", such as specific siliceous algae, characteristic of various natural environmental conditions even since the last Ice Age. Changes in the siliceous algal composition became discernible as early as the 1950's and the changes since then are usually very dramatic.

When waters are subject to acidification the process takes place essentially in three stages:

— In the *first stage there* is no marked or persistent lowering of the pH because of the available buffering capacity in the drainage basin; however, in due course the content of bicarbonate ion levels will decline.

— In the *second stage*, when the bicarbonate content has gone low enough, large influxes of hydrogen ions can no longer be neutralized; the pH value becomes unstable and begins to decline rapidly; and,

— In the *third state* the pH value has decreased and subsequently stabilized at around 4.5, even if the precipitation is more acidic, and the influx of hydrogen ions continues.

Several factors can influence the susceptibility of lakes and watercourses to acidification, including:

— the location of the lake in the drainage basin area to the waterbody surface area;

— the ability of the soil to neutralize acids;

— the extent of humic content in the inflowing waters, and

— the water resident time.

As a result of ongoing acidification, there is often a decline in, or even elimination of, the fish populations. In more general terms, a reduction in the number and variety of plant and animal species, or changes in, and replacement of, certain aquatic organisms occur. The direct cause of many fish kills in a acid lakes seems to be aluminium poisoning.

The concentration of this element, which has a strongly toxic effect on many aquatic organisms, increase dramatically in the water as acidification progrèsses. The mobility and concentrations of other toxic metals, such as cadmium, mercury and since, are also enhanced in acidic waters as a result of increased leaching from the surrounding soils in the drainage basin. The only long-term solution to combat acidification is to dramatically lower the sulphur and nitrogen emissions to the atmosphere. Scientists have estimated this reduction must be around 80 and 50 per cent, respectively, based on the critical load approach. In the meanwhile, attempts to replenish bicarbonate supplies in lake waters, thereby counteracting the acidification of lakes, have been intimated in large-scale liming programmes, mainly with lime additions directly into lakes, but also on the land surface in the drainage basins in extreme cases. Despite some early success, these programmes are being reconsidered with regard to their acute negative effects on the remaining biota.

In the early 1960's, Rachel Carson, in her book *Silent Spring*, alerted the world to the disruption of ecosystems by the uncontrolled release of halogenated hydrocarbon pesticides as a result of agricultural and public health activities. As a consequence of her discoveries, many Northern hemisphere countries began to strongly regulate the use of biocides in the early 1970's. She correctly predicted negative impacts on higher trophic level organisms, due to pesticides. The regulatory activities charted a new course in environmental protection. For the first time, chemical use began to be restricted to maintain the integrity of biological communities.

Atmospheric and oceanic concentrations of halogenated hydrocarbon pesticides are mainly made up of industrially used materials, and exhibit similar values in both the Northern and Southern hemispheres. Such data indicate continued human use of these toxic materials. The data emphasize the crucial need for global-scale environmental monitoring and control of these environmentally-persistent substances. The most effective course of action would be to conduct a monitoring programme, using appropriate indicator organisms, with the goal of ascertaining whether or not aquatic and terrestrial ecosystems may be threatened by present day usages. Further, the compilation of data on the production and use of these chemicals also is most important for assessing their present day distributions.

Persistent, slowly degraded organic pollutants of human origin are widely distributed in the environment, and have properties that result in their accumulation in organisms. It is difficult to anticipate their eventual distribution and fate. Thus, their environmental effects are hard to interpret and relate to the sources. Substances with the potential to become pollutants are introduced into the environments in either an active or passive manner.

Pesticides are actively dispersed within more or less defined areas to limit or eradicate animals or plants interfering with the well-being of humans or production of food and fibers. They are further distributed by natural transportation mechanisms. Thus, it is not surprising that these compounds can be transported to areas which are remote from the sites of their intended use. The best known example is DDT, whose use as an insecticide has resulted in world-wide contamination, with unforeseen effects.

It is, however, more alarming that serious ecological effects have been documented for chemicals never intended to be distributed in the environment. For example, PCB's are one group of the many substances used as components in various industrial products and applications, which have subsequently contaminated the global ecosystem. There are reasons to believe there are other chemicals with similar properties to DDT and PCB's circulating in the environment. In fact, the major part of the chlorinated, organic materials found in many organisms have yet to be identified, and their effects assessed.

Atmospheric transportation is one mechanism that explains the appearance of pollutants far from their known source. They are precipitated to the Earth's surface via dry and wet deposition. However, comparing their distribution and levels in terrestrial and aquatic ecosystems, the most contaminated organisms typically are found in the aquatic environment. Because these substances usually have a pronounced hydrophobic character, their ubiquitous appearance in the aquatic food web, in contrast to their lesser impact on terrestrial ecosystems, is still not satisfactorily understood.

There may exist mechanisms that allow airborne residues to settle more efficiently on the water surface than on the ground. Interfaces, such as those between air and water, and between sediments and water, seem to be crucial in the transfer of pollutants between abiotic and biotic materials in the aquatic environment. Pollutants are trapped and enriched in the thin surface mycrolayer that covers most bodies of water, and aldo in the surface sediments of lakes and oceans. Low water solubilities, in combination with high lipid/water partition coefficient seem to determine the rate and extent of organic pollutant adsorption at these interfaces. Thus, the same chemical properties that directly affect bioaccumulation and biomagnification of pollutants in organisms and in food webs, are also of prime importance in pollutant adsorption process elsewhere in aquatic systems.

Organisms living close to interfaces, are therefore continuously exposed to higher concentrations of organic contaminants than those living in the water column environment. In addition, processes in the surface microlayer may allow dissolved pollutants to becoming incorporated in particles, thus making them more available for food chain transport. Since many organisms use the surface water and/or bottoms of lakes and oceans as habitats during part of their life cycles, such exposure might result in biological affects. A better knowledge of mechanisms governing the transfer and transport of the persistent pollutants in the aquatic ecosystem is therefore required to predict and initiate the appropriate measures to restrict or mitigate their biological effects.

Some substances, once believed to be harmless, have subsequently proved to cause large scale and unforeseeable damage to aquatic organisms. These substances are of various origins and composition, but are together classed as stable or persistent. They have three decisive properties in common. They are either.

— not readily degradable.

— toxic to living organisms; and;

— bioaccummuable.

Examples of these types of pollutants are stable organic compounds, mainly halogenated hydrocarbons and organo-metallic compounds. Several of these compounds have been used, and continue to be used, as pesticides in many countries. The well-known PCB's, with wide industrial application, are also chemically-similar compounds. Organo-metallic compounds are those containing both carbon and metals, the most well-known being organotin compounds such as anti-fouling preparations for boat hulls, pot constructions. fishing gear, etc. Dioxins and dibenzofurans are not directly manufactured, but can form during the production, use or burning of organic matter in the presence of chlorine. They are produced in most combustion processes, even natural ones such as forest fires. Dioxins have been shown to be emitted to the environment from sources such as flue gas from waste incinerators, iron and steel works, vehicle exhausts, effluents from pulp and paper mills and coal-fired power stations. Dioxins are a group of 210 chemically-identical compounds. Twelve of these are considered to be extremely toxic; the so-called "dirty dozen". The expression "TCEE equivalents" is used to indicate the combined toxic effect of various dioxins, with reference to the quantity of 2,3,7,8-TCDD that would have the same effect.

Dioxins are sometimes called "the most dangerous poisons that exist". Their presumed extreme toxicity has been questioned lately, because of lack of consistent evidence of this effect. By no means, they certainly are acutely toxic. However, by comparison, the tetanus toxins produced by the bacillus *Clostridium tetan* is considered to be a thousand times more poisonous than dioxins. Furthermore, toxins produced by the bacillus *Bacillus botulinus*, which can cause severe food-poisoning, can be 10,000 times more poisonous than dioxins.

Over the years it has been observed that several mammals have suffered a marked decline because of increased pollution from man-made substances. Their bioaccuation capacity makes highest trophic-level predators specifically vulnerable. PCB's have substantially reduced selected seal populations, because of a variety of effects including: changed uterine conditions, skin disorders, claw changes, intestinal ulcers, kidney damage, adrenocortical hyperplasia and skeletal leisons.

Special emphasis has been placed on uterine disorders in the females, specifically tumors and stenosis of the uterus. Females that have pups can pass these organochlorine compounds to their pups in their milk. Disturbed hormone production can also result in metabolic disorders and impairment of the immune system, in both males and females. DDT and DDE, and toxaphene have caused damage to fishes, birds and mammals. These substances are toxic to fish in very low concentrations.

DDT and DDE may cause cancer in mammals. In predatory birds, like the white-tailed sea eagle, osprey and guillemot, these persistent compounds have caused sterility. Where birds have been able to produce and lay eggs, they have often failed to hatch because of the shells being abnormally thin and brittle. The main reason why birds have been particularly affected is that they lack mechanisms to eliminate DDT and DDE, and toxaphene from their bodies. Thus, increasingly high concentrations can therefore build up in their tissues. Chlorinated organic compounds have been found to cause damage to fishes and benthic animals, including fin erosion, skeletal deformities, fewer iarvae and fry, deformed gills, impaired immune systems, disturbed osmoregulation, jaw deformities and skin ulcers. Chlorinated organic compounds have also affected the survival of common mussels and amphipos crustanceans, and have caused changes to algal communities.

Shortly after the turn of the century, as oil began to replace sail and steam as the principal energy source for ship propulsion, and because of the increased demand for transportation of oil, raw materials and gods to support the industrialization process, the potential for the pollution of the oceans was recognized. Every year, approximately 3.5 million tonnes of oil are released into the world's oceans, representing one metric tonne of oil spilled for every thousand tonnes of oil extracted.

Oil gets into the sea in natural and man-induced ways. Oil releases can be divided about equally between land-based sources and sea-based sources-Land-based sources could be managed by coastal states via regulatory actions. Sea-based pollution, on the other hand, is linked mainly to maritime transportation, and requires international action. The most dramatic form of input of oil into the sea results from accidents often in form of oil tankers springing a leak, or a "blow-out" from an oil platform in an offshore field. Such incidents result in the release of large quantities of oil in a short time, which can be carried far from the scene of the accident by currents and winds, and which usually causes widespread damage. It has often been reported that oil contamination in the form of dissolved and dispersed petroleum residues is present almost everywhere in the world's oceans. Oil is an organic compound that is not readily soluble in water. Mineral oils are produced from crude oil, which is a mixture of different hydrocarbons containing small amounts of nitrogen, sulphur and traces of about 50 other elements.

Depending on the composition and amount of oil discharged, the duration of the discharge, the time of the year it occurs, the water and air temperatures, weather conditions, species composition in the area affected, etc., the amount of damage caused can vary in a given situation. As far as accidents involving major oils concerned, it has been found that the biggest environmental threats in more temperature waters are to sea birds, benthic organisms and the animals living in, and dependent on, the beaches and rocky shores.

The water column and its animal life actually a appearance to be able to recover relatively quickly after pollution ceases. Benthic animals on the other hand, cannot escape, and either have to be able to adapt to the hydrocarbons or else die. Considerable uncertainty exists concerning the accumulation of petroleums hydrocarbons in benthic sediments. Sea-birds are affected in two ways by acute oil discharges.

First, birds in the area become oiled, making their plumage useless as thermal insulation thereby causing hypothermia and death. Second, the oil severely impairs the shore zones as food sources. Thus, when a major oil spill occurs, sea-bird populations are the ones to be hit earliest and hardest by the oil patches and slicks floating on the surface of the water. Marine pollution problems in the developed countries are fairly well-researched and quantified. In contrast, marine pollution problems in developing countries are generally less well understood or acknowledged than these of developed countries.

Many developing countries are situated in tropical zones, and their marine biotypes have different susceptibilities to pollutants and environmental stresses. It might be speculated that marine pollution problems in developing countries would be less severe, due to a lower degree of industrialization and the generally sparser populations.

A romantic image of tropical seas with clear turquoise waters, palm-fringed beaches and coral islands springs to mid. Indeed, by global standards the seas of many developing countries are relatively uncontaminated. However, there are localized instances of acute marine pollution in most developing countries. These damage the marine environment and resources, and constitute dangers to public health.

Those instances are "not spot" of marine pollution. The principal causes to pollution are uncontrolled disposal of sewage and industrial effluents, often mixed together. To make matters worse, there is usually a severe lack of data on the pollutant levels and fluxes, an inadequate understanding of the seriousness of the consequences, and an insufficient legal framework to take measures to eliminate pollution. Urbanization is increasing very rapidly in many developing countries.

Disposal of large quantities of untreated sewage from coastal cities often leads to contamination of shallow inshore waters with pathogenic bacteria and versus, endangering public health. In addition, organic substances and nutrient overload may lead to eutrophication in the adjacent marine habitats. Many developing countries have an urgent desire to industrialize as rapidly as possible. Pollution control measures may be viewed as a hindrance to this process. Industrial effluents are often unregulated and unmonitored, and toxic compounds may be released into the environment without regard to their negative impacts. There is a short-sighted inclination to try to attract foreign investment by offering tax breaks and tax environmental regulations; this may be further exacerbated by corrupt tendencies.

Agricultural chemicals such as DDT and other pesticides, are applied indiscriminately in some cases, and conveyed to the sea by runoff. Oil pollution threatens marine biotopes, particularly in the Caribbean Sea, Red Sea, Arabian Gulf and parts of West Africa Mangroves and sea-birds are especially prone to oil, and beaches may be anesthetically spoiled. Major damming of rivers and shoreline engineering alter sedimentation patterns, often resulting in increased erosion. Coralline-sand extraction can cause serious erosion problems on some small islands.

6

Marine Pollutants

The activities of man have exaggerated the problem in the sense of causing a marked increase in the amount of pollutant present. Common pollutants associated with the marine environment are the following:

Pathogens

Pathogenic materials are the living organisms that can produce sickness or biological unbalance in either plants or animals within the ocean itself or in humans who either contact oceanic waters or eat the organisms caught in the water. These include a wide variety or bacteria, protozoa, viruses and fungi. The most common of these are normally associated with human waste products and are found in sewage. However, other pathogens may occur in non-waste disposal areas where environmental conditions are such that the proper conditions are present for growth and reproduction.

Sediments

Sediments are always present to some extent in the marine environment. Generally speaking, concentration of suspended solids increases with proximity to the coast, with the maximum occurring in the riverine and estuarine environment. As man impinges on the coastal regions, his construction and agriculture efforts generally tend to increase erosion and therefore increase the amount of sediment in suspension. These sediments have a marked effect on plant growth since they block out a large portion of the light normally reaching greater depths and therefore decrease photosynthetic activity. In some cases rooted plants are completely destroyed by this process.

As sediments are deposited on the bottom they will cover up bottom dwelling organisms (benthos) such as oysters and may even smoothes them under extreme conditions. In addition to destroying bottom dwelling life, deposited sediments tend to make the water shallower so that, in regions travelled by ships, periodic dredging is required. Dredging and the disposal of dredged material have their own set of environmental problems which will be discussed later.

The sediments of concern are primarily inorganic silts and clays since the larger particles such as sand and gravel do not remain in suspension for any monegligible period of time. They result from soil being washed from land areas into sea, in many cases because man has changed the character of the affected area by agricultural or construction activities. Once the sediments settle to the bottom they may be responded in shallow water by natural causes, such as storms, or by man as an operator of a power boat. The relative importance of recreational vessels in maintaining turbid conditions in shallow water is not well known at this time.

Solid waste

The disposal of solid waste is a critical urban problem

at the present time primarily because areas suitable for the dumping of the sevoluminous materials are becoming scarcer, especially when transportation costs are considered. Due primarily to low transportation costs the ocean has been used as a dumping ground for solid waste for centuries. The solid waste most frequently marine dumped is sludged materials left over as a by-product from domestic sewage treatment. However the unused products of industry and the used-up products of society are also discharged into the sea. If the product discharged at sea contains materials which may be leached into the oceanic environment, a serious problem could develop, especially if the materials are toxic. However, if the solid materials are inert, a little forethought may result in some benefit to the marine environment. Artificial fishing reefs, for example, have been very successful in certain areà, especially for small fish.

On the other hand, solid waste materials also can serve as a pollutant in the sense of destroying habits when this materials is dumped into marsh or wetland area. Until recent years marshes and wetlands were assumed to have no practical value, but recently we have found these areas to serve as breeding grounds for most of the commercial species of fish along with many other organisms important in the food chains of all marine creatures. Thus there is a growing movement not only to save the wetlands from further destruction but also in many cases to attempt to rehabilitate these areas of extreme biological importance.

Excess Heat

Excess heat, when added to the marine environment, changes ambient conditions, and these changes may be detrimental to the organisms present. The amount of heat that is detrimental and the extent of the degradation is determined by a number of factors to be discussed later. The primary source of this heat is, of course, from electrical generating plants, whether they by fossil fuelled or nuclear powered.

Fresh Water and Brine

Although fresh water may be in great demand ashore, too much of it in the ocean obviously will produce a marked environmental change within a small area. This change may be caused by poorly designed storm drainage systems, water diversion networks associated with dams, and effluent of some industrial process. Excessive fresh water usually is not a critical problem but it could be one if the effluents were directed into a sensitive area.

The introduction of brine into the marine environment is similar in its effect to that of fresh water except in the opposite direction. The organisms acclaimed to a particular salinity now find themselves in a more saline environment which could cause permanent damage. Brine is a by-product of desalination plants, but changes in the salinity regime also can produced by changes in estuarine channel depths necessitate by shipping considerations.

Toxics

Toxic inorganics are materials commonly used in industry, many of them primarily to control the growth of algae or to destroy pathogens. Chlorine is an excellent example of this. In larger quantities this material is relatively harmless; however, in larger quantities it may be quite destructive. The key here apparently is how much and how often. There are perhaps 35 to 40 commonly used toxic inorganics and these should be very closely controlled by the user.

The toxic organics are the most disturbing of the modern day chemicals commonly discharged either purposefully or accidentally into the marine environment. These include the biocides such as fungicides, herbicides, insecticides, rodenticides, and also the additional organics including halogenated hydrocarbons, petroleum and industrial chemicals. The most disturbing toxic organics are the pesticides such as DDT and ketone which have the unfortunate characteristic of being more soluble in oil than in water so that they tend to collect within the fatty tissues of marine organisms. They are also very stable compounds which do not deteriorate very easily over a long period of time.

These find way into the ocean both as manufacturing effluent and as runoff after utilization. Perhaps the most disturbing aspect of there toxic organics is that there are hundreds available with many more being produced by the chemical industry without any real knowledge of their long term effects.

Petroleum

Although petroleums may be classed as a toxic organic, it is a naturally occurring materials and is biodegradeable, given enough time. Petroleum in its natural state is a very complex organic materials containing a large number of separate compounds, each of which seems to have it own effect on the biosphere. These effects are not too well known and opinions within the scientific community range from one extreme to the other with respect to the toxicity of the material. It is a aesthetically disleasing of nothing else. Petroleum finds its way into the marine environment due to accidents such as tanker damage or transfer loss, natural seepage, offshore production losses, losses associated with refineries, from runoff originating as drippings or disposal of used automobile lubricants, and unburned hydrocarbons emitted into the atmosphere as internal combustion exhaust.

Nutrients

Nutrients are what are commonly called fertilizers, those chemicals required by plants. The most common of these are the compounds of nitrogen and phosphorous. They exist in the natural environment at all times and some of them are recycled naturally by decaying living organisms. However, the activities of man have added to the total nutrient load of almost all coastal areas. When nutrient levels get out of hand, plants grow unchecked so that decaying plants exist in such great numbers that the oxygen supply becomes rapidly depleted. These nutrients are present in domestic sewage effluents, agricultural runoff, and the little understood but apparently important non-point source runoff from urban areas.

Radioactivity

Radioactive materials are not only discharged to the marine environment by nuclear power plants, fuel production and reprocessing plants, and uranium activities such as the burning of coal, when coal is burned it emits radioactive particles to the atmosphere which are then washed into the sea at a greater rate than any known nuclear power plants at this time. Other sources of radioactivity are the natural background, weapons testing, mine drainage, accidental spillage, and a few isolated industries.

One of the partially unsolved problems associated with the use of nuclear energy for electrical power is the long term storage or disposal of spent fuels. This storage must be in an area such that there are no pathways back to man, and deep oceans have been suggested as meeting this criterion.

Oxygen Demand

Oxygen demand materials are those which require oxygen for degeneration and therefore steal oxygen which would normally be utilized by marine animals. Thus if too many oxygen demand materials are placed in the marine environment, the animal population will be markedly decreased due to the lack of oxygen. Sewage sludge and any other organic waste materials, even that resulting from excessive plant growth due to an over supply of nutrients, are examples of common oxygen demand materials.

Acids and Bases

The discharge of acid and bases to the marine environment can be quite disturbing to the natural ecological balance of the systems. The normal pH of oceanic water is somewhere around 8.0, slightly basic. This is maintained by the carbonate system wherein carbon dioxide is moved back and forth through a chemical reaction to bicarbonate and carbonic acid. If a large amount of acid or base is introduced into the system, the carbonate reaction will be offset and an important element of the environment will be affected. In addition, there are large synergistic effects associated with pH. Most toxic materials, for example, increase their toxicity under condition of low pH.

The sources of acidic or basic material are primarily industrial with some of this material reaching the marine environment from accidental discharges and the rupturing of tankers.

Aesthetic Considerations

Aesthetically displeasing materials include all the stuff one finds in the ocean that is unpleasant to look at or to smell. Tar balls, floatables, gas (often hydrogen sulphide) producing materials, and colouring, agents are some examples of pollutants affecting the sense, although in some cases these materials presents no real threat to the ecology of an area, when the area is being used for recreation, the quality of the surroundings becomes very important. Thus even though an aesthetically unpleasant area may still be useable for many activities, it is one which probably generates the most public response because no special instruments are required to measure the degradation; it is obvious. We thereafter find that aesthetic considerations very often are more important to the average person than those that may be more damaging from an ecological point of view.

Management Problems

Even though the major pollutants have been delineated the management of marine pollution turns out to be quite complex. The reason for this is that the marine environment is used by man in many different ways and this multi-use has a number of ramifications. In the first place each oceanic activity pursued by man may produce a whole spectrum of pollutants. A moving ship, for example, may not only discharge pollutants in the form of waste products from the people living aboard, oil from pumping its bilges, and heat from the discharge of its condensers, it may also require depending of a harbour channel. This may produce a salinity change in addition to sedimentation problems associated with the maintenance dredging required.

Each pollutant may come from many different users. The nutrients which primarily seem to come from the effluent of sewage disposal plants also may come from storm drainage of urban areas in the form of waste products of domestic animals, along with runoff from agricultural areas that have been fertilized by either commercial fertilizers or farm animals.

Complicating the situation still further is the fact that pollutants sometimes affect each other. An interesting example of this occurs in baltimore. Maryland a rather large, industrial city located on a small arm of the Chesapeake Bay. A significant portion of the effluents. It turns out that the waste ferrous sulphate from the steel plant combines with the phosphate in the sewage plant effluent to form a precipitate. Thus the phosphate ends up on the bottom of baltimore Harbour rather than dissolved in the waters of Chesapeake Bay. In this case it appears that an industrial; effluent is utilized profitably (although accidentally) to decrease the input of a pollutant comprising one of the larger pollution problems in the Chesapeake Bay.

Another example of the effect of one pollutant on another is the attraction of heavy metals to suspended sediments. Most of the heavy metals in coastal waters seems to be swept out of the water by sinking sedimentary particles and end up in the bottom deposits. This may or may not be desirable. If the heavy metals then find their way into bottom dwelling organisms which, in turn, find their way into a food chain pathway to man, then this obviously is not desirable. A third example of this synergistic effect of two or more pollutants is the effect of oil on pesticides, combined with sediments. As indicated previously, pesticides in the main are more soluble in oil then they are in water so that if there is oil present in oceanic water, it will tend to concentrate any pesticides that also may be present. Oil also has an affinity for sediments and as it collects on the suspended particles, their weight is increased to the point where they sink to the bottom. Portions of the inshore marine environment thus are covered with sediments very rich in both oil and pesticides. Any management activity therefore must be very careful in controlling one pollutant not to disturb the conditions of another so that a greater problem is not generated as a result of some "solution".

The introduction of foreign material into the marine environment is not always detrimental to man or to the environment either. The construction of fishing reefs was mentioned previously as one example of man's improving the environment by introducing foreign materials. Another example of this is the generation of wetlands in some instance due to man's carelessness. In many areas the increased erosion produced by construction activities has resulted in large areas of siltation where these eroded sediments have been deposited in the shoreline areas. After stabilisation, populations of marsh grass have been seen to spring up in many of these newly crated areas. In the main there has been no planning for this type of rehabilitation, but recent experimental work indicates that production of marshlands may very well be a common tool of the estuarine planner of the future.

Pollution Control Costs

It should be constantly kept in mind that wastes are never destroyed. Waste materials, whether liquid, solid or gaseous, either can be moved from one location to a other or can have their form or chemical composition altered. But the material is still there. Some authors have suggested the term "waste placement" be used instead of "waste disposal". Nothing is ever consumed; it is just used for a while and then pushed aside. Entropy is increased but there is no decrease in mass, and there is usually on increase in the amount of energy required to keep the system going. This is why recycling is so attractive. The advantages in terms of energy and natural resource requirements along with the usual decrease in pollutants, are very strong. This is why recycling is so attractive. The advantages in terms of energy and natural resource requirements, along with the usual decrease in pollutants, are very strong. The key appears to be cost, with must of the cost setting in the area of transportation. When the cost of recycled materials in low enough to be competitive with new material then recycling will be increased to the point where it becomes a common part of every product that we use. Cost is a major part of every pollution problem. For example, ocean dumping has been criticized by many to the point where the U.S. Environmental Protection agency is attempting to stop it completely. In this context ocean dumping usually means dumping in the near coastal zone: within 10 or 15 miles of the area where these waste are generated. One satisfactory solution would be to require a distance of a thousand miles from the coast before dumping could proceed. Here, the pathways back to man would be extremely difficult and highly improbable. However, the cost of transporting this material such a great distance is, at this time, more than society is willing to pay so that this does not appear to be a viable solution.

Effects of marine pollution

The opportunities to study the effects of oil presented by continuous natural seepage, refinery effluent, oil rig discharges, etc., on the one hand, and the more massive short-term injections of oil arising from oil rig blowouts and tanker accidents on the other, are different, and differences exist even within these two broad classes. It may therefore by though that results obtained in one case may not be applicable in the others. It is thus worthwhile to consider types differences and to assess the extent to which results obtained at the various sites and incidents may be of universal application. The first point to note in this endeavour is that oil does not dissolve in water. It floats on the sea surface as a thin layer when spilled or otherwise discharged because it is less dense than water and insoluble in it. This thin layer tends to break into droplets by wave action and these droplets become dispersed in the volume of sea water beneath the slick.

Photochemical and biological oxidation of the sicks and of the dispersed oil droplets take place producing oxygenated derivatives of the original oil components and these may form true solutions in water. Thus the area of sea covered by the surface slick is proportional to the magnitude of the spillage, but the concentrations in the sea arise from the slow dispersion of droplets of oxygenated derivatives. Sea water concentrations are therefore a function of mass transfer rates from slick to water and not a function of the quantity spilled.

Sea water concentrations are in fact independent of the quantity spilled, provided a surface layer has formed above the sea water volume in question. If more or less oil is spilled or otherwise introduced to the sea the result is more or less sea affected rather than that a given volume is affected to a greater or lesser extent. Oil concentrations are therefore controlled by the in solubility of the oil and mass transfer rates from surface slicks to the underlying sea. In the absence of detailed knowledge of mass transfer rates it is not possible to calculate the resulting concentrations, but upper limits can easily be established. Thus if the slick thickness to which the oil spreads and from which it subsequently disperses to the water is 0.1 mm, then the maximum concentration which can achieved if the oil were instantaneously dispersed uniformly in the top metre of sea would be 100 ppm.

Concentrations over other depth ranges and for other thicknesses are of course pro data. It must be concluded therefore that is we leave aside for the time being the possible environmental effects of continuous oil slicks on the sea surface which occur when the capacity of the aqueous phase for oil is exceeded, we can discuss the other oil concentration-related aspects in the same manner whether a surface slick is present or not and whether the oil in question across from a natural seep, a blowout, cargo tank rupture or operational discharge from ship, oil rig or refinery. Generally speaking, we have limited our discussions to those materials introduced into the marine environment that are the direct result of man's activities, and with a few minor exceptions we shall continue to limit our discussions of pollution to those activities of man and to consider the deleterious effects of natural occurrences.

Pollutant types

There are three basic type of pollutants: the pathogenic, the aesthetic, and the ecomorphic. Pathogenic pollutants are those which cause disease. This disease may be fatal if the pollutant is a lethal poison. Aesthetic pollutants are those pollutants causing a change in the environment displeasing to the eye, ear, or nose of man. Ecomorphic pollutants, on the other hand, are those pollutants which produce a change in the physical characteristics of the environment in such a way that there may be drastic changes in the structure or composition of the biosphere. Obviously, these three types of pollutants are not of equal import.

Pathogenic pollutants are certainly much more serious than the other two; however, ecomorphic pollutants are often an indicator of more serious types of pollution to follow . Furthermore, since pollution is man-produced and the effects are suffered by man, aesthetic problems are certainly of interest. Nevertheless in any management situation when trade-offs are required, it will certainly be necessary to rank different types of pollutants so that society can determine how it would like to spend is limited funds of time, effort, and money.

Acute effects

Let us look first at the pathogenic pollutants since these are obviously the most important. The effects of pathogenic pollutants are either acute or chronic. Acute effects are those which occur in a relatively short period of time while chronic effects may take time to be noticed, as in the case of carcinogenic pollutants, or the effect may be noticed immediately but continued for a very long period of time. The acute effects are the easiest to determine because of the short time between administration and affection. The easiest way of measuring acute effect is by feeding the pollutant in question to test organisms, such as since or selected fish, and observing the dosage required to will 50% of the organisms involved. This is usually done by feeding a pollution of test organisms increasing amounts of the pollutant, and for each dosage the number of individuals that succumb is noted.

Another way of examining acute effect is to observe the effect of a given pollutant concentration on organisms over a somewhat longer period of time, noting how long it takes for given dosage to produce mortalities. This say be done by giving a predetermined concentration of the pollutant to the test animals and observing how long it takes to kill half of them.

Charonic effects

With the asymptotic values, suggests another concept : the threshold value. There appears to be a dose size for each pathogen below which the pollutant has no effect. The concern with threshold values for various pollutants is one aspect of the study of chronic effects. Chronic effects are the most difficult to measure because of the time involved; in some cases cancers have developed as long as 25 years after initial exposure to the carcinogenic agent. Nevertheless, measurements have been made and for many materials threshold value seems to describe the data reasonably well. Most experiments need some measure of the effect on the organisms other than death, so that many different measures are used. These are : deformity in the growth of organisms, damage to particular organs, change in heartbeat or breathing rate, genetic damage to individuals, change in the rate of increase of a population, life expectancy of individuals within a particular population, and fecundity of females with the population. Unfortunately, and index may be very descriptive of the effect of a pollutant on a particular species, but it may be completely ineffective in describing what happens when this pollutant comes in contact with other species.

Synergism

Another complication in the examination and quantification of pathogenic pollutants is the phenomenon of synergism. A synergistic effect occurs when the combined effect of two or more materials acting together is greater than would be expected from the simple sum of the individual effects. Temperature, for example, is a very strong synergistic parameter, generally enhancing most pollutant effects as temperature is increased. The same is true of salinity and dissolved oxygen. Some pollutants, on the other hand, tend to decrease the effects of others, as might be in the case of a strong acid and a strong base present at the same time. Other pollutants may cause strong pathogens to be precipitated out of the water column or to be collected on sediments, so that in either case they end up on the bottom. Thus it is extremely important in the analysis of any pollutant to be aware of the other materials present and their synergistic tendencies. Within the marine biosphere many organisms are affected by various pollutants. Whether or not a particular organism is affected by any given pollutants will depend on any variable. For example, many pollutants are found only in he water column while others, such as some of the pesticides and heavy metals, are adsorbed onto suspended sediments and usually find their way to the bottom within a relatively short period of time.

Consequently, these latter types would tend to affect those organisms living on the bottom or feeding from bottom organisms more then they would affect the organisms living within the water column, such as free swimming fish. Also of import in determining the effectiveness of a particular pollutant on living organisms is its relative solubility in water and oil. Pollutants more soluble in oil will tend to find their way to organisms that have a larger content of oil in their body issues. This is particularly true of some of the pesticides which are more soluble in oil than water.

The individual habits of marine organisms also affect their susceptibility to a particular pollutant. Feeding habits with respect to time of day, portion of water column for aged, type of material ingested, and the method of digestion utilized all determine to a great extent the types of pollutant the organism will be exposed to. Similarly spawning habits determine the type of area and time of year in which a species is particularly sensitive to subtle changes in the environment. These changes affect not only the parents but also the offspring, and may be even their progeny.

Other habits not having to do with spawning also help to determine whether an organism will be exposed to particular pollutants. Weather the organism is sensitive to light or sound, for example, will often determine whether it is attracted to a particular out-fall. Thus we find that a pure and simple cause and effect relationship between a pollutant and an organism is not enough to determine completely the actual response of the organism in the real world. Laboratory results might be completely refused in the field simply because the organism does not respond to extraneous characteristics of the environment under natural conditions in the same manner in which it did in the laboratory.

Once some of the pollutant has been ingested by marine organisms, the major concern of man is the possibility of this pollutant appearing on his dinner table and causing a pathogenic response. Obviously if a fish ingests a pollutant and a human eats that fish, then that person will have ingested a does of that pollutant and there will probably be some danger. The question is, "How much?" In order to arrive at an approximation of the actual amount of undesired material finding its wax into the reader's stomach, one mush follow the pollutant through a number of steps. Most organisms living in the sea tend to concentrate materials existing in the sea to much greater values that they are in the ocean itself. For example, a diatom, a small form of marine algae having a silicate frustule, has a body concentration of silicon about 40 thousand times as great as the oceanic waters from which the organism derives all of its material. Thus the diatom concentrates silicon very effectively so that if we eat diatoms, a large portion of our diet would be glassy. Similarly, other organisms, including fish, will concentrate other materials even if these do not naturally occur in the environment. But this amplification or concentration does not stop with one step. We must continually keep in mind the fact that an organism does not exist by itself in the marine environment.

Any organism is dependent upon many other organisms for its existence. An edible fish, for example, might very well subsist on smaller fish which, in turn, might subsist on small zooplankton, which, in turn, may subsist on phytoplankton. There may be 5 to 10 individual links in a food chain leading to man, and there is the distinct possibility that for each one of these links a concentration of the pollutant occurs. Thus the total pathway to man for the pollutant might be a rather tortuous one, but it might result in a very high concentration of the pollutant material in the fish. This in itself may be of no concern to the individual unless he ingests the fish and if so, how often and how much he consumes.

It is not enough simply to know that there is some pollutant present in marine organisms : one also should know how much is present, and in addition two other facts are required. This first is the accepted maximum level of ingestion of the pollutant before harm results, and the second is the amount of fish that can be eaten before this level is reached. In this way it might very well be possible to have a particular kind of fish one or two times a year with perfect safety, while if it is eaten once a day, it might very well have a toxic effect.

Ecomorphic pollutants

There are many different types of pollutants that may be classified as ecomorphic, while some pollutants fall into all three of the classes stipulated above and many fall into at least two. Sediment is a pollutant whose effect is primarily that of changing the environment since it is not pathogenic and very often is not aesthetically displeasing, although it can be. As it settles to the bottom, it will tend to bury the organisms that live on the bottom, such as cysters and clams, and eventually smother them. Sediment also tends to fill in marsh areas, killing the marsh grass, and completely changing the habitat. Since marsh areas are breeding grounds for small fish and an important ecological link in most of the oceanic life, any destructive process such as this is bound to markedly change the marine biological environment. On the other hand, in some cases where man's activities have produced large amounts of erosion and sediment has been brought down by rivers into estuaries, some estuarine areas have been filled enough to support marsh grasses.

In some cases excess erosion can produce marsh lands rather than destroy them. Whenever there is a depth change in an estuarine or coastal area, the effects are many. They range from changing the biological environment so that larger fish will no longer live in the shol areas to affecting the total circulation pattern of the area. But suffice it to say that changing depth in many cases does change the manner in which salt and fresh water mix in the coastal area and also the amount of flushing present in a particular region. When the sediment is in suspension it also has an effect on the eco-system, the most obvious aspect being a change in transparency. By making the water more opaque, light will not penetrate as deeply as before so that the thickness of the layer of water in which plants grow will be decreased.

If the water is fairly shallow to begin with, this decrease in transparency may very well result in the inability of rooted plants to grow and some marsh lands may be destroyed. The effect of sediment, then is two-fold: changing both bottom and water properties. Both of these effects tend to change the physical characteristics of the ecosystem. Another ecomorphic pollutant is oil, although oil sometimes produces toxic effects. The result of oil coating bird feathers is a well known physical effect. The oil does not poison birds; it simply makes it impossible for them to fly and consequently many of them die. A film of oil on the surface will also decrease the amount of sunlight entering the water and, similarly, will limit the exchange of oxygen from the atmosphere. In addition to the aesthetic and pathogenic effects of oil, there are thus also ecomorphic effects. The toxic effects of various nitrogen compounds are well known but fertilizers and other nutrients washed into the sea have a nontoxic effect on marine waters. These materials will do just what they are designed to do make plants grow, whether these plants be terrestrial or aquatic plants. The toxic effects of various nitrogen compounds are well known but fertilizers and other nutrients washed into the sea have a nontoxic effect on marine waters. These materials will do just what they are designed to do : make plants grow, whether these plants be terrestial or aquatic plants.

Those plants on the bottom of the blanket will tie, due to lack of light, and those rooting plants will utilize oxygen in their decay processes. Even though there are more plants than before, producing more oxygen in the process of photosynthesis, so many of them are dying and decaying the result is to decrease the dissolved oxygen. This phenomenon is called "Eutrophication."

Another ecomorphic pollutant that seems to be receiving a lot of attention lately is heat. Usually supplied to the marine environment form electrical power plants or other industrial sources, this heat will increase the water temperature and may result in different kinds of damage to marine organisms. Since most mutations are caused to thermal activity under normal conditions, the possibility of genetic damage is real. It is estimated that about 90% of the mutations occurring normally are thermally caused, while only about 10% are caused by radiation.

Aesthetic pollutants

The last type of pollutant mentioned above was aesthetic pollutants. Aesthetic pollutants are those which offend the human senses and as such are considered by many to be unimportant. In many environmental problem areas, though, the aesthetic considerations often receive more attention by environmentally oriented citizens than some of the pathogenic pollutants. This is simply because the aesthetic pollutants are visible and what can be seen, smelled, or heard appears much more bothersome than that which is hidden, even though the hidden pollutant might be much more dangerous to life. Consequently, any scheme for controlling marine pollution must include some consideration of the aesthetic pollutants if it is to succeed.

An excellent strategy seems to be to focus on the aesthetic pollutants and use them as a mechanism to gather momentum to clean up the rest of the pollution problems. Power transmission cable has caused more than one power company grief because of the environmental consideration given the local citizens who are concerned about the appearance of power cables running across the countryside. Oil wells, especially the offshore variety visible from resort areas, are of great concern to most environmentalists. The same thing is true of equipment required for dredging operations and the spoil areas resulting from these operations.

To some people, especially those living in relatively pristine environments near the water, boats can also be an aesthetic pollutant, especially those that cause waves and noise. Effluents that cause the colour of the sea to change to increase the amount of suspended sediments also may be considered aesthetic pollutants. It simply is not as pleasant to go swimming in water that is cloudy and contains colouring material different from what one would expect in a normal, natural body of water. In essence, any change from the pristine environment appears to many to be aesthetic pollution. Obviously we are living in an unreal world if we think the marine environment can be maintained in an unspoiled form.

It should be borne in mind that many complaints about aesthetic pollution come from individuals who would father live in the primeval environment not realizing that it would not be available to them unless the commercial world about them supported it. There appears to be a dichotomy wherein try to maintain the unspoiled environment in certain areas while letting others become over utilized.

Nevertheless, there is a growing movement to include in the cost of every project a relatively small sum to improve its aesthetic qualities. This is, of course, exactly the same philosophy that is applied to the control of other forms of pollution. Additional money is spent in a chemical process, for example, to control the pollution-producing properties of the effluent since society believes that this additional sum of money is desirable expenditure. It may similarly be maintained that the expenditure for aesthetic pollution control is desirable as it also will tend to increase the quality of life. This paragraph briefly state those portions of these studies that are relevant to determining the effects of oil on marine wetlands. Also, the literature and cut personal experiences with oiled marine wetlands are synthesized to allow an evaluation of methods or protection, cleanup, and restoration attempts that have been carried out in marine wetlands.

Effects of oil spills on marshes and mangroves

Oil impacts to marshes will vary with a number of factors including the amount of oil, type and magnitude of cleanup activities, type of oil, physical and biological structure of the marsh, latitude, and season. Subsequent persistence of damages and recovery of the system also depend on numerous physical, chemical, and biotic factors, including weathering rate and degree of removal or retention of oil, availability of propagules (seeds or vegetative), successional processes, sediment erosion/acceleration, and restrorative activities by man. Plants can be affected in several ways. Physical smothering by oil can lead to reduced transpiration, respiration, and photosynthesis. Absorption of toxic oil fractions through the leaves or roots may cause poisoning of the plant by disrupting cell membranes and cellular organelles. Some species such as *juncusmaritimus is gerarii,* and Spartina anglica exhibit epidermal or cellular resistance to oilds. There is a considerable range of sensitivity to oil. Some species are resistant even to repeated spills (e.g., salicornea sp. Many of the more resistant species are also perennials with large root systems that enable them to grow back following oil damage to aerial portions.

Oils vary in their toxicity, according to the content of lowboiling compounds, unsaturated compounds, and aromatics. In general, the higher the concentration of these constituents, the more toxic the oil. It is self evident that the amount of oil and frequency of oiling will effect the degree of damage, but it is less obvious that viscosity of the oil is important. With light oil, there is a physical limit to the amount that will "stick" to a shore, with subsequent tides redistributing oils.

In contrast, the viscosity of heavy oils often allows retention of large volumes and many cause mortality not through toxicity but through smothering. Heavy oils also tend to be more persistent and to extend the duration of damage, thus slowing recovery. Since and sediment structure of the marsh considerably affect the degree of damage and potentials for recovery. In the United States, Europe, and elsewhere marshes may be narrow fringing bands along the high water mark, especially in areas where tides are small, or marshes may be broad vegetational belts (occasionally many hundreds of meters wide) in estuaries or on sheltered coasts, especially where tidal ranges are large.

Extensive marshes may not be completely covered even to massive spills, as oil will tend to affect the sides of the creeks and drainage channels first and then progress into the marshes plateau. Where vegetation it tall and dense (e.g., in a spartinetum of juncetum), considerable volumes of all may be completely oiled, and after severe damage, there may be no source of propagules for recovery. In such area, restorative action may be the only means of marsh re-establishment in the short term.

Sediment characteristics, including particle size distribution and drainage patterns, considerably affect potential for oil retention. Marshes in North America and European be found in sediments ranging from medium grainted sands to very fine silts where more than 95% of sediment particles are less than 63 in diameter. Sands tend to be more freely drainging and more easily penetrated by oils as shoots can occur.

If oil penetrates anaerobic sediments weathering is reduced or stops, and the oil may be retained in unchanged form for considerable periods of time, reducing or preventing plant regrowth. However, where oil is weathered before or after incorporation, even very high levels may not prevent plant regrowth. Growth in solicornia sp., *suaeda maritima, Aster tripolium* and *Spartina anglica* has been reported run areas where levels of total aliphatic hydrocarbons of up to 5,875 μg/ g were found.

Seasonal changes in the marsh may considerably affect the extent of oil damage. Oiling before or during flowering can cause reduced flowering and seed production. This may delay flowering and seed production (Dicks, unpublished data). During winter months many species die back and oil may affect only dead and decaying vegetation; however, in spring and summer growth, new shoots and germinating seedlings are particularly vulnerable. In some cases, a major problem following oil damage to vegetation has been loss of sediment stability followed by erosion (e.g., Isle Grande, France following the Amoco Cadiz oil spill). Where extensive rhizomatous roots mats ramify the sediments or where vegetation cover is continuous (e.g., in denise Spartina Stands), sediments may remain stable even when vegetation has been killed. In low marsh colonized mainly by annual species (e.g., Salicornica) or where vegetation is sparse, root mats may be insufficient to prevent erosion.

Where erosion occurs, lowering of marsh level may prevent re-establishment of vegetation. Erosion may also follow damage to creek systems after cleanup activities (e.g., during the Amoco Cadiz spill that affected the Isle Grande marshes. The importance of slat marshes in prevention of coastline erosion is well established and may be of prime importance in some areas. Because of the preceding considerations, basin forest may have variable characteristics. Generally, however, basin forests are well developed with canopy heights that may reach 15-20 m.

Riverine forests: This forest type develops along the edges of estuaries, often as far as the inland extent of the saline intrusion. It is best developed, however, in the lower course of the estuary where water flows are moderate to high and high nutrient inputs prevail. This combination of adequate freshwater and nutrient inputs allows the development luxriant stands.

On the periphery of the forest, the dominant species is the Rhizophora mangrove. This is an area where there is greater kinetic energy by due to the combination of river flow and tidal motion. The complex root system of Rhizophora, with its extraordinarily developed adventitious ("stilt") roots, allows the establishment of large trees on very unstable, soft soiled. In the inner forest, mixed stands of Laguncularia and Avicennia occur. Rieverine forests are highly productive with litter fall rates in excess of 4 g/m/day. Canopy heights reach 20 m in the best-developed forests.

Fringe forests: This type occurs along the seaward edge of forests lining protected shorelines. There is usually a strong horizontal gradient in tropography as well as a significant gradient in turbulence and tidal amplitude. Energy derived from the tides and waves decays rapidly inland where tidal flooding is further reduced by the rise in the mangrove floor.

The reduced flusing inland results in the establishment of a physiochemical gradient in water quality, toward the outer edge of the fringe, where greater energy levels prevail, the large, heavy seedlings of Rhizophora become established. Inland this way and tidal energy dissipates, and in the higher, less flushed parts of the fringe, Avicennia becomes the dominant species. Since frings are exposed, they are subjected to periodic destruction buy storms, waves, or scouring by strong current as. During storms large amounts of debris may be deposited in the outer firinge, reducing circulation to the inner firinge and the basins inland.

Overwash forests: These forests are formed on small island or projections from land masses (peninsulas) they are characterized by intense flushing by daily tides. The high flushing rates do not allow the formation of strong salinity gradients nor the accumulation and aggradation of the soil or of nutrients factors that usually lead to a succession of species toward the interior. True overwash forests are thus monospecific (cominated by rhizophora). The amount of flushing and nutrient availability are critical factors that determine the structure and the rate of overwash forests. They, overwash islands in coastal oligotrophic waters may not be as developed as those inside coastal lagoons where higher nutrient accumulation is possible. Excessive flushing leads to erosion and loss of the forest whereas extremely low flushing rates lead to accumulation of debris and vertical aggradation inside the forest with reduced flushing rates toward the core of the island. These islands thus evolve into firings and basin forests.

Dwarf forests: Dwarf forest are found in marginal environments where their structural development is limited by edaphic factors, probably the unavailability of nutrients, Mature trees in these forests are usually less than 3 m tall. Salinity is not the limiting factor. Although the vegetation is limited in high, leaf size is not reduced as usually happens when mangroves are under the influence of a chronic stressor. This type of forest is different from those that may be considered scrub forests and that develop under the influence of chronic stressor, such as high salinity or cold stress. The dominant species in Dwarf forest in Florida and Puerto Rico is Rhizophora.

Worldwide, where some documentation of impact to mangroves has been observed and reported. Most of the earlier reports are anecdotal with little or no quantification as to the levels of oil contamination; the actual types of oil stranded in the forests; the aerial extent of mangroves oiled, and actual numbers, sizes, or aerial coverage of mangroves killed or stressed by the oil spill. In addition, the species of mangroves involved was often not mentioned. In addition to impacts to the trees themselves, the final component of the ecosystem is usually treated by noting dead or stressed animals at the time of the spill, or attempting to quantify losses or changes by one-shot sampling. In particular, the sampling of infauna, in many of these cases, has not taken into account the normal seasonal variations in infaunal species and numbers.

All these problems may lead to widely different observations of the "impact" of a spill by different investigators. Due to the fact that floating oil is transported by waves and currents and strands on shorelines, low-wave energy ecosystems such as mangroves forests are routinely sites where oil accumulates after a spill. In addition, the inaccessibility of most mangrove forests makes oil removal very difficult, if not impossible, and the fine-grained and peaty anaerobic sediments characteristic of mangrove forests may reduce the rate of microbial breakdown of oil. These factors, plus the burrowing activities of crustaceans characteristic of mangrove forests, can lead to persistent, high levels of oil contamination not only on the soil's surface but also deep in the sediments in the mangrove root core, and mangroves can be killed.

Marine oil pollution

Marine oil pollutants originating from domestic and industrial sources and from agricultural operations due to high inputs of heavy metals, hydrocarbons, pesticides fungicides, insecticides have spread to coastal areas through rivers run off, via the atmosphere, direct discharges or dumping into the sea where the most of the active primary and secondary production direct, are being polluted, causing serious damage to aquatic ecosystems. Oil spill on ocean waters kills birds, fouls beaches, and poisons marine life. Hasan Jawaid Khan gives an account of these deadly oil spills, the damage they bring about and the ways by which an oil slick is contained tense of thousand of sea birds acted with oil shivering and dying on the beaches. At least a thousand sea otters succumbing in the oil with their livers and kidneys fatally impaired. And an unknown number of seals, whales and porpoises poisoned.

Even before the tragic images of the deadly oil spill on the Alaskan coast could fade from memory, the specture of an oil spill is back again to haunt us-only this time it is much too bigger. The enormous oil slick in the Gulf region, 30 times more than the Alaskan episode, threatens to set into motion an unprecedented ecological disaster that may take decades to fix. Ironically, the oil that drives millions of vehicles round the world, sometimes drives countless marine animals to a most cruel death, crude oil when refined drives automobiles and airplanes, runs factories and farm equipments, provides gas for heating and cooking and is a source for making drugs, cosmetics and fertilizers. But when crude oil spills on to ocean waters it spells death for marine animals and disaster for the ocean ecology.

There has always been a danger of major oil spills acquiring near a coastal area with supertankers being increasingly used to carry industrial and heating oils. Several of these huge ships have been grounded and cracked open by the seas, their vast cargoes spilling out heavy oil into the oceans where currents can carry it many miles before it disperses and gradually sinks to the floor. Sometimes the currents carry the oil toward land where it fouls beaches and kills marine life. The world first woke up to the disastrous consequences of an oil spill when on 18 March 1967 a Librarian tanker, Terry Canyon, ran a ground on the southwest cast of Great Britain, near the entrance to the English Channel, spilling 60,000 tons crude oil into the sea. Oil splittered on to 160 kilometers of coastline killing countless number of fish and birds. Two years later, in January 1969 occurred the second major oil spill off the coast of Santa Barbara in the United States when an offshore oil well below out resulting in the discharge of oil at the rate of 1,000 gallons per hour causing extensive damage to the coast.

In 1978, in the much publicized Amoco Cadiz disaster 68 million gallons of oil was dumped all along the French coast. And then on March 24, 1989 the supertanker Exxon Valdez belonging to the Exxon corporation, the largest petroleum company in the world, plied on to a reef off the coasts of Alaska. Through five gashed in its hull the 30,000 ton super tanker spilled over 11 million gallons of oil into the clean water of Alaska's Prince William Sound. As the oil hit 1,930 kilometers of shoreline. 100,000 seabirds died including 150 rare species of baldeageles. An unknown number of dead seals sank to the bottom of the ocean. And at least 1,000 sea otters perished. Even a few deer and a couple of bears that fed near the shoreline were found dead. Closer home, Indian coasts have also been witness to a few tanker disasters, none too serious thought. In July 1973, 3,000 tons of oil washed on to the Gujarat coast when an oil tanker, cosmos pioneer, ran around. In 1974 an American oil tanker Transhuron colided with one of the atolls of the Lacadives spilling 5,000 tons of special furnance oil causing extensive damage to marine life.

Similarly destruction was witnessed when the oil tanker Lajpat spilled thousands of tons of oil along the Bombay coast. The last time an oil spill threatened the India coast was in June 1989 when a Malteese tanker M.T., Puppy collided with a British vessel. The Maltese tanker spilled over 5,500 tons of furnance oil into the open seas off Bombay. At that time the fear of contamination of fish brought the fish industry to virtual halt at people stopped buying fish for fear it might cause cancer.

But not all the petroleum that gets into the marine environment is through oil spills. Natural seeps have been discharging petroleum into the marine environment for millions of years in amounts substantially greater than those resulting from present offshore production activities. More than 200 submarine oil seeps have been identified worldwide. An assessment of petroleum pollution of the world's oceans by the national Academy of Sciences, Washington, estimated that between 1.7 and 8.8 million metric tons of oil enter the oceans annually.

Oil spills are by far the major contributors to this pollution. While other categories of pollution have shown a fifty per cent decrease, oil spills have been on the rise. But what is it that makes crude oil shore so deadly? Crude oil is rarely used in the form of product at the offshore wells but it is converted in refineries into a wide range of products such as gasoline, kerosene, diesel fuel, jet fuel, domestic and industrial fuel oils and petrochemicals feedstocks. Until the oil is refined it contains potentially dangerous components.

Crude oil is primarily made up of compounds of carbon and hydrogen called hydrocarbons. These hydrocarbons may be paraffins parafin oil is used as a fuel in heaters and lamps cycloparaffins (naphthenes) and aromatic compounds in varying proportions. Crudes founds in easter and aid western sections of the United States are predominantly paraffinic, while those found along the Gulf coast are usually naphthnic. Crude oil also contains varying amounts of sulphur compounds, a small amount of nitrogen and very little oxygen or olefins which are unsaturated hydrocarbons. Nickel and vanadium are present in all crudes in high concentration. Iron may be found in inorganic form as a result of corrosion of pipes and containers used to produce and transport oil.

Paraffins like methane and ethane are asphyxiants, that is, cause suffocation. Some paraffins are central nervous system depressants. Liquid paraffins can remove oil from exposed skin and cause dermatitis or pneumonia in lung tissue. However, these are the least toxic of the hydrocarbons. The effects of cycloparaffins are much like those of the paraffins except that unsaturated cycloparaffins are more toxic than the saturated ones, breathing high concentrations of their vapour can result in Irritation and an aesthesia, the most toxic of the hydrocarbons are the aromatic hydrocarbons. Inhalation of the vapour can cause acute intoxication. Benzone is particularly toxic and long-term exposure can cause anemia and leukopenia even at low concentrations.

Sulphur compounds present in crude oil can also be toxic. Carbonyl sulfide is dangerously poisonous. It is lethal to rats at 2900 ppm (parts per million). The mechanisms of toxic action appears to involve its breakdown to hydrogen sulfide. It acts principally on the central nervous system, with death resulting mainly from respiratory paralysis. Sulphur in the form of aromatic thiophenes, benzothiophenes, can be moderately toxic. These damage the livers and kidneys. Certain sulphur compounds like sercaptan can also be lethal. Although the long-term effects of an oil spill are not so well known, the Alaskan oil spill provided an opportunity to study the short-term effects. As the 11 million gallons of oil spilled by the Exxon Valdex hit the shores, seabirds started shivering and dying. The oil had broken down the natural insulating oils and waxes which shield the birds from water. As a result hypothermia (abnormally low body temperature) set in and the birds started dying. About 150 rare species of bald eagles also became victims when they ingested oil, seaven giving on oily seabird carcasses. Cleaning away the oil from the birds has not been very successful as it causes a severe strain on the birds. However, the

British Wildlife Rescue Association has designed wool sweaters which absorb oil from the stricken birds. The sweaters have already been used to clean birds in the North sea and were found to be more effectively than cleaning with detergents. About 1,000 sea others died after their far became saturated with oil and provided no insulation. Others developed respiratory ailments as volatile components of the oil weakened membranes in their lungs. Some suffered liver and kidney damage caused by ingesting oil while cleaning their coasts. Firstly were found to be the least affected. When fish from the oil spillage sites were tested no hydrocarbons were found in their flesh. The fish are efficient at converting hydrocarbons they ingest into metabolities which are then everted from the liver to the gall bladder.

Moreover, because of their mobility the fish escape large-scale contaminated as they are able to avoid heavily contaminated areas. When oil spills on to ocean waters it spreads rapidly over the surface.

The force of gravity causes the lighter oil to seek a constant level by spreading horizontally on the heavier water The movement of the oil is caused by the combined action of wind, surface currents waves and tides. Oil on water normally moves at about 1/30th of the wind speed. With large amounts of oil, as with accidental spills, the oil drift is largely independent of spill volume, spreading, or weathering. Since the thick portion of the slick drifts faster than the thin portion a heavy oil accumulation forms the leading edge of an advancing slick. As the oil spreads it comes under the influence of several weathering processes that ultimately break down a spill with time. The first of these is evaporation which is dominant soon after oil is released. Evaporation is determined by wind velocity, nature of the roughness, and temperature. Almost 50 per cent of oil is lost through evaporation during an oil silk's lifetime. Some of the light, low-bowling hydrocarbons, such as benzene, toluene, and xylene are lost through evaporation. Their removal decreases toxicity of the oil to marine life. Muce of the oil that evaporates is photooxized in the atmosphere and some of it may return to the seas as atmospheric fallout.

A very small fraction of the oil dissolves in the water in the early stages of an oil spill. Lower-molecular-weight compounds tend to be the most soluble. However, this process is very insignificant. Natural dispersion also removes some oil from the water. In this process, small droplets of oil which are larger than dissolved molecules, are incorporated into the water in the form of dilute oil-in-water suspension. Crude oil contains trace amounts of altrogen, sulfur, and oxygen-bearing compounds which can act as natural surfactants. These surfactants reduce the oil-water interfacial tension allowing the oil to break up and to disperse into droplets more readily.

A part of the oil is also broken down by microbial degradation. Microorganisms present in the water have a great capacity to utilize hydrocarbons present in the oil as in energy source. This process especially speeds up when the oil disperses. Some organisms may also ingest dispersed oil droplets and subsequently deposit them as fecal pollets. Emulsification is yet another weathering process in which water is incorporated into the floating oil forming a water-in-oil emulsion. Such emulsions, which may contain from 20 to 80 per cent water, are often very viscous and referred to as "mousse" once mousse formation starts, cleanup operation run into difficulties as it is almost impossible to pump.; Ultimately the mouse is broken up by wind and wave action into tar balls that may wash ashore.

However, breaking up of an oil spill takes time. And the longer the oil continues to flat on water the more damage it does to the marine environment therefore, cleaning to an oil spill fast assumes prime importance. An oil spill can be cleaned up by mechanical removal of the oil, by the use of chemical and microbial surfactants, by using absorbants, or by burning the oil slick.

Spills can be dealt with more easily if they are confined to a small area on the water surface. For this, mechanical booms or barriers are spread around on oil slick to check its progress and prevent it form hitting the shoreline. But sometimes high waves may splash the oil over the booms. The oil may even pass below the booms once it has piled against the barrier. So after the oil has been contained by the booms it is sucked up from the surface of the sea by vessel known as skimmers.

Skimmers now available generally fall into one of two categories. The first, mechanical surface skimmers, remove the top layers of the water and oil from the surface but they are not very effective if there are high waves. They gulp large amounts of water unless some provision is made to allow the weir suction port to follow the water surface. A second type of skimmer operates on the principle of selective wetting of a surface by oil rather than by water. Rotating metal disk or conveyor belts dip into the water, a surface layer of oil removed. The spilled oil can also be treated with dispersants. These chemicals are sprayed from aircrafts or ships. Dispersants cause the oil to spread further and disperse in a manner similar to the way soap removes oil from one's hands allowing the oil to be emulsified and washed away with water. A dispersant contains a surfactant, a solvent, and a stabilizer. The solvent usually comprises the bulk of the sispersant and enables the surface-active agent or surfactant to mix with, and penetrate into the oil slick and form an emulsion. The stabilizer fixes the emulsion and prevents it from coalescing once it is formed.

Dispersion increase the slick surface area and allows a rapid increase in the rate or microbial decomposition. But although dispersants are effective in diffusing a slick, these chemicals are toxic to marine life. And, since the emulsified out droplets sink into the water body, oil stays in the waters with its toxic components such as benzene and toluene entering the food chain with disastrous long-term effects. Absorbents are also used to facilitate the cleaning up of oil spilts. When they are applied to the slick, they absorb the oil and prevent it from spreading, and when the absorbent material is removed from the water, the oil is removed. Natural materials such as peat moss, straw, sawdust, and pine bark can be used. Synthetic absorbents include polyethylene, polystyrene, polypropylene, and polyurethane. Of all synthetic absorbents, polyurethane is the most promising.

Burning oil slicks on the open seas has generally been less successful because the more volatile light fractions evaporate quickly from the oil slick. Also, the water removes heat faster than it can be created to support the combustion. But burning oil slicks also leads to extensive air pollution. By far the safest way of rating an oil slick is by using biological agents for degrading oil. These microbial surfactants are sprayed from the air. They mix with the oil, emulsify it and disperse it throughout the water body so thinly that it no longer remains hazardous. However, not every clean-up method can clear up all oil spills. Clean-up methods are chosen on a case by methods are chosen on a case-by-case basis. But whatever the method, it is important that the efforts are mounted as soon as the oil spills is discovered. For the longer it takes for the cleaning up to start, the more distance the oil travels. And as the oil charts its destructive course it fouls beaches, kills marine animals and contaminates the food chain.

According to H.J.K, the massive oil slick in the Gulf is making history. With the total spillage of oil in the Gulf waters now standing at more than 330 million gallons, it is already 30 times more than the quantity spilled by the Exxon Valdez on the shores of Alaska. The oil slick that now stretches over an area more than 80 km long and 20 km wide is moving south at a speed of 20 km a day. Having already hit the Saudi shores, affecting birds and marine life, the slick is now threatening the shores of Bahrain, Gatar and the United Arab Emirates. Apart from killing marine life the oil also threatens to disrupt the deslination plants on the western coast of the Gulf that provide nearly half the water to Arabian states.

The enormous oil slick will disrupt the already fragile ecosystem of the region. According to the world conservation Monitoring Centre in Cambridge, between 1 million and 2 million birds will die as a result of the gulf oil spillage. Some species may never recover. Cormorants coates with oil have already started dying on the Saudi beaches. Dolphins may escape contamination as they seem to be able to sense a spill and street clear of it. The dugong or sea-cows will be affected with their food supply of sea or grass getting contaminated. The three already endangered species of turtles the green, leatherback and hawks bill may be seriously affected. Coral reefs housing a diverse variety of fish maybe destroyed. The oil is likely to affect the mangroves of Iran and a number of valuable shrimp fisheries.

No immediate threat to the Indian coastline is perceived so far according to oil experts. The oil split from the Al-Ahmadi terminal is export quality Kuwaiti crude, extremely light and fluid. Hence, much of it would evaporate. In the first 24 hours, 35 per cent of the crude is likely to evaporate and in the next 10 days about 45 per cent. Even if some of the oil manages to find its way out of the Gulf, much of it would be broken up by the rough tropical waters of the Arabian Sea. Due to burning of the oil in the Gulf and attempts for its removal, a very small quantity of tar balls may eventually hit the Indian coast. These tar balls can just be collected and set on fire. Biman Basu made survey on Gulf oil spill and he pointed out that the oil spill in the Gulf is the largest so far, spreading over 700 sq km, it does not pose any pollution threat to Indian waters.

"This is not so much environmental terrorism as an environmental crime." Said Worldwatch founder Less Brown, "We need a code of ethics like the Geneva Convention (governing treatment of prisoner of war) for the environmental filed. The Gulf could die in a matter of months." Ancient warriors knew how to use the environment as a weapon. Corpses were catapulted into besieged cities to spread disease; water supplies were diverted to cause drought or floods; wells were poisoned. The Romans spread salt on the fields of Carthage to deny food to their enemies; Russian troops defeated Napoleon's army by torching the earth as they retreated, destroying all crops animals and human dwellings.

Prime Minister Winston Churchill planned to spread burning oil on Britain's beaches to block any German invasion in the Second World War. In the same war the Dutch opened up their sea dikes to flood their own land in a bid to stop the advancing Nazi troops.

The U.S. Forces in Vietnam also practised environmental warfare when they sprayed Agent Orange to defoliate vaste stretches of forest land deprive Viet Cong guerillas of protective cover. The spraying destroyed large number of animals that lived in the forests, polluted waterways with the reputedly, cancer-causing chemical dioxin, and Vietnamese exposed to defoliated areas reported increased rates of miscarriages and birth deformities. Heydemann, Science Counsellor in the US Embassy in New Delhi, the oil may not come out of the Gulf for years because of the current patterns in the region. Ben Barber studied that the gaint oil slick released into the waters of the Gulf during the war has been denounced as "environmental terrorism" which along with deliberately set oil well and refinery fires, could alter the region's ecology for the years to come.

Yet, since Biblical times, armies have destroyed the environment to deny and enemy food, water or shelter. "The phenomenon is not new there have been efforts to degrade the environment as part of war fare for sometime," said Mr. Chris Flavin an analyst with the Washington based environmental think-tank, Worldwatch institute. But modern technology has upped the ante", he added "There s a much greater impact." The estimated 460 million gallons of oil released in to the shallow waters of the Gulf is by for the world's greatest oil spill. Spreading south from off the Kuwaiti and Saudi coasts towards Bahrain and Gatar, it threatens millions of sea birds and marine life forms, including the rare dugong or sea cow, the mammal that supposedly gave rise to the legend of the mermaid. Since the war ended in 1975, low-value bamboo and grasses have invaded defoliated areas, preventing the regrowth of valuable hardwood forests. The U.S. also seeded clouds over Asia to try to alter Vietnam's rainfall and make supply trains to muddy to use, said Prof. George Rathjens of the Massachusetts Institute of Technology. A political science teacher who has specialised in nuclear weapons and environmental issues, he said some modern military planners have proposed cloud seeding to divert rainfall from an enemy's crops. In addition to the releases of oil into the Gulf, several Kuwaiti oil refineries were set on fire in what may have been an attempt to raise a smoke shield against attacking aircraft. Some scientists have warned that such huge fires could block out sufficient sunlight to disrupt monsoon rains as far away as South Asia. The worst-case scenario warned that massive famine could result. Prof. Rathjens, however said it is unlikely the fires would result in the phenomenon known as "Nuclear Winter" the predicated effect on the planet of an atomic war.

Ballerini-D and J.P. Vandecasteele studied the aims essentially at quantifying the processes of microbial degradation of crude oil in optimal conditions compatible with a marine environment. Our purpose, specifically, was to determine the proportion of crude which could undergo biological degradation, and to improve our knowledge of the biodegradation kinetics of the various hydrocarbon families which constitute a crude oil. This work was performed in laboratory reactors where various physiochemical parameters such as pH temperature, stirring speed and air flow rate were strictly controlled. The study was conducted first in batch then in continuous cultures.

The composition of the mineral medium used for the culture was chosen by taking the average composition of the Atlantic Ocean as a basis (1) and enriching it in nitrogen, phosphorus and iron. The concentrations of these three elements were respectively raised from 0.5 to 235 mg/L for nitrogen, from 0.007 to 26.7 mg/L for phosphorus and from 0/001 to 0.4 mg/L for iron and the pH of this medium was adjusted to 8.1 the average pH of seawater.

In order to approximate the conditions existing at sea, where evaporation is not negligible (2) we mainly used crude oil which had been topped at 240 degree C. In the present case, we used a residue of an Arabian light crude, obtained by distillation under reduced pressure, in which all the fractions distilling below 240 degree C had been removed.

In the alkaline distribution of Arabian light crude oil topped at 240 degree C n-paraffins of chain length below C 14 have been completely removed. In oil spills at sea, all compounds with a number of carbons below 15 disappear after a residence time of about 10 days.

Mineral medium

Salts	Concentration (g/L)
Sodium Chloride	23.9
Magnesium Chloride	10.8
Calcium Chloride	1.15
Potassium Chloride	0.74
Sodium Sulphate	0.40
Sodium Sulphate	0.023
Sodium Bromide	0.117
Sodium Fluoride	0.002
Sodium Bicarbonate	0.196
Silican Dioxide	0.022
Sodium Oxide	0.022
Ferrous Sulphate	0.002
Ammonium Chloride	0.9
Potassium Hydrogen Phosphate	0.15

On the residue obtain evaporation, separation of the three main classes of compounds of crude oil, saturated hydrocarbons, aromatic hydrocarbons and resins is performed either by thin layer chromatography on silica gel or by liquid chromatography on a silica gel column using cyclohexane as the elution solvent.

The sum of the weights of the four fractions recovered in this procedure always represents 90 to 100% of the initial weight of the total oil sample. On the saturated and aromatic fractions, more detailed analyses using gas chromatography and mass spectrometry are then performed.

The isolation and selection of the strains of microorganisms used were performed starting from marine silt and sand samples collected at places hit by crude oil spills.

The first enrichment cultures were performed by successive transfers in liquid medium to which 2 g/L of crude had been added, first in shaken flasks and, soon afterward, in laboratory fermentors in order to obtain perfectly defined culture conditions.

Coral reefs and petroleum infrastructure

Coral reefs are structures created and maintained by the establishment and growth of populations of hermatypic corals and coraline algae. They may be comprised of wave resistant emergent of submerged reefal zones, or a combination of both. Geomorphically barrier and fringing reef protect the insular and continental coastlines that they border from erosion. Reef rock that forms terrestrial substratum on islands and recently uplifted coastal margins is often the sole or major component of limestone. Geologically older reef formations are found far inland and may serve as porous, oil bearing strata.

Reefs typically provide habitat for a large variety of attached plants and epifauna, infauna mobile invertebrates, and fishes. The large numbers of economically important species they support make reefs locally important to commercial sport fisheries. The resultant high diversity and abundance of reef associates and the functional and spatial dominance of corals and coralline algae are the essential characteristics of coral reefs. Coral reefs are circumglobal in the tropics and subtropics between the northern and southern hemispheric 18.5 degree climatic isotherms. A majority of coral species and the most diverse and prolific reefs occur in Indo-West pacific seas. Tropical West Atlantic and Eastern Pacific reefs are generally less diverse in terms of carosals and reef associates, but are functionally quite as important.

In a recent interview of the impact of oil upon corals, Ray pointed out that extensive tanker traffic and oil-related activity occurs within the biogeographic zones occupied by coral reefs. Sufficient information exists to enable the production of detailed maps showing the location of coral reefs in relation to petroleum infrastructure. Such maps may be a useful aid in the identification of high risk areas. Two areas that have well developed reefs and much petroleum activity are given as examples in this discussion.

Biological effects

Having now made the effort to consider from theoretical point of view the system which it is thought may give rise to biological effects, it is no time to consider whether these effects can actually be observed under the conditions which prevail in the marine environment.

The marine environment is, however, subject to a wide range of influences the effects of which may swamp any effects which may be due to pollution. This is the well-known signal/noise ratio problem commonly encountered in the physical sciences. On the other hand, if studies are conducted in the laboratory the results can be no more than indicators of what will happen in the real world because it is quite impossible to reproduce the marine environment in the laboratory. Thus on the one hand we have the problem that the data obtained in what may be well-regulated laboratory experiments, in which the pollution parameter may be isolated for study, do not give results necessarily applicable to the marine environment, and on the other we have real environment studies in which the pollution effects are not isolatable and are usually swamped by other more influential effects. The review also covers results obtained by exposing organisms to oil in the laboratory. Here again there are difficulties. Often the concentrations used in order to observe an effect are higher than could possibly be experienced in the marine environment itself or are continued for greater periods of time. Again, even when the concentrations are comparable, it is impossible to extrapolate to the real situation.

It is quite clear that one can measure in the laboratory lethal and sub-lethal effects on organisms exposed to dissolved oil components and disoerbed droplets of oil in the water column. It is also clear that the concentrations of oil in the water column at real spills can be broadly comparable to those in the laboratory studies. In addition similar effects, both lethal and sub-lethal, on planktonic species can be observed at sea under real spills.

When one attempts to evaluate the significance of those observations, however, in the only manner possible or meaningful, *viz,* by attempting to observe subsequent changes in fish populations, no such changes are discernible. There are a number of quite reasonable explanations for this state of affairs. Thus even if plankton populations were reduced significantly under oil slicks, phytoplankton is in continuous production and is rapidly restored as the oil alike moves on. Even if fish egg and larval stage numbers were similarly reduced it is fact that very few would have reached maturity anyway. The losses caused by the oil merely cause losses which would otherwise have taken place naturally.

The conclusions reached above regarding plankton in general do not of course rule out the possıbility that larger marine organisms may be affected. When this possibility is considered, however, it is found that free-moving fish and crustacea are largely unaffected. Sedentary crestacea on the other hand may be subject to smothering with an oil layer deposited by the outgoing tide. Grazing molluscs and, of course, sea-weeds are liable to similar fate while filter-feeding molluscs can ingest oil in separating out food particles. Generally mortality is highest with fresh oil, weathered oil having little effect. In any case the effects are transient as regards populations and depuration occurs rapidly with filter feeders when exposed to clean water. Some species are not sufficiently mobile to escape, do not posses shells by which to isolate themselves or have other protective coatings. Worms living in sandy or muddy beaches may be killed if oil components penetrate the substratum. Of course, oil will not penetrate across the water-table interface and so this will occur mainly in well-drained beaches.

With birds it can be concluded that soluble and dispersed oil components will have no effect and we have now reached a pure example of the effects of physical coating. There is no doubt that this form of pollution has a very serious effect at least on individual birds, but here again the Royal Commission has not been able to demonstrate conclusively that there is any threat to populations. There is, however, considerable cause for concern, particularly in relation to major spills close to a breeding colony onshore. It is obvious that oiled birds are one of the main vehicles of public awareness of oil pollution and arouse widespread feelings of pity and revulsion.

There seems little possibility of affecting large marine mammals such as the cetaceans. Seals on the other hand may become oiled as they leave and reenter the sea and this could result in loss of insulation. It has been noted, however, that seal populations around the UK are generally stable and that grey seal numbers have been increasing dramatically for the past 50 years.

In the early 1970s attention was given to the possibility that polyaromatic hydrocarbons present in oil pollution might concentrate in the tissues of marine organisms and that those concentrations might increase up the food web to levels which could induce cancer in man. Research results now available, however, indicate that in common with other petroleum-derived hydrocarbons these compounds are rapidly released when the organisms are exposed to clean water and it is extremely unlikely that they could accumulate in the manner originally feared.

It has also been shown that these compounds are in any case the inevitable products of the combustion of most types of organic material such as wood, garden rubbish and even tobacco, and as such are widely distributed in the environment. Furthermore they are present in many foods and it is therefore possible to show on the basis of dietary studies that the consumption of sea food would be unlikely to provide more than 2-3% of the normal intake. Recent research has also failed to establish a connection between this form of pollution and cancer in the marine animals themselves and it is extremely unlikely, to say the least, that ingestion of cancerous tissue from animals could cause cancer in man in any case.

The aims and objective of oil spill response should therefore be to protect amenity, fishery and wildlife resources and the efforts expended should ideally have some relationship to the quantification of threat to those resources if nothing is done. If nothing is done to respond to an oil slick far enough at sea for it to disperse through natural forces before it reaches shore, then minimum impact on the environment will result since there will be no amenity loss, and no effect on inshore fisheries. The oil will disperse far at sea when its effect is least. The only possibility of quantifiable damage resulting would be if high concentrations of seabirds became affected.

If natural dispersion forces are unable to remove the oil from the sea surface before it reaches shore, then, in addition to seabirds, inshore fisheries, the flora and fauna of the inshore zone and amenity are at risk. In terms of quantified risk, therefore, there is no likely to be greater environmental impact than in the previous example. It is reasonable therefore to make greater efforts to respond in this case than in the previous one. It should however, be realised that efforts should be made to deal with the oil in the lower - risk are, i.e., at sea, before it reaches the comparatively high - risk area, i.e., the inshore zone. If it is possible to prevent oil reaching the high-risk zone, minimum damage will result. If response occurs only when the oil has reached the high-risk zone then the damage will already have occurred and one is then no longer preventing damage but only attempting to assist the area to recover from the damage it has already sustained. It is therefore clearly preferable to deal with the oil in low risk areas before it reaches those of high risk. If this is impossible, then the aim should be to return the damaged areas to their original state as quickly as possible and the best way to assist in this will be to remove the oil as quickly as possible if natural processes are considered to be too slow.

There are three possible responses to oil spills at sea.

— It can be decided to leave the oil to be dispersed by natural processes.

— The natural dispersion rate may be increased by the use of chemical.

— Attempts may be made to remove the oil from the sea surface by mechanical means.

The nil response option will be possible when no resources are threatened and natural dispersion rates are fast enough to remove the oil from the surface before any resource comes under threat. The use of chemical dispersants should be seen as a means to increase natural dispersion rates so that resources are less likely to come under threat.

It is of course preferable to remove the oil completely from the environment, and so mechanical recovery devices are favoured provided they will work sufficiently to deal with the oil in the low—risk zones before it reaches those of high risk. It is generally accepted that if recovery is into possible far at sea in a given situation, it may be preferable to remove the oil completely from the environment, and so mechanical recovery devices are favoured provided they will work sufficiently to deal with the oil in the low-risk zones before it reaches those of high risk.

It is general accepted that if recovery is not possible far at sea in a given situation, it may be preferable to disperse the oil there and so prevent damage later in a high-risk sheltered zone than to wait and attempt to recover it when it has reached the high-risk sheltered zone. The latter option will not prevent damage. It will merely remove the oil after the damage is done. Such belted action will of course assist in the recovery of the area affected.

Clearly oil does not remain permanently on the sea surface. The pollutant may disperse into the water column either completely or partially under the action of natural forces and or it may come shore. If the oil is spilled close to shore there is little opportunity for natural dispersion before the slicks reach shore. In such circumstances beach pollution seems inevitable. However, even in the Amoco Cadiz it has been estimated that some 50% of the spillage dispersed into the water column in the prevailing conditions of high natural agitation rather than stranding on the beaches. With the advent of North Sea oil exploration and production, efforts were made to estimate the quantities likely to reach shore by considering natural dispersion rates in relation to the speed of travel on wind and tide. It had been concluded that for Ekofisk oil only very small percentages of the original spillages have any chance of polluting beaches.

Thus although natural dispersion does take place, it cannot be relied upon in general to remove the pollutant from the sea surface before it reaches shore. The extent to which natural dispersior will assist is a function of oil type, quantity spilled and distance from shore of the spillage source. It is important to recognise at this point that dispersants are simply as means of increasing the natural dispersion rate so that sufficient before it reaches the showe. Certainly it is necessary to treat an in which this is an advantage. Thus the spreading phenomenon itself is form of dispersion. In fact it is two-dimensional dispersion and all that remains to be done is to add the third dimension, i.e., to disperse the surface oil into the body of the sea. Oil concentrations measured under chemically dispersed oil slicks and under the naturally dispersing Ekofish Bravo oil slicks were much lower than 100 ppm because the oil, of course, disperses, throughout the sea water to even greater depths than 1m.

Further experiments on this topic have been carried out on Kuwait crude oil at experimentally controlled thicknesses, with the fan-jet nozzle arrangement used for dispersant efficiency testing at sea. Here slicks up to 1 mm in thickness were produced in order to produce high initial concentrations in the water by use of appropriately enhanced dispersant discharge rates. Maximum possible concentration in the top metre on dispersal of a 1 mm thick slick would be 1000 ppm as opposed to the 100 ppm arising from the normal 0.1 mm thick case. The aim of these experiments was to study rates of dilution of the dispersed oil into the sea following treatment. Wind speeds on this occasion were 8-10 knots with sea state 2-3.

With this degree of agitation, observed concentrations were low, suggesting rapid transportation of oil to greater depths by natural turbulence. When these results are compared with the theoretical concentration of 1000 ppm. If all the oil remained uniformly dispersed in the top metre, there is a strong suggestion that initial concentrations in surface waters are reduced by dilution to greater depths. The results of these chemical dispersion experiments in calm and slightly rougher conditions suggest that while initial concentrations might be higher than for natural dispersion, subsequent dilution is rapid, even for slick thicknesses ten times thicker than those normally treated. As a result the persistence of significant amounts of oil in the surface waters is likely to be of shorter duration if dispersant are used than if they are not.

Sampling of the oil carried on board ship

It has already been stated that the best way of establishing that a pollution sample originated from a suspect ship is to compare the results of chemical analysis of the pollutant with that of the oil carried by the ship. In fact it is the only way. Such is the complexity of individual oils and the wide variety of potential sources of distinct oils that it is quite impossible on the basis of a pollutant sample to state the source of that pollutant. Generally speaking, the best that can be done with an unreferenced sample is to say that it is a fresh crude oil, a weather crude oil, a light or heavy fuel oil or tank washings. This is quite insufficient to associate it with a particular source.

This being so, it is necessary in a case of suspected operational discharge to sample all the oils on board including bunker fuel and lubricating oil. This may involve sampling all the tanks, though reference to the cargo manifest may help to reduce the amount of required sampling. Similarly in a shipping casualty it is useful to sample all oils on board since damage to the vessel can result in the release of an variety of oils.

Sampling from the sea and beaches

In collecting samples of liquid oil from the surface of the sea, scare is necessary to ensure that oil is indeed being collected and that the result is not simply a sample of dirty water in an oil contaminated container. Where the pollutant is a relatively thick layer of water-in-oil emulsion it is easier than if the pollutant is fresh oil present to about 0.1 mm thick or even less, but in all cases it is easier to collect water than oil. The use of a container with a bottom outlet and tap is helpful in collecting sufficient oil since with such a device water can be drained off and sampling repeated if necessary. A funnel can be used in this way, using the finger to release the water and retained the oil.

Alternatively where the oil layer is very thin or is in the form of many small isolated globules of oil or emulsion, it may be possible to use adsorption pads. These may be of Teflorn, steel or polyurethane. The oil sticks to the pad when it is placed lightly on the oil-contaminated sea surface. The pad is then placed in a sealed air tight container for transport to the laboratory. Oil can be removed from the pad by use of a suitable solvent and this operation can be carried out either before transportation to the laboratory or after arrival there.

Everything that has been said in the chapters or at-sea oil spill response holds also for inshore waters However, there are a number of additional points o specific relevance to the inshore situation. As oil approaches the shore, the efforts made to combat it either by dispersants or by mechanical recovery means will of necessity be conducted closer and closer to shore, and if these efforts are inadequate the oil will eventually strand on the shoreline. The extent to which the oil stands will depend on the extent to which it is treatable at sea and this in turn will depend on soil size, oil type and the proximity to shore of the original spillage.

So far, beach-cleaning costs per tonne are considered to be so high as to justify operations at sea. For the moment it will be assumed that if activities at sea were justified, they presumably still are close to shore. The next step is to consider dispersants and mechanical recovery separately with a view to establishing whether their ought to be in reasons for discontinuing activities commenced at sea simply because the oil is coming closer and closer to shore, and alternatively the extent to which it might actually be easier to carry out the desired operations now that the oil slicks may be reaching more sheltered waters.

It has been stated elsewhere that crude .oils which spread on the sea surface after spillage form water-in-oil emulsions in which oil is the continuous phase and the water is present as small droplets dispersed throughout the oil. Such emulsions are more viscous than the original oils and have non-Newtonian properties, i.e. they are thixotropic and their flow rates are a function of the stress applied. Thus under the influence of wave action they may have viscosity which permits pumping, but once in a storage tank they will increase in viscosity by standing still and be virtually impossible to remove from the tank when the time comes to do so.

A dispersion of two immiscible liquids is thermodynamically unstable, tending to reduce its free energy by reducing the interfacial area between the two phases by droplet coalescence. Droplet coalescence occurs to a limited extent between rising droplets, but eventually coalescence of droplets in the more densely packed region under the phase boundary and with in the growing continuous phase itself assumes more importance. Finally two separate continuous phases are formed, the separation having been achieved by gravity acting on components of differing density.

Emulsions by contrast are quasi-stable systems in which coalescence is inhibited, often by the presence of a third component, present usually at comparatively low concentration and which is adsorbed on the droplet surfaces. This component is known as an emulsifying agent or emulsifire. Naturally occurring emulsifiers give rise to water-in-oil emulsions.

7

Protection of Marine Environment

The following set of guidelines is addressed to Governments with a view to assisting them in the process of developing appropriate bilateral, regional and multilateral agreements and national legislation for the protection of the marine environment against pollution from land-based sources. They have been prepared on the basis of common elements and principles drawn from relevant existing agreements and drawing upon experience already gained through their preparation and implementation, Principal among these agreements are the United Nations Convention on the Law of the Sea (Part XII), the Paris Convention for the Prevention of Marine Pollution from Land-Based Sources, the Helsinki Convention on the Protection of Marine Environment of the Baltic Sea Area, and the Athens Protocol for the Protection of the Mediterranean Sea against Pollution from Land-Based Sources.

These guidelines are suggested as a broad framework for the development of similar agreements in these regions ere such agreements are called for; for the guidance Governments in areas which may not presently be covered by any regional agreements; and for the preparation in the longer term, should the need arise, of global convention on pollution from land-based sources signed to strengthen international institutional arrangements to ensure the harmonization and application of global and regional rules, criteria, standards and recommended practices and procedures and to review the effectiveness of measures taken.

The guidelines are of a recommendatory nature. They are presented as a checklist of basic provisions rather than a model agreement, from which Governments may select, adapt of elaborate, as appropriate, to meet the needs of specific regions. They are without prejudice to the elaboration of cross-sectoral guidelines/principles within the framework of the programme for the development and periodic review of environmental law, as recommended by the UNEP Ad Hoc Meeting of Senior Government Official Expert in Environmental Law.

Definitions

For the purposes of these guidelines:

(a) "Pollution" means the introduction by man, directly or indirectly, of substances or energy into the marine environment which results or is likely to result in such deleterious effects as harm to living resources and marine ecosystems, hazards to human health, hindrance to marine activities, including fishing and other legitimate uses of the sea, impairment of quality for use of sea water and reduction of amenities.

(b) "Land-based sources" means:

(i) Municipal, industrial or agricultural sources, both fixed and mobile, on land, discharges from which reach the marine environment, in particular: From the coast, including from outfalls discharging directly into the marine environment and through run-off;

Through rivers, canals or other water-courses, including underground water-courses; and via the atmosphere.

(ii) Sources of marine pollution from activities conducted on offshore fixed or mobile facilities within the limits of national jurisdiction, save to the extent that these sources are governed by appropriate international agreements.

(c) "Marine environment" means the maritime area extending, in the case of water-courses up to fresh water limit and including inter-tidal zones and salt-water marshes;

(d) "Freshwater limit" means the place in watercourses where, at low tide and in a period of low freshwater flow, there is an appreciable increase in salinity due to the presence of sea-water.

Basic obligation

States have the obligation to protect and preserve the marine environment. In exercising their sovereign right to exploit their natural resources, all States have the duty to prevent, reduce and control pollution of the marine environment.

Discharges affecting other States or areas beyond the limits of national jurisdiction

States have the duty to ensure that discharges from land-based sources within their territories do not cause pollution to the marine environment of other States or of areas beyond the limits of national jurisdiction.

Adoption of measures against pollution from land-based sources

States should adopt, individually or jointly, and in accordance with their capabilities, all measures necessary to prevent, reduce and control pollution from land-based sources, including those designed to minimize to the fullest possible extent the release of toxic, harmful or noxious substances, especially those which are persistent, into the marine environment. States should ensure that such measures take into account internationally agreed rules, criteria, standards and recommended practices and procedures.

In taking measures to prevent, reduce and control pollution from land-based sources, States should refrain, in accordance with international law, from unjustifiable interference with activities carried out by other States in the exercise of their sovereign rights and in pursuance of their duties in conformity with internationally agreed rules, criteria, standards and recommended practices and procedures.

Co-operation on a global, regional or bilateral basis

States should undertake, as appropriate, to establish internationally agreed rules, criteria, standards and recommended practices and procedures to prevent, reduce and control pollution from land-based sources, with a view to co-ordinating their policies in this connection, particularly at the local and regional level. Such rules, criteria, standards and recommended practices and procedures should take into account local ecological, geographical and physical characteristics, the economic capacity of States and their need for sustainable development and environmental protection, and the assimilative capacity of the marine environment, and should be reviewed from time to time as necessary.

States not bordering on the marine environment should co-operate in preventing, reducing and controlling pollution of the marine environment originating or partially originating from releases within their territory into or reaching water basins or water-courses flowing into the marine environment or via the atmosphere. To this and, States concerned should as far as possible and, as appropriate, in co-operation with competent international organizations, take necessary measures to prevent, reduce and control pollution of the marine environment from land-based sources.

If discharges of a water-course which flows through the territories of two or more States or forms a boundary between them are likely to cause pollution of the marine environment, the States concerned should cooperate in taking necessary measures to prevent, reduce and control such pollution.

Duty not to transfer or transform pollution from land-based sources

In taking measures to prevent, reduce and control pollution from land-based sources, States have the duty to act so as not to transfer directly or indirectly, damage or hazards from one area to another or transform such pollution into another type of pollution.

Specially protected areas

States should consistent with international law, take all appropriate measures, such as the establishment of marine sanctuaries and reserves, to protect certain areas to the fullest possible extent from pollution, including that from land-based sources, taking into account the relevant provisions of Annex 1.

States should, as practicable, undertake to develop, jointly or individually, environmental quality objectives for specially protected areas, conforming with the intended uses, and strive to maintain or ameliorate existing conditions by comprehensive environmental managements practices.

Scientific and technical co-operation

States should co-operate, directly and/or through competent international organizations, in the fields of science and technology related to pollution from land-based sources, and exchange data and other scientific information for the purpose of preventing, reducing and controlling such pollution, taking into account national regulations regarding the protection of confidential information. They should, in particular, undertake to develop and co-ordinate to the fullest possible extent their national research programmes and to co-operate in the establishment and implementation of regional and other international research programmes.

Assistance to developing countries

States should, directly and/or through competent international organizations, promote programmes of assistance to developing countries in the fields education, environmental and pollution awareness training, scientific research , transfer of technology and know-how, for the purpose of improving the capacity the developing countries to prevent, reduce and control pollution from land-based sources and to assess its effect on the marine environment.

Such assistance should include:

(a) Training of Scientific and technical personnel;

(b) Facilitation of the participation of developing countries in relevant international programmes

(c) Acquisition, utilization, maintenance an production by those countries of appropriate equipment; and

(d) Advice on, and development of, facilities for education, training, research, monitoring and other programmes.

States should directly and/or through competent international organizations, promote programmes of assistance to developing countries for the establishment, as necessary, of infrastructure for the effective implementation of applicable internationally agreed rules, criteria, standards and recommended practices and procedures related to the protection of the marine environment against pollution from land-based sources, including the provision of expert advice on the development of the necessary legal and administrative measures.

Development of a comprehensive environmental management approach

States should undertake to develop, as far as practicable, a comprehensive environmental management approach to the prevention, reduction and control of pollution from land-based sources, taking into account relevant existing programmes at the bilateral, regional or global level and the provisions of Annex 1. Such a comprehensive approach should include the identification of desired and attainable water-use objectives for the specific marine environments.

Monitoring and data management

States should endeavour to establish directly or, whenever necessary through competent international organizations, complementary or joint programmes for monitoring, storage and exchange of data, based, when possible, on compatible procedures and methods, taking into account relevant existing programmes at the bilateral, regional or global level and the provisions of Annex III, in order to:

(a) Collect data on natural conditions in the region concerned as regards its physical, biological and chemical characteristics;

(b) Collect data on input of substances or energy that causes or potentially causes pollution emanating from land-based sources, including information on the distribution of sources and the quantities introduced to the region concerned;

(c) Assess systematically the levels of pollution along their coasts emanating from land-based sources and the fate and effects of pollution in the region concerned; and

(d) Evaluate the effectiveness of measures in meeting the environmental objectives for specific marine environments.

Environmental assessment

States should assess the potential effects/impacts, including possible transboundary effects/impacts, of proposed major projects under their jurisdiction or control, particularly in coastal areas, which may cause pollution from land-based sources, so that appropriate measures may be taken to prevent or mitigate such pollution.

Development of control strategies

States should develop, adopt and implement Programmes and measures for the prevention, reduction and control of pollution from land-based sources. They should employ an appropriate control strategy or combination of control strategies, taking into account relevant international or national experience, as described in Annex I.

States should, as appropriate, progressively formulate, and adopt, in co-operation with competent international organizations, standards based on marine quality or on emissions, as well as recommended practices and procedures, taking into account the provisions of Annex 1.

Where appropriate, states should undertake to establish priorities for action, based on lists of substances from which pollution should be eliminated and of substances from which pollution should be strictly limited on the basis of their toxicity, persistence, bioaccumulation and other criteria as elaborated in Annex II, or in relevant international agreements.

Pollution emergencies arising from land-based sources

States and, as appropriate, competent international organizations, should take all necessary measures for preventing and dealing with marine pollution emergencies from land-based sources, however caused, and for reducing or eliminating damage or the threat of damage therefrom. To this end states should, as appropriate, individually or jointly, develop and promote a national and international contingency plans for responding to incidents of pollution from land-based sources and should co-operate with one another and, whenever necessary, through competent international organizations.

Notification, information exchange and consultation

Whenever releases originating or likely to originate from land-based sources within the territory of a State are likely to cause pollution to the marine environment of one or more other States or of areas beyond the limits of national jurisdiction, that State should immediately notify such other State or States, as well as competent international organizations, and provide them with timely information that will enable them, where necessary, to take appropriate action to prevent, reduce and control such pollution. Furthermore, consultations deemed appropriate by States concerned should be undertaken with a view to preventing, reducing and controlling such pollution.

National law and procedures

Each State should adopt and implement national laws and regulations for the protection and preservation of the marine environment against pollution from land-based sources, taking into account internationally agreed rules, criteria, standards and recommended practices and procedures, and take appropriate measures to ensure .compliance with such laws and regulations.

Paragraph 1 is without prejudice to the right of States to take more stringent measures nationally or in co-operation with each other to prevent, reduce and control pollution from land-based sources under their jurisdiction control.

Each State should, on a reciprocal basis, grant equal access to and non-discriminatory treatment in its courts, tribunals and administrative proceedings to persons in other States who are or may be affected by pollution from land-based sources under its jurisdiction control.

Liability and compensation for pollution damage emanating from land-based sources

States should ensure that recourse is available in accordance with their legal systems for prompt and adequate compensation or other relief in respect of damage caused by pollution of the marine environment by natural or juridical persons under their jurisdiction.

To this end, States should formulate and adopt appropriate procedures for the determination of liability for damage resulting from pollution from land-based sources.. Such procedures should include measures for addressing damage caused by releases of a significant scale or by the substances referred to in guideline 13, paragraph 3.

Implementation reports

States should report, as appropriate, to other States concerned, directly or through competent international organizations, on measures taken, on results achieved and, if the case arises, on difficulties encountered in the implementation of applicable internationally agreed rules, criteria, standards and recommended practices and procedures, to this end, States designates national authorities as focal points for the reporting of such measures, results and difficulties.

Institutional arrangements

States should ensure that adequate institutional arrangements are made at the appropriate regional or global level, for the purpose of achieving the objectives of these guidelines, and in particular for promoting the formulation, adoption and application of international rules, criteria, standards and recommended practices and procedures, and for monitoring the condition of the marine environment.

The function of such institutional arrangements should include:

(a) Periodic assessment of the state of the specific marine environment concerned;

(b) Formulation and adoption, as appropriate, of a comprehensive environmental management approach consistent with the provisions of guideline 7 and 10;,

(c) Adoption, review and revision, as necessary of the lists referred to in guideline 13;

(d) Development and adoption, as appropriate, of programmes and measures -consistent with the provisions of guidelines 10 and 13;

(e) Consideration, where necessary, of the reports and information submitted in accordance with guidelines 15 and 18;

(f) Recommendation of appropriate measures to be taken for the prevention, reduction and control of pollution from land-based sources, such as assistance to developing countries, the strengthening of regional mechanisms of cooperation, consideration of aspects of transboundary pollution, and the difficulties encountered in the implementation of agreed rules; and

(g) Review of the implementation of relevant internationally agreed rules, criteria,' standards and recommended practices and procedures, and of the efficacy of the measures adopted and advisability of any other measures.

Annex I

Strategies for protecting, preserving and enhancing strategic the quality of the marine environment

Introduction

In controlling marine pollution from land-based ,sources, and overall approach to the uses and the natural values of the marine environment should be taken, while 11 considering the needs of populations and industries waste disposal. It is important to note that for many of Waste, the use of the marine environment is only e option among several. However, in some instances, marine disposal may be a feasible alternative. This ,document describes a number of strategies which can be employed to protect the marine environment against Pollution from land-based sources and, where-necessary, restore areas that have been affected. The goal is to protect the marine ecosystem by maintaining its quality within acceptable levels as determined on the basis of scientific, institutional, social and economic factors, It should be recognized that there are many activities competing to derive benefits from the marine environment, None of these activities, save the perpetuation of a marine ecosystem as a vital component of global life support, should be regarded as having guaranteed rights. Compromise and consideration of all alternatives must always be considered. Consequently, in the course of the decision-making process determining the use of a particular sector of the marine environment, social, economic and political factors, as well as natural environmental factors must be taken into account.

Once decision makers have determined the desired present, interim and long terms uses, and associated objectives for a water body, a number of control strategies may be employed to achieve those objectives. Flexibility will be an important consideration in the strategies or regulatory instruments implemented for various water bodies, reflecting their different environmental capacities and other properties and differences in regional socioeconomic conditions. The principal strategies in use are based on marine quality standards, on emission standards and on environmental planning. Experience shows that a combination of strategies is often needed. Practical constraints may prevent full implementation of a strategy based on quality standards. Where such an approach cannot be fully implemented, other strategies should be employed.

Control strategies

Pollution control strategies in use have been categorized according to:

— those based on marine environmental quality standards,

— those based on emission standards,

— those based on environmental planning.

Priorities for control are often established by the classification of substances into a black and a grey list substances are assessed according to the criteria described in Annex II. States undertake to eliminate pollution 41 those substances in the black list and strictly to limit pollution by those in the grey list.

Strategies based on marine quality standards

Such strategies relate directly to quality of water, biota or sediments that must be maintained for a desired level of quality and intended use. Several applications of such quality-based strategies exist.

Direct derivation from quality objectives

Technical assessments are conducted to determine the maximum allowable inputs that will ensure the desired levels of environmental quality are met. The assessments consider the fates and affects of various contaminants, amounts of input, and the existing natural characteristics of the relevant marine ecosystem. Numerical standards are then established to which concentrations measured in the receiving environment may be compared. They are usually more restrictive than numbers derived from the technical assessment to allow for monitoring and enforcement capabilities and safety requirements. They may apply to water, sediment, fish or the tissues, health or community composition of organisms in the marine ecosystem.

Monitoring is required to detect changes and compliance with the standards. Changes in the items monitored, after adjustment for natural fluctuation, may signal a need further to reduce inputs and vary existing standards and controls.

No change above ambient

Standards are set based on existing levels which Must not be exceeded. This strategy is employed in situations where the aim is to prevent any increase in prevailing specific contaminant levels. It is an interim strategy to allow time to develop a solid scientific base on which more precise quality criteria may be employed for a specific use. It does not imply an existing state of the environment that is satisfactory, nor does it eliminate the need for its improvement.

Dilution

Some contaminants discharged at the source are assumed to attenuate as they spread, from that source. Dynamic characteristics of the receiving environment are employed to determine rate and level of dilution. Standards are derived from measured parameters taken at given distances from the discharging source. The strategy may accept short-term or local excess of a potential pollution at the source of discharge. Application is generally used with effluent that is considered biodegradable, and avoided where scientific evidence suggests that the effluent may accumulate in a given receiving environment.

Loading allocations

These impose priority of control on the larger sources in consideration of the most cost-effective solution. Allowable discharges are measured in terms of the total allowable for an entire receiving environment regardless of specific site quality. Application is suited to relatively self-contained receiving environments such as lagoons and semi-enclosed bodies of water. It allows flexibility of contaminant output in that certain sources may emit more than adjacent ones as long as loading limits are not exceeded. All these strategies may employ criteria for water, air or sediment quality, as well as criteria related to specific marine life. Receiving environment quality standards are most prevalent for uses, e.g. swimming, direct harvesting of fish for human consumption, where sound scientific criteria exist to determine levels of harm. Emissions of potential pollutants are usually controlled to ensure that the desired quality is achieved. If the quality needs to be upgraded, additional controls are placed on allowable emissions.

Strategies based on emission standards

These strategies may be based on:

— a general principle to control pollution,

— achievable technology,

— distribution of control costs,

— enforceability.

They differ from strategies based on marine quality is that the standards set are not primarily determined by the level of contaminant in the environment.

Technology-based standards

These standards are usually applied on a sectoral basis, thus providing a means of imposing similar costs .Across a particular sector. Alternatively, they may be ,determined on a case-by-case basis. The standards will need to be reviewed periodically the light of developing technology.

Standards may be based on:

Best practicable technology

This reflects the application of demonstrable and sound treatment technology or spectrum of technologies which affordable by the sector concerned.

Best available technology

This reflects state-of-art technology in use in contaminant control. In general, the standards set would reflect a more stringent level of control as compared to best practicable technology. Application is generally for control of emissions of the most noxious substances to protect a sensitive environmental use.

As low as reasonably achievable

This is mainly applied to radionuclides and is based on the principle of "optimization". This, as defined by the international Commission on Radiological Protection, requires radiation doses to be kept to levels that are "reasonable achievable", by technological improvements and by suitable choice among alternative options. "Reasonably achievable" takes into account both the ease with which the technology can be applied and the balance between the benefits, in terms of dose reduction, and social and economic costs of its application.

In a situation where stringent protection of sensitive marine environment is deemed appropriate, consideration may be given to the denial of any release of a contaminant to the environment.

Uniform regional emission standards

Such standards are usually applied in situations where there are existing pollution problems of a similar nature and there is urgent need to reduce pollution. They do not give primary consideration to the nature of sources, their economic base, or the receiving environment.

Planning strategies

Planning strategies allow an approach to the management and protection of particular environments which may involve restrictions on, or modification of, activities and sites as well as discharges.

Activity management

Certain activities are deemed inappropriate or inconsistent with the value or use of an environment. Consideration should be given to whether the activity is essential, and if so, whether it can be accommodated elsewhere or in a different manner.

Use designation

Use of the receiving environment is the determining factor for pollution control standards as well, as the basis for regulations or guidelines affecting other activities. For example, if the desire is to maintain or develop a shellfish harvest (a socio-economic decision) then quality standards and uses are developed with, this in mind.

The application may result from the perceived threat to an established economic base, or cultural value, or, a conscious effort to change the existing use of the receiving environment.

Environmental assessments of activities

Siting of any activity significantly affecting the marine environment is subject to a comprehensive analysis and assessment of :

— The ecological characteristics of the receiving environment,

— the direct and indirect potential effects/impacts of the activity on the environment; and, as appropriate,

— the direct and indirect potential effects/impacts on the environment of any reasonable alternative to the activity.

Regional planning

Plans are drawn up for particular region, taking into account socio-economic and ecological factors, which are then used as a basis for development.

Coastal zone management

The strategy employs planning capabilities to make best use of the coastal zone.

It is not uses or source specific but area specific assessed as components of a coastal zone planning is based on regional socio-economic and ecological considerations. Zoning and other land-use restrictions or modifications are major regulatory tools. Many state employ the use of regional planning authorities of councils, given the task to manage overall resource planning within A particular coastal area.

Watershed or drainage basin planning

This strategy acknowledges that a large proportion of pollution enters the marine environment via watercourses. It does not necessarily account for inputs via the atmosphere, though air management areas have also been employed for control purposes.

Through consideration of socio-economic an environmental factors utilizing a drainage system as the boundary limit, the desired uses and level of quality that can be attained for any given marine water body are determined.

Pollution via watercourses is controlled through regulation of points and diffuse sources of such pollution within the given watershed.

Specially protected areas

This strategy involves the identification of unique or pristine areas, rare or fragile ecosystems, critical habitats and the habitat of depleted, threatened or endangered species and other forms of marine life.

Those areas to be protected or preserved from pollution, including that from land-based sources, are selected on the basis of a comprehensive evaluation of factors, including conservational ecological, recreational, aesthetic and *scientific values.*

State should notify an appropriate international organization of the establishment of and any modification to such areas, with a view to that data being included in an inventory of specially protected areas.

Control Instruments

This section outlines the various types of mechanism which can be invoked to implement control strategies.

Regulations

Regulations are developed pursuant to establishing legislation and can exist in form such as:

Emissions standards (air/water)

Standards based on best practicable technology, best available technology, geographical area, etc.,

Environmental quality standards

Standards for the receiving environment which vary according to its intended use.

Guidelines of practice

These are descriptions of practices and abatement technologies that may be developed to meet the pollution control needs of various point and non-point sources. They provide a listing of basic requirements that may be implemented or adopted by industry or local authorities.

Permits

Legislation may require a discharger to have a permit to satisfy the requirements for the release of pollutants. These requirements can be based on standards in the form of emission control regulations, guidelines, codes of practice or specific requirement derived from environmental quality standard prescribed to protect the receiving environment.

Equipment standards certification

Environmental considerations may be incorporated directly in association with particular equipment. To this end, the equipment, or configuration of equipment may be designed, manufactured, tested and certified to comply with the requirements for source releases of pollutants.

Product controls

If a particular substance, or assemblage of substances in the form of a commercial product is deemed to be of environmental significance, a restriction on the product in the form of production, use, as well as export/import may be implemented.

Planning restrictions

Under planning law or practice, restrictions 'may be placed on the use of certain land.

Economic measures

These may take a variety of forms, e.g. tax incentive, subsidies and effluent charges. To be effective, the incentive offered must be strong enough or the charge levied high enough to persuade the discharger of user that it is in his own financial interest to limit his discharge or use of the substance concerned.

Factors Influencing Choice of Strategies and Control Instruments

There is a wide range of strategies and control instruments which can be utilized by a state either individually or in combination to address pollution, of the marine environment from land-based sources. A number of factors may influence such a choice. In general terms, they may be categorized as economic, scientific/technical or social/cultural/political.

Economic

— General economic conditions and trends (deficit, balance of trade, inflation etc.),

— Availability of public financing,

— Availability of external funding,

— Unemployment

— Economic viability of various sectors,

— Polluter-pays principle,

— Availability of institutions and infrastructure.

Scientific/Technical

Availability-accessibility of scientific data, including.

— Physical characteristic affecting flushing and mixing,

— Natural nutrient cycles and geochemical, cycles,

— Biological processes and nature of communities.

Availability/ accessibility of technology, including.

— Basic information on industry types, total effluent releases, and specific data on waste stream constituents.

— Availability of expertise,

— Capability for monitoring,

— Existing engineering infrastructure

— Experience with implementation of strategies or instruments elsewhere,

— Sensitivity of ecosystems to be affected,

— Climatic consideration,

Current level of pollution of the receiving environment and identified trends, in municipal agricultural and industrial waste releases.

Social/cultural/political

— Infrastructure,

— Existing and proposed uses of the marine environment,

— Political realities,

— Social/cultural awareness of the population,

— Perception of environmental, social and cultural values.

Annex II

Classification of substances

Substances may be classified into a black list of those substances pollution from which should be eliminated and grey list of those substances pollution from which should be strictly limited and reduced.

The basic criteria to be taken into account in allocating substances to one of these lists are:

(a) persistence,

(b) toxicity to bio-accumulation,

(c) tendency to bio-accumulation.

These criteria are not necessarily of equal importance for a particular substance or group of substances. Other factors such as location and quantities of the discharge may need to be considered.

Black List

Substances may be included in this list:

(a) because they are not readily degradable or rendered harmless by natural processes; and

(b) because they may either:

  (i) give rise to dangerous accumulation of harmful material in the food chain, or endanger the welfare of living organism causing undesirable changes in the marine ecosystems, or interfere seriously with the harvesting of set foods or with other legitimate uses of the sea and because it is considered that pollution by these substances necessitates urgent action.

The substances that fulfil criteria may include:

— certain organic biocides (e.g. organohalogen compounds and substances which may form such compounds in the marine environment);

— persistent hydrocarbons of petroleum origin;

— certain metals and their compounds (e.g. mercury);

— persistent synthetic materials which may

seriously interfere with any legitimate use of the sea;

— Radioactive materials;

— Substances in respect of which it has been proved that they possess carcinogenic properties in or via the aquatic environment;

— Materials in whatever form (e.g. solids, liquids, semi-liquids, gases, or in a living state) produced for biological and chemical warfare.

Grey List

Substances may be included in this list because, although exhibiting similar characteristics to the substances in the black list and requiring strict control, they seem less noxious or are more readily rendered harmless by natural processes. The substances to which this may apply include:

— Organic biocides not included in the black list;

— Hydrocarbons of petroleum origin and their derivatives not included in the black list;

— Certain elements and their compounds (e.g. fluorides and cyanides);

— Organic and synthetic organic materials, other those included in the black list, which are likely to produce harmful effects on marine organisms or to make ~edible marine organisms unpalatable, as well as chemicals which may lead to the formation of such substances in the marine environment;

— Acid and alkaline compounds of such composition and in such quantities that they may seriously impair the quality of the marine environment;

— Substances which though not producing toxic effects, may become harmful because of the concentrations or quantities in which they are discharged, or which are liable to reduce amenities seriously or to endanger human life or marine organisms or to impair other legitimate uses of the sea;

Pathogenic micro-organisms which are or may become harmful because of the concentrations and quantities in which they are discharged or which are liable to endanger human life or marine organisms, or impair other legitimate uses of the marine environment and the coastal waters in particular.

Annex III

Monitoring and Data Management

In the Protection of the marine environment against pollution from land based sources, monitoring can be defined as the measurement of the pollutant or its effects either man or elements or the marine resources for purposes of assessing and controlling exposure to the pollutant. Thus monitoring is used first to assess the d for pollution prevention measures and subsequently effectiveness of any protection measures introduced. If monitoring is to meet these objectives and be cost-effective it must be carefully designed and implemented.

Resources to be protected

One of the first thing to ascertain is what resources need protecting in the area concerned and the various pollutant sources and ways in which each could possibly be threatened. For example, the well-being of a nature, reserve, fish hatchery of fish resource might be threatened by the variety of substances. Similarly, the suitability of fish or shell-fish for human consumption might be affected by other substances such as mercury of arsenic which may adversely affect man, whilst not affecting fisheries.

Information on inputs

It is also important at an early stage to establish for each area the activities already practised and the pollutants likely to reach the sea via point, non-point and riverine sources.

A knowledge of the resources to be protected and which pollutants are most likely to affect them will allow attention to be focused on those substances which appear most likely to be of concern, thereby reducing the amount of effort devoted to establishing a data base, on inputs. Information on inputs can also be used to focus environmental monitoring efforts on those pollutants most likely to be encountered in each area. If possible the scale of input should also be established, at least in order of magnitude terms. This will normally be fairly easy but in more accurate qualification will require improvements in the quality of data on both concentration and flow.

Information on inputs from direct discharges may be determined from descriptions of unit processes in use. If permit programmes have been established, information on controlled pollutants should be available from the permitting authority. Inputs from non-point sources are generally estimated by employing accepted formulae describing land use in the watershed and the associated run-off. In estimating point and non-point sources inputs, the pollutants of concern may include a broad range of substance for example, toxicants and nutrients.

Establishing baseline concentrations

Having decided what needs to be monitored, on the basis of what resources must be protected and which pollutants are likely to be of interest, the concentrations actually present in the environment can be established. This information can then be used to assess those protection measures necessary and/or their effectiveness. The need for control measures my be judged either by comparison of the concentrations found with some form of water quality criteria, for example maximum permissible concentration, or with similar data from other areas known not to be contaminated.

When baseline concentrations are being ascertained, the most appropriate substrate should be selected. Three options exist: water, biota and sediments, only rarely should it be necessary to analyse samples of all three. The choice will depend on the pollutant concerned, the water quality criteria selected and the nature of the pathways exposed. For example, water would be most suitable for nutrients, biochemical oxygen demand (BOD), pH and certain metals, but biota would be more appropriate for polychlorinated biphenyles (PCBs) or mercury, and undisturbed sediments can be particularly useful in time or spatial trend assessments.

Ongoing monitoring

Monitoring will be required to establish the effectiveness of pollution protection measures. Even if no reductions in inputs are deemed necessary it may be desired to check that the situation does not deteriorate. Whatever their purpose, monitoring programmes should designed to consider the receiving capacity of the environment as well as inputs. This means considering present water quality in relation to the desired quality, the scale of environmental protection measures taken in relation to the existing concentrations, nature of the pollutants present, the scale of their input and their removal processes. On this basis it will be possible to define what should be monitored and with what frequency.

Sampling and analysis

The number of samples collected and their nature should represent the substrate being monitored. Water quality, biological tissues and sediments can all be very variable even over short distances and the sampling strategy should, when necessary be tested statistically to ensure it is sound. The programme design should take account of the hydrographic characteristics of the area so as to avoid sampling the same body of water at different places as it moves under the influence of a current. Finally, the sample collected must be adjusted to the form in which the pollutant occurs in the environment or in the discharge streams.

Once a suitable sampling programme has been designed, it may be possible to bulk samples for analysis in order to reduce the analytical workload and costs. This will inevitably lead to the loss of some information and should only be considered if the complexity of the analytical technique demands it and/or the loss of information can be tolerated or if the monitoring is only to be used to pick up abnormalities such as in compliance monitoring.

Resource monitoring

In addition to monitoring the pollutants of interest in the selected substrate, it is essential that the state of the resource(s) be monitored. However, if adverse changes do occur it should not be assumed the protection measures taken were inadequate. For example, fish stocks decline due to fishing effort as well as pollution and undesirable plankton blooms occur for reasons other than nutrient enrichment. Biological effects monitoring is desirable but very few techniques can be applied routinely on a wide scale and most give unspecific responses. Once suitable effects monitoring techniques are available, they may be more attractive alternatives than purely chemical monitoring in environmental matrices.

Data and data management

Before the data from any monitoring programme are used, it is important that confidence limits be established and reported in order to ensure that the confidence with which recorded numbers are handled and interpreted is not misplaced. It is also necessary to decide how the data should be handled for future reference and use.

Limitations in the data and the extent to which they can be tolerated

The results obtained from any monitoring programme will be subject to errors of accuracy and precision, the size of which must be quantified. If precision is high and accuracy poor then all results for a set of analyses of the same sample will be very close together, for example, differing by no more than one per cent though they may differ from the true result by much more, possibly by as much as an order of magnitude. Some errors will derive from the nature of the samples. There can be minimized by proper statistical design of the sampling procedures and attention to the collection of uncontaminated samples.

All analytical procedures have inherent errors in precision and accuracy. To a greater or lesser extent either or both types of error can be compounded by operator or laboratory errors, which are often not recognized. However, by use of good analytical equipment and methods and by following a rigorous analytical quality assurance scheme, it should be possible to achieve high accuracy and precision for all analytical-data, and allow qualification of the scale errors.

Intercomparability requirements

In most cases where monitoring programmes are operated on a multilateral basis it is essential that the results obtained by all contributors are truly comparable.

Establishing comparable monitoring programmes may prove difficult. However, it is desirable that targets be set for comparability of the data. Analytical comparability is only one aspect of monitoring data. The actual programmes run by different countries must also be comparable. It obviously will not be possible to compare results from three countries if one analyses water, another a fish species and another sediments. Even when agreement is reached on whether to sample water, biota or sediments it will be necessary to agree for example, which species of fish should be used, whether the water should be filtered before analysis or whether whole sediment should be analysed or only a particular size fraction.

Requirements for analytical quality control

It may be impossible to arrange that all contributors use identical analytical procedures. Even if they do, for the reasons given previously, intercomparability is not guaranteed. To establish whether differences do exist and to minimize them, a programme of intercalibration is essential. Each laboratory should assure the quality of its data by participating in intercalibration exercises and analysing at intervals reference materials containing certified concentrations of the pollutants of interest in appropriate matrices and concentrations.

Data storage, retrieval and exchange

Depending on the scale of the monitoring programme various methods of data storage and transfer may be appropriate. It is essential that the design of the storage/ retrieval system be carefully worked out to reflect the end use of the data both in its raw and interpreted form. The most efficient method in many respects is to use a computer. It is essential that the limitations of any set of data be instantly recognized when it is retrieved. To this end, information such as performance in a recognized interealibration exercise, analysis of reference material, etc. should be retrievable with the data. Ideally the data ,should be freely accessible by all contributors and the ,scientific community in general. However, if a country or group of countries wish certain types of data to be available only to a limited audience that wish must be safeguarded. Regions may exhibit different, natural, background or baseline concentration, have different resources to be protected and be exposed to different pollutants. As a consequence their monitoring programmes might differ. For example, different fish species might be used as indicators permissible limits might differ according to exposure patterns and different targets might be set for sampling and analytical accuracy. Therefore it will probably be more practical and effective, at least initially to organize monitoring programmes and data storage on a, regional rather than a global basis.

8

Convention on the High Seas

Geneva, 29 April 1958

The States Parties to this Convention,

Desiring to codify the rules of international law relating to the high seas,

Recognizing that the United Nations Conference on the Law of the Sea, held at Geneva from 24 February to 27 April 1958, adopted the following provisions as generally declaratory of established principles of international law,

Have agreed as follows:

Article 1

The term high seas means all parts of the sea that are not included in the territorial sea or in the internal waters of State.

Article 2

The high seas being open to all nations, no State may validly purport to subject any part of them to its sovereignty. Freedom of the high seas is exercised under the conditions laid down by these articles and by the other rules of international law. It comprises, inter alia, both for coastal and noncoastal States;

1. Freedom of navigation;
2. Freedom of fishing;
3. Freedom to lay submarine cables and pipelines;
4. Freedom to fly over the high seas.

These freedoms, and others which are recognized by the general principles of international law, shall be exercised by all States with reasonable regard to the interests of other States in their exercise of the freedom of the high seas.

Article 3

1. In order to enjoy the freedom of the seas on equal terms with coastal States, States having no sea-coast should have free access to the sea. To this and States situated between the sea and a State having no sea-coast shall by common agreement with the latter and in conformity with existing international convention accord;

   a) To the State having no sea-coast, on a basis of reciprocity, free transit through their territory; and

   b) To ships flying the flag of that State treatment equal to that accorded to their own ships, or to the ships of any other States, as regards access to seaports and the use of such ports.

2. States situated between the sea and a State having no sea-coast shall settle, by mutual agreement with the latter, and taking in to account the rights of the coastal State of transit and the special conditions of the State having no sea-coast, all matters relating to freedom of transit and equal treatment in ports, in case

such States are not already parties to existing international conventions.

Article 4

Every State, whether coastal or not, has the right to sail ships under its flag on the high seas.

Article 5

1. Each State shall fix the conditions for the grant of its nationality to ships, for the registration of ships, in its territory, and for the right to fly its flag. Ships have the nationality of the State whose flag they are entitled to fly. There must exist a genuine link between the State and the ship; in particular, the State must effectively exercise its jurisdiction and control in administrative, technical and social matters over ships flying its flag.
2. Each State shall issue to ships to which it has granted the right to fly its flag documents to that effect.

Article 6

1. Ships shall sail under the flag of one State only and, save in exceptional cases expressly provided for in international treaties or in these articles, shall be subject to its exclusive jurisdiction on the high seas. A ship may not change its flag during a voyage or while in a port of call, save in the case of a real transfer of ownership or change of registry.
2. A ship which sails under the flags of two or more States, using them according to convenience, may not claim any of the nationalities in question with respect to any other State, and maybe assimilated to a ship without nationality.

Article 7

The provisions of the preceding articles do not prejudice the question of ships employed on the official service of an inter-governmental organization flying the flag of the organization.

Article 8

1. Warships on the high seas have complete immunity from the jurisdiction of any State other than the flag State.
2. For the purposes of these articles, the term warship means a ship belonging to the naval forces of a State and bearing the external marks distinguishing warships of its nationality, under the command of an officer duly commissioned by the government and whose name appears in the Navy List, and manned by a crew who are under regular naval discipline.

Article 9

Ships owned or operated by a State and used only on government non-commercial service shall, on the high seas, have complete immunity from the jurisdiction of any State other than the flag State.

Article 10

1. Every State shall take such measures for ships under its flag as are necessary to ensure safety at sea with regard inter alia to;
   a) The use of signals, the maintenance of communications and the prevention of collisions;
   b) The manning of ships and labour conditions for crews taking into account the applicable international labour instruments;

c) The construction, equipment and seaworthiness of ships.

2. In taking such measures each State is required to conform to generally accepted international standards and to take any steps which may be necessary to ensure their observance.

Article 11

1. In the event of a collision or of any other incident of navigation concerning a ship on the high seas, involving the penal or disciplinary responsibility of the master or of any other person in the service of the ship, no penal or disciplinary proceedings may be instituted against such persons except before the judicial or administrative authorities either of the flag State or of the State of which such person is a national.

2. In disciplinary matters, the State which has issued a master's certificate or a certificate of competence or licence shall alone be competent, after due legal process, to pronounce the withdrawal of such certificates, even if the holder is not a national of the State which issued them.

3. No arrest or detention of the ship, even as a measure of investigation, shall be ordered by any authorities other than those of the flag State.

Article 12

1. Every State shall require the master of the ship sailing under its flag, in so far as he can do so without serious danger to the ship, the crew or the passengers-,

    a) To render assistance to any person found at sea in danger of being lost;

b) To proceed with all possible speed to the rescue of persons in distress if informed of their need of assistance, in so far as such action may reasonably be expected of him;

c) After a collision, to render assistance to the other ship, her crew and her passengers and, where possible, to inform the other ship of the name of his own ship, her port of registry and the nearest port at which she will call.

2. Every coastal State shall promote the establishment and maintains of an adequate and effective search and rescue service regarding safety on and over the sea and—where circumstances so require—by way of mutual regional arrangements co-operate with neighbouring States for this purpose.

Article 13

Every State shall adopt effective measures to prevent and punish the transport of slaves in ships authorized to fly its flag, and to prevent the unlawful use of its flag for that purpose. Any slave taking refuge on board any ship, whatever its flag, shall *ipso facto* be free.

Article 14

All States shall co-operate to the fullest possible extent in the repression of piracy on the high seas or in any other place outside the jurisdiction of any State.

Article 15

Piracy consists of any of the following acts:

1. Any illegal acts of violence, detention or any act of depredation, committed for private ends by the crew or the passengers of a private ship or a private aircraft, and directed;

a) On the high seas, against another ship or aircraft, or against persons or property on board such ship or aircraft;

b) Against a ship, aircraft, persons or property in a place outside the jurisdiction of any State;

2. Any act of voluntary participation in the operation of a ship or of an aircraft with the knowledge of facts making it a pirate ship or aircraft;

3. Any act of inciting or of intentionally facilitating an act described in sub-paragraph 1 or sub-paragraph 2 of this article.

Article 16

The acts of piracy, as defined in article 15, committed by a warship, government aircraft whose crew has mutinied and taken control of the ship or aircraft are assimilated to acts committed by a private ship.

Article 17

A ship or aircraft is considered a pirate ship or aircraft if it is intended by the persons in dominant control to be used for the purpose of committing one of the acts referred to in article 15. The same applies if the ship or aircraft has been used to commit any such act, so long as it remains under the control of the persons guilty of that act.

Article 18

A ship or aircraft may retain its nationality although it has become a pirate ship or aircraft. The retention or loss of nationality is determined by the law of the State from which such nationality was derived.

Article 19

On the high seas, or in any other place outside the jurisdiction of any State, every State may seize a pirate ship or aircraft, or a ship taken by piracy and under the control of pirates, and arrest the persons and seize the property on board. The courts of the States which carried out the seizure may decide upon the penalties to be imposed, and may also determine the action to be taken with regard to the ships, aircraft or property, subject to the rights of third parties acting in good faith.

Article 20

Where the seizure of ship or aircraft on suspicion of piracy has been effected without adequate grounds, the State making the seizure shall be liable to the State the nationality of which is possessed by the ship or aircraft, for any loss or damage caused by the seizure.

Article 21

A seizure on account of piracy may only be carried out by warships or military aircraft, or other ships or aircraft on government service authorized to that effect.

Article 22

1. Except where acts of interference derive from powers conferred by treaty, a warship which encounters a foreign merchant ship on the high seas is not justified in boarding her unless there is reasonable ground for suspecting;

    a) That the ship is engaged in piracy; or

    b) That the ship is engaged in the slave trade; or

    c) That, though flying a foreign flag or refusing

to show its flag, the ship is, in reality, of the same nationality as the warship.

2. In the cases provided for in sub-paragraphs [a], [b] and [c] above, the warship may proceed to verify the ship's right to fly its flag. To this end, it may send a boat under the command of an officer to the suspected ship. If suspicion remains after the documents have been checked, it may proceed to a further examination on board the ship, which must be carried out with all possible consideration.

3. If the suspicions prove to be unfounded, and provided that the ship boarded has not committed any act justifying them, it shall be compensated for any loss or damage that may have been sustained.

Article 23

1. The hot pursuit of a foreign ship may be undertaken when the competent authorities of the coastal State have good reason to believe that the ship has violated the laws and regulations of that State. Such pursuit must be commenced when the foreign ship or one of its boats is within the internal waters or the territorial sea or the contiguous zone of the pursuing State, and may only be continued outside the territorial sea or the contiguous zone if the pursuit has not been interrupted. It is not necessary that, at the time when the foreign ship within the territorial sea or the contiguous zone receives the order to stop, the ship giving the order should likewise be within the territorial sea or the contiguous zone. If the foreign ship is within a contiguous zone, as defined in article 24 of the Convention on the Territorial Sea and the Contiguous Zone, the pursuit-may only be undertaken it there has

been a violation of the rights, for the protection of which the zone was established.

2. The right of hot pursuit ceases as soon as the ship pursued enters the territorial sea of its own country or of a third State.

3. Hot pursuit is not deemed to have begun unless the pursuing ship has satisfied itself by such practicable means as may be available that the ship pursued or one of its boats or other craft working as a team and using the ship pursued as a mother ship are within the limits of the territorial sea, or as the case may be within the contiguous zone. The pursuit may only be commenced after a visual or auditory signal to stop has been given at a distance which enables it to be seen or heard by the foreign ship.

4. The right of hot pursuit may be exercised only by warships or military aircraft, or other ships or aircraft on government service specially authorized to that effect.

5. Where hot pursuit is effected by an aircraft;

   a) The provisions of paragraphs 1 to 3 of this article shall apply mutatis mutandis;

   b) The aircraft giving the order to stop must itself actively pursue the ship until a ship or aircraft of the coastal State, summoned by the aircraft, arrives to take over the pursuit, unless the aircraft is itself able to arrest the ship. It does no suffice to justify an arrest on the high seas that the ship was merely sighted by the aircraft as an offender or suspected offender, if it was not both ordered to stop and pursued by the, aircraft itself or other aircraft or ships which continue the pursuit without interruption.

6. The release of a ship arrested within the jurisdiction of a State and escorted to a port of that State for purposes of an enquiry before the competent authorities may not be claimed solely on the ground that the ship, in the course of its voyage, was escorted across a portion of the high seas, if the circumstances rendered this necessary.
7. Where a ship has been stopped or arrested on the high seas in circumstances which do not justify the exercise of the right of hot pursuit, it shall be compensated for any loss or damage that may have been thereby sustained.

Article 24

Every State shall draw up regulations to prevent population of the seas by the discharge of oil from ships or pipelines or resulting from the exploitation and exploration of the seabed and its subsoil, taking account of existing treaty provisions on the subject.

Article 25

1. Every State shall take measures to prevent pollution of the seas from the dumping of radioactive waste, taking into account any standards and regulations which may be formulated by the competent international organizations.
2. All States shall co-operate with the competent international organizations in taking measures for the prevention of pollution of the seas or air space above, resulting from any activities with radio active materials or other harmful agents.

Article 26

1. All States shall be entitled to lay submarine cables and pipelines on the bed of the high seas.

2. Subject to its right to take reasonable measures for the exploration of the continental shelf and the exploration of its natural resources, the coastal State may not impede the laying or maintenance of such cables or pipelines.

3. When laying such cables or pipelines the State in question shall pay due regard to cables or pipelines already in position on the seabed. In particular, possibilities of repairing existing cables or pipelines shall not be prejudiced.

Article 27

Every state shall take the necessary legislative measures to provide that the breaking or injury by a ship flying its flag or by a person subject to its jurisdiction of a submarine cable beneath the high seas done wilfully or through culpable negligence, in such a manner as to be liable to interrupt or obstruct telegraphic or telephonic communications, and similarly the breaking of injury of a submarine pipeline or high-voltage power cable shall be punishable offence. This provision shall not apply to any break or injury caused by persons who acted merely with the legitimate object of saving their lives or their ships, after having taken all necessary precautions to avoid such break or injury.

Article 28

Every State shall take the necessary legislative measures to provide that if persons subject to its jurisdiction who are the owners or a cable or pipeline beneath the high seas, in laying or repairing that cable or pipeline, cause a break in or injury to another cable or pipeline, they shall bear the cost of the repairs.

Article 29

Every State shall take the necessary legislative measures to ensure that the owners or ships who can prove that they have sacrificed an anchor, a net or any other fishing gear, in order to avoid injuring a submarine cable or pipeline, shall be indemnified by the owner of the cable or pipeline, provided that the owner of the ship has taken all reasonable precautionary measures beforehand.

Article 30

The provisions of this Convention shall not affect conventions or other international agreements already in force, as between States Parties to them.

Article 31

This Convention shall, until 31 October 1958, be open for signature by all States Members of the United Nations or of any other specialized agencies and by any other State invited by the General Assembly of the United Nations to become a Party to the Convention.

Article 32

This Convention is subject to ratification. The instruments of ratification shall be deposited with the Secretary-General of the United Nations.

Article 33

This Convention shall be open for accession by any States belonging to any of the categories mentioned in article 31. The instruments of accession shall be deposited with the Secretary-General of the United Nations.

Article 34

1. This Convention shall come in to force on the thirtieth day following the date of deposit of the

twenty-second instrument of ratification or accession with the Secretary-General of the United Nations.

2. For each State ratifying or acceding to the Convention after the deposit of the twenty-second instrument of ratification or accession, the Convention shall enter into force on the thirtieth day after deposit by such State of its instrument of ratification or accession.

Article 35

1. After the expiration of a period of five years from the date on which this Convention shall enter into force, a request for the revision of this Convention may be made at any time by any Contracting Party by means of a notification in writing addressed to the Secretary-General of the United Nations.

2. The General Assembly of the United Nations shall decide upon the steps, if any, to be taken in respect of such request.

Article 36

The Secretary-General of the United Nations shall inform all States Members of the United Nations and the other States referred to in article 31;

a) Of signatures to this Convention, and of the deposit of instruments of ratification or accession, in accordance with articles 31, 32 and 33;

b) Of the date on which this Convention will come into force, in accordance with article 34;

c) Of requests for revision in accordance with article 35.

Article 37

The original of this Convention, of which the Chinese, English, French, Russian and Spanish texts are equally authentic, shall be deposited with the Secretary-General of the United Nations, who shall send certified copies thereof to all States referred to in article 31.

In Witness Whereof the undersigned Plenipotentiaries, being duly authorized thereto by their respective Governments, have signed this Convention.

Done at Geneva, this twenty-ninth day of April one thousand nine hundred and fifty-eight.

Convention on Fishing and Conservation of Living Resources of the High Seas (1958)

Geneva, 29 April 1958

The States Parties to this Convention

Considering that the development of modern techniques for the exploitation of the living resources of the sea, increasing man's ability to meet the need of the world's expanding population for food, has exposed some of these resources to the danger of being over-exploited,

Considering also that the nature of the problems involved in the conservation of the living resources of the high seas is such that there is a clear necessity that they be solved, whenever possible, on the basis of international co-operating through the concerted action of all the States concerned,

Have agreed as follows:

Article 1

1. All States have the right for their nationals to engage in fishing on the high seas, subject (a) to

their treaty obligations, (b) to the interests and rights of coastal States as provided for in this Convention, and (c) to the provisions contained in the following articles concerning conservation of the living resources of the high seas.

2. All States have the duty to adopt, or to co-operate with other States in adopting, such, measures for their respective nationals as may be necessary for the conservation of the living resources of the high seas.

Article 2

As employed in this Convention, the expression "conservation of the living resources of the high seas" means the aggregate of the measures rendering possible the optimum sustainable yield from those resources so as to secure a maximum supply of food and other marine products. Conservation programmes should be formulated with a view to securing in the first place a supply of food for human consumption.

Article 3

A State whose nationals are engaged in fishing any stock or stocks of fish or other living marine resources in any area of the high seas where the nationals of other States are not thus engaged shall adopt, for its own nationals, measures in that area when necessary for the purpose of the conservation of the living resources affected.

Article 4

1. If the nationals of the two or more States are engaged in fishing the same stock or stocks of fish or other living marine resources in any area or areas of the high seas, these States shall, at the request of any of them, enter into negotiations with a view to prescribing by

agreement for their nationals the necessary measures for the conservation of the living resources affected.

2. If the States concerned do not reach agreement within twelve months, any of the parties may initiate the procedure contemplated by article 9.

Article 5

1. If, subsequent to the adoption of the measures referred to in articles 3 and 4, nationals of other states engage in fishing the same stock or stocks of fish or other living marine resources in any area or areas of the high seas, the other States shall apply the measures, which shall not be discriminatory in form or in fact, to their own nationals not later than seven months after the date on which the measures shall have been notified to the Director-General of the Food and Agriculture Organization of the United Nations. The Director-General shall notify such measures to any State which so requests and, in any case, to any State specified by the State initiating the measure.

2. If these other States do not accept the measures so adopted and if no agreement can be reached within twelve months, any of the interested parties may initiate the procedure contemplated by article 9. Subject to paragraph 2 of article 10, the measures adopted shall remain obligatory pending the decision of the specified commission.

Article 6

1. A coastal State has a special interest in the maintenance of the productivity of the living resources in any area of the high seas adjacent to its territorial sea.

2. A coastal States is entitled to take part on an equal footing in any system of research and regulation for purposes of conservation of the living resources of the high seas in that area, even through its nationals do not carry on fishing there.

3. A State whose nationals are engaged in fishing in any area of the high seas adjacent to the territorial sea of a State shall, at the request of that coastal State, enter into negotiations with a view to prescribing by agreement the measures necessary for the conservation of the living resource of the high seas in that area.

4. A State whose nationals are engaged in fishing in any area of the high seas adjacent to the territorial sea of a coastal State shall not enforce conservation measures in that area which are opposed to those which have been adopted by the coastal State with a view to prescribing by agreement the measures necessary for the conservation of the living resources of the high seas in that area.

5. If the States concerned do not reach agreement with respect to conservation measures within twelve months, any of the parties may initiate the procedure contemplated by article 9.

Article 7

1. Having regard to the provisions of paragraph 1 of article 6, any coastal States may, with a view to the maintenance of the productivity of the living resources of the sea, adopt unilateral measures of conservation appropriate to any stock of fish or other marine resources in any area of the high seas adjacent to its territorial sea, provided that negotiation to that effect with the other States

concerned have not led to an agreement within six months.

2. The measures which the coastal State adopts under the previous paragraph shall be valid as to other States only if the following requirements are fulfilled:

   a) That there is a need for urgent application of conservation measures in the light of the existing knowledge of the fishery;

   b) That the measures adopted are based on appropriate scientific findings;

   c) That such measures do not discriminate in form or in fact against foreign fishermen.

3. These measures shall remain in force pending the settlement, in accordance with the relevant provisions of this Convention, of any disagreement as to their validity.

4. If the measures are not accepted by the other states concerned, any of the parties may initiate the procedure contemplated by article 9. Subject to paragraph 2 of article 10, the measures adopted shall remain obligatory pending the decision of the special commission.

5. The principles of geographical demarcation as defined in article 12 of the Convention on the Territorial Sea and the Contiguous zone shall be adopted when coasts of different States are involved.

Article 8

1. Any State which, even if its nationals are not engaged in fishing in an area of the high seas not adjacent to its coast, has a special interest in the conservation of the living resources of the high seas in that area, may request the State or State

whose nationals are engaged in fishing there to take the necessary measures of conservation under articles 3 and 4 respectively, at the same time mentioning the scientific reasons which in its opinion make such measures necessary, and indicating its special interest.

2. If no agreement is reached within twelve months, such State may initiate the procedure contemplated by article 9.

Article 9

1. Any dispute which may arise between States under articles 4, 5, 6, 7 and 8 shall, at the request of any of the parties, be submitted for settlement to a special commission of five members, unless the parties agree to seek a solution by another method of peaceful settlement, as provided for in Article 33 of Charter of the United Nations.

2. The members of the commission, one of whom shall be designated as chairman, shall be named by agreement between the States in dispute within three months of the request for settlement in accordance with the provisions of this article. Failing agreement they shall, upon the request of any State party, be named by the Secretary-General of the United Nations within a further three-months period, in consultation with the States in dispute and with the President of the International court of Justice and the Director-General of the Food and Agriculture Organisation of the United Nations, from amongst well-qualified persons being nationals of States not involved in the dispute and specializing in legal, administrative or scientific questions relating to fisheries, depending upon the nature of the dispute to be settled. Any vacancy arising

after the original appointment shall be filled in the same manner as provided for the initial selection.

3. Any State party to proceedings under these articles shall have the right to name one of its nationals to the special commission, with the right to participate fully in the proceedings on the same footing as a member of the commission, but without the right to vote or take part in the writing of the commission's decision.
4. The commission shall determine its own procedure, assuring each party to the proceedings a full opportunity to be heard and to present its case. It shall also determine how the costs and expenses shall be divided between the parties to the dispute, failing agreement by the parties on this matter.
5. The special commission shall render its decision within a period of five months from the time it is appointed unless it decides, in case of necessity, to extend the time limit for a period not exceeding three months.
6. The special commission shall in reaching its decision, adhere to these articles and to any special agreements between the disputing parties regarding settlement of the dispute.
7. Decisions of the commission shall be by majority vote.

Article 10

1. The special commission shall, in disputes arising under article 7, apply the criteria listed in paragraph 2 of that article. In disputes under articles 4, 5, 6 and 8 the commission shall apply the following criteria, according to the issues involved in the dispute:

a) Common to the determination of disputes arising under articles 4, 5 and 6 are the requirements.

(i) That scientific findings demonstrate the necessity of conservation measures;

(ii) That the specific measures are based on scientific findings and are practicable; and

(iii) That the measures do not discriminate, in form or in fact, against fishermen of other States:

(b) Applicable to the determination of disputes arising under article 8 is the requirement that scientific findings demonstrate the necessity for conservation measures, or that the conservation programme is adequate, as the case may be.

2. The special commission may decide that pending its award the measures in dispute shall not be applied, provided that, in case of disputes under article 7, the measures shall only be suspended when it is apparent to the commission on the basis of *prima facie* evidence that the need for the urgent application of such measures does not exist.

Article 11

The decisions of the special commission shall be binding on the States concerned and the provisions of paragraph 2 of Article 94 of the Charter of the United Nations shall be applicable to those decisions. If the decisions are accompanied by any recommendations, they shall receive greatest possible consideration.

Article 12

1. If the factual basis of the award of the special commission is altered by substantial changes in

the conditions of the stock or stocks of fish or other living marine resources or in methods of fishing, any of the States concerned may request the other States to enter into negotiations with a view to prescribing by agreement the necessary modifications in the measures of conservation.

2. If no agreement is reached within a reasonable period of time, any of the States concerned may again resort to the procedure contemplated by article 9 provided that at least two years have elapsed from the original award.

Article 13

1. The regulation of fisheries conducted by means of equipment embedded in the floor of the sea in areas of the high seas adjacent to the territorial sea of a State may be undertaken by that State where such fisheries have long been maintained and conducted by its nationals, provided that non-nationals are permitted to participate in such activities on an equal footing with nationals except in areas where such fisheries have by long usage been exclusively enjoyed by such nationals. Such regulations will not, however, affect the general status of the areas as high seas.

2. In this article, the expression "fisheries conducted by means of equipment embedded in the floor of the sea" means those fisheries using gear with supporting members embedded in the sea floor, constructed on a site and left there to operate permanently or, if removed, restored each season on the same site.

Article 14

In articles 1, 3, 4, 5, 6 and 8, the term "nationals" means fishing boats or craft of any size having the nationality of the State concerned, according to the law of that State, irrespective of the nationality of the members of their crews.

Article 15

This Convention shall, until 31 October 1958, be open for signature by all States Members of the United Nations or of any of the specialized agencies and by any other State invited by the General Assembly of the United Nations to become a Party to the Convention.

Article 16

This Convention is subject to ratification. The instruments of ratification shall be deposited with the Secretary-General of the United Nations.

Article 17

This Convention shall be open for accession by any States belonging to any of the categories mentioned in article 15. The instruments of accession shall be deposited with the Secretary-General of the United Nations.

Article 18

1. This Convention shall come into force on the thirtieth day following the date of deposit of the twenty-second instrument of ratification or accession with the Secretary-General of the United Nations.

2. For each State ratifying or acceding to the Convention after the deposit of the twenty-second instrument of ratification or accession, the Convention shall enter into force on the thirtieth day after deposit by such State of its instrument of ratification or accession.

Article 19

1. At the time of signature, ratification or accession, any State may make reservations to articles of the Convention other than to articles 6, 7, 9, 10,11 and 12.

2. Any contracting State making a reservation in accordance with the preceding paragraph may at any time withdraw the reservation by a communication to that effect addressed to the Secretary-General of the United Nations.

Article 20

1. After expiration of a period of five years from the date on which this Convention shall enter into force, a request for the revision of this Convention may be made at any time by any contracting party by means of a notification in writing addressed to the Secretary-General of the United Nations.

2. The General Assembly of the United Nations shall decide upon the steps, if any, to be taken in respect of such request.

Article 21

The Secretary-General of the United Nations shall inform all States Members of the United Nations and other States referred to in article 15:

a) Of signature to this Convention and of the deposit of instruments of ratification or accession, in accordance with articles 15,16 and 17;

b) Of the date on which this convention will come into force, in accordance with article 18;

c) Of requests for revision in accordance with article 20;

d) Of reservations to this Convention, in accordance with article 19.

Article 22

The original of this Convention, of which the Chinese, English, French, Russian and Spanish texts are equally authentic, shall be deposited with the Secretary-General of the United Nations, who shall send certified copies thereof to all states referred to in article 15.

In Witness Whereof the undersigned plenipotentiaries, being duly authorized thereto by their respective governments have signed this Convention.

Done at Geneva, this twenty-ninth day of April one thousand nine hundred and fifty-eight.

9

Helsinki Convention on the Protection of Marine Environment of the Baltic Sea Area (1974)

The States Parties to this Convention

Conscious of the indispensable economic, social and cultural values of the marine environment of the Baltic Sea Area and its living resources for the peoples of the Contracting Parties;

Bearing in mind the exceptional hygrographic and ecological characteristics of the Baltic Sea Area and the sensitivity of its living resources to changes in the environment;

Noting the rapid development of human activities at the Baltic Sea Area, the considerable population living within its catchment area and the highly urbanized and industrialized state of the Contracting Parties as well as their intensive agriculture and forestry;

Noting with deep concern the increasing pollution of the Baltic Sea Area, originating from many sources such as discharges through rivers, estuaries, outfalls and pipelines, dumping and normal operations of vessels as well as through airborne pollutants;

Conscious of the responsibility of the Contracting Parties to protect and enhance the values of the marine environment of the Baltic Sea Area for the benefit of their peoples;

Recognizing that the protection and enhancement of the marine environment of the Baltic Sea Area are tasks that cannot effectively be accomplished by national efforts only but that also close regional cooperation and other appropriate international measures aiming at fulfilling these tasks are urgently needed;

Noting that the relevant recent international conventions even after having entered into force for the respective Contracting Parties do not cover all special requirements to protect and enhance the marine environment of the Baltic Sea Area;

Noting the importance of scientific and technological cooperation in the protection and enhancement of the marine environment of the Baltic Sea Area, particularly between the Contracting Parties;

Desiring to develop further regional cooperation in the Baltic Sea Area; the possibilities and requirements of which were confirmed by the signing of the Convention of Fishing and Conservation of the Living Resources in the Baltic Sea and the Belts, Gdansk 1973;

Conscious of the importance of regional intergovernmental cooperation in the protection of the marine environment of the Baltic Sea Area as an integral part of the peaceful cooperation and mutual understanding between all European States;

Have Agreed as follows;

Article 1

Convention Area

For the purposes of the present Convention "the Baltic Sea Ara" shall be the Baltic Sea proper with the Gulf of Bothnia, the Gulf of Finland and the entrance to the Baltic Sea bounded by the parallel of the Skaw in the Skagerrak at 57° 44' 8" N. It does not include internal waters of the Contracting Parties.

Article 2

Definitions

For the purposes of the present Convention:

"Pollution" means introduction by man, directly or indirectly, of substances or energy into the marine environment including environment, including estuaries, resulting in such deleterious effects as hazard to human health, harm to living resources and marine life, hinderance to legitimate uses of the sea including fishing, impairment of the quality for use of sea water, and reduction of amenities;

"Land-based pollution" means pollution of the sea caused by discharges from land reaching the sea waterborne, airborne or directly form the coast, including Outfalls froth pipelines;

(a) "Lumping" means:

(i) any deliberate disposal at sea of wastes or other matter from vessels, aircraft, platforms or other man-made structure at sea;

(ii) any deliberate disposal at sea of vessels, aircraft, platforms or other man-made structures at sea;

(b) "Dumping" does not include:

(i) the disposal at sea of wastes or other matter incidentals to, or derived from the normal operations of vessels aircraft, platforms or other man-made structures at sea and their equipment, other than wasted or other matter transported by or to vessels, aircraft, platforms or other man-made structures at sea, operating for the purpose of disposal of such matter or derived from the treatment of such vessels or other matter on such vessels, aircraft, platforms or structures;

(ii) placement of matter for a purpose other than the mere disposal thereof , provided that such placement is not contrary to the aims of the present Convention;

"Vessels and aircraft" means waterborne or airborne craft of any type whatsooever. This expression includes hydrofoil boat.%, air-cushion vehicles, submersibles, floating craft whether self-propelled or not, and fixed or floating platforms;

"Oil" means petroleum in any form including crude oil, fuel oil, sludge, oil refuse and refined products;

"Harmful substance" means any hazardous, noxious, or other substance, which, if introduced into the sea, is liable to cause pollution;

"Incident" means an event involving the actual or probable discharge into the sea of harmful substance, or effluents containing such a substance.

Article 3

Fundamental principles and obligations

1. The Contracting Parties shall individually or jointly take all appropriate legislative, administrative or other relevant measures in order to prevent and abate pollution and to

protect and enhance the marine environment of the Baltic Sea Area.

2. The Contracting Parties shall use their best endeavours to ensure that the implementation of the present Convention shall not cause an increase in the pollution of sea areas outside the Baltic Sea Area.

Article 4

Application

The present Convention shall apply to the protection of the marine environment of the Baltic Sea Area which comprises the water-body and the sea-bed including their living resources and other forms of marine life.

Without prejudice to the sovereign rights in regard to their territorial sea, each Contracting Party shall implement the provisions of the present Convention within its territorial sea through its national authorities.

While the provisions of the present Convention do not apply to internal waters, which are under the sovereignty of each contracting Party, the Contracting Parties undertake, without prejudice to their sovereign rights, to ensure that the purposes of the present Convention will be obtained in these waters.

The present Convention shall not apply to any warship, naval auxiliary, military aircraft or other ship and aircraft owned or operated by a State and used, for the time being, only on government non-commercial service.

However, each Contracting Party shall ensure, by the adoption of appropriate measures not impairing the operations or operational capabilities of such ships and aircraft owned or operated by it, that such ships and aircraft act in a manner consistent, so far as is reasonable and practicable, with the present Convention.

Article 5

Hazardous Substances

The Contracting Parties undertake to counteract the introduction, whether airborne, waterborne or otherwise, into the Baltic Sea Areas hazardous substances as specified in Annex I of the present Convention.

Article 6

Principles and obligations concerning land-based pollution

The Contracting Parties shall take all appropriate measures to control and minimize land-based pollution of the marine environment of the Baltic Sea Area.

In particular, the Contracting Parties shall take all appropriate measures to control and strictly limit pollution by noxious substances and materials in accordance with Annex 11 of the present Convention. To this end they shall, inter alia, as appropriate, cooperate in the development and adoption of specific programmes, guidelines, standards or regulations concerning discharges, environmental quality, and products containing such substances and materials and their use.

The substances and materials listed in Annex II of the present Convention shall not be introduced in to the marine environment of the Baltic Sea Area in significant quantities without a prior special permit, which may be periodically reviewed, by the appropriate national authority.

The appropriate national authority will inform the Commission referred to in Article 12 of the present

Convention of the Quantity, quality and way of discharge if it considers that significant quantities of substances and materials listed in Annex II of the present Convention were discharged.

The Contracting Parties shall endeavour to establish and adopt common criteria for issuing permits for discharges.

To control and minimize pollution of the Baltic Sea Area by harmful substances the Contracting Parties shall, in addition to the provision of Article 5 of the present Convention, aim at attaining the goals -And applying the criteria enumerated in Annex III of the -present Convention.

If the discharge from a watercourse, flowing through the territories of two or more Contracting Parties or forming a boundary between them, is liable to cause pollution of the marine environment of the Baltic Sea Area, the Contracting Parties concerned shall in common take appropriate measures in order to prevent and abate such pollution.

The Contracting Parties shall endeavour to use best practicable means in order to minimize the airborne pollution of the Baltic Sea Area by noxious substances.

Article 7

Prevention of pollution from ships

1. In order to protect the Baltic Sea Area from pollution by deliberate, negligent or accidental release of oil, harmful substances other than oil, and by the discharge of sewage and garbage from ships, the Contracting Parties shall take measures as set out in Annex IV of the present Convention
2. The Contracting Parties shall develop and apply

uniform requirements for the capacity and location of facilities for the reception of residues of oil, harmful substances other than oil including sewage and garbage, taking into account inter alia the special needs of passenger ships and combination carriers.

Article 8

Pleasure craft

The Contracting Parties shall, in addition to implementing those provisions of the present Convention which can appropriately be applied to pleasure craft, take special measures in order to abate harmful effects on the marine environment of the Baltic Sea Area of pleasure craft activities. The measures shall inter alia deal with adequate reception facilities for wastes from pleasure craft.

Article 9

Prevention of dumping

1. The Contracting Parties shall, subject to Paragraphs 2 and 4 of this Article, prohibit dumping in the Baltic Sea Area.
2. Dumping of dredged spoils shall be subject to a prior special permit by the appropriate national authority in accordance with the provisions of Annex V of the present Convention.
3. Each Contracting Party undertakes to ensure compliance with the provisions of this Article by vessels and aircraft:
   (a) registered in its territory or flying its flag;
   (b) loading, within its territory or territorial sea, matter which is to be dumped; or
   (c) believed to be engaged in dumping within its territorial sea.

4. The provisions of this. Article shall not apply when the safety of human life or of a vessel or aircraft at sea is threatened by the complete destruction or total loss of the vessel or aircraft, or in any case which constitutes a danger to human life, if dumping appears to be the only way of averting the threat and if there is every probability that the damage consequent upon such dumping shall be so conducted as to minimize the likelihood of damage to human or marine life.
5. Dumping made under the provisions of Paragraph 4 of this article shall be reported and dealt with in accordance with Annex VI of the present Convention and shall also be reported forthwith to the Commission referred to in Article 12 of the present Convention in accordance with the provisions of Regulation 4 of Annex V of the present Convention.
6. In case of dumping suspected to be in contravention of the provisions of this Article the Contracting Parties shall co-operate in investigating the matter in accordance with Regulation 2 of Annex IV of the present Convention.

Article 10

Exploration and exploitation of the sea-bed and its subsoil

Each Contracting Party shall take all appropriate measures in order to prevent pollution of the marine environment of the Baltic Sea Area resulting from exploration or exploitation of its part of the sea-bed and its subsoil or form any associated activities thereon. It shall ensure that adequate equipment is at hand to start an immediate abatement of pollution in that area.

Article 11

Co-operation in combating marine pollution

The Contacting Parties shall take measures and cooperate as set out in Annex VI of the present Convention in order to eliminate or minimize pollution of the Baltic Sea Area by oil or other harmful substances.

Article 12

Institutional and organizational framework

1. The Baltic Marine Environment Protection Commission, hereinafter referred to as "the Commission", is hereby established for the purposes of the present Convention.

2. The chairmanship of the Commission shall be given to each Contracting Party in turn in alphabetical order to the names of the States in the English language.

The Chairman shall serve for a period of two years, aid cannot during the period of his chairmanship serve as representative of his country.

Should the chairmanship fall vacant, the Contracting Party chairing *the Commission* shall nominate a successor to remain in office until the term of chairmanship of that Contracting Party expires.

3. Meetings of the Commission shall be hold at least once a year upon convocation by the Chairman. Upon request of a Contracting Party, provided it is endorsed by another Contracting Party, the Chairman shall, as soon as possible, summon an extraordinary meeting at such time and place as the Chairman determines, however, not later than ninety days from the date of the submission of the request.

4. The first meeting of the Commission shall be called by the Depositary Government and shall take place within a period of ninety days from the date following the entry into force of the present Convention.

5. Each Contracting Party shall have not one vote in the Commission. Unless otherwise provided under the present Convention, the Commission shall take its decisions unanimously.

Article 13

The duties of the Commission shall be;

(a) To keep the implementation of the present Convention under continuous observation;

(b) To make recommendations on measures relating to the purposes of the present Convention,

(c) To keep under review the contents of the present Convention including its Annexes and to recommend to the Contracting Parties such amendments to the present Convention including its Annexes as may be required including changes in the lists of substances and materials as well as the adoption of new Annexes;

(d) To define pollution control criteria, objectives for the reduction of pollution, and objectives concerning measures, particularly according to Annex III of the present Convention;

(e) To promote inclose cooperation with appropriate governmental bodies, taking into consideration subparagraph; (f) of this Article, additional measures to protect the marine environment of the Baltic Sea Area and for this purpose:

(i) to receive, process, summarize and disseminate from available sources relevant scientific, technological and statistical information; and

(ii) to promote scientific and technological research;

(f) To seek, when appropriate, the services of competent regional and other international organizations to collaborate in scientific and technological research as well as other relevant activities pertinent to the objectives of the present Convention;

(g) To assume such other functions as may be appropriate under the terms of the present Convention.

Article 14

Administrative provisions for the Commission

1. The working language of the Commission shall be English

2. The Commission shall adopt its Rules of Procedure.

3. The office of the Commission, hereafter referred to as the "Secretariat", shall be in Helsinki.

4. The Commission shall appoint an Executive Secretary and make provisions for the appointment of such other personnel as may be necessary, and determine the duties, terms and conditions of the Executive Secretary.

5. The Executive Secretary shall be the chief administrative official of the Commission and shall perform the function that are necessary for the administration of the present Convention, the work of the Commission and other tasks entrusted to the Executive Secretary by the Commission and its Rules of Procedure.

Article 15

Financial provisions for the Commission

1. The Commission shall adopt its Financial rules.

2. The Commission shall adopt an annual or biennial budget of proposed expenditures and budget estimates for the fiscal period following thereafter.

3. The total amount of the budget, including any supplementary budget adopted by the Commission, shall be contributed by the Contracting Parties in equal parts, unless the Commission unanimously decides otherwise.

4. Each Contracting Party shall pay the expenses related to the participation in the Commission of its representatives, experts and advisers.

Article 16

Scientific and technological cooperation

1. The Contracting Parties undertake directly, or when appropriate through competent regional or other international organizations, to cooperate a the fields of science, technology and other research, and to exchange date as well as other scientific information for the present Convention.

2. Without prejudice to Paragraphs 1,2 and 3 of Article 4 of the present Convention the Contracting Parties undertake directly, or when appropriate, through competent regional or other international organizations to promote studies, undertake, support or contribute to programmes aimed at developing ways and means for the assessment of the nature and extent of pollution, pathways, exposures~ risks and remedies in the Baltic Sea Area, and particularly to develop alternative methods of treatment, disposal and

elimination of such matter and substances that are likely to cause pollution of the marine environment of the Baltic Sea Area.

3. The Contracting Parties undertake directly, or when appropriate through competent regional or other international organizations', and on the basis of the information and data acquired pursuant to Paragraphs 1 and 2 of this Article, to cooperate in developing intercomparable observation methods, in performing baseline studies and in establishing complementary or joint programmes for monitoring.

4. The organization and scope of work connected with the implementation of tasks referred to in the preceding Paragraphs should primarily be outlined by the Commission.

Article 17

Responsibility for damage

The Contracting Parties undertake, as soon as possible, jointly to develop and accept rules concerning responsibility for damage resulting from acts of omissions in contravention of the present Convention, including, inter alia, limits of responsibility, criteria and procedures for the determination of liability and available remedies.

Article 18

Settlement of disputes

1. In case of a dispute between Contracting Parties as to the interpretation or application of the present Convention, they should seek a solution by negotiation. If the Parties concerned cannot reach agreement they should seek the good offices of or jointly request the mediation by a third Contracting Party, a qualified international organization or a qualified person.

2. If the Parties concerned have not been able to resolve their dispute through negotiation or have been unable to agree on measures as described above, such disputes shall be, upon common-agreement, submitted to an ad hoc arbitration tribunal, to a permanent arbitration tribunal, or to the International Court of Justice.

Article 19

Safeguard of certain freedoms

Nothing in the present Convention shall be construed as infringing upon the freedom of navigation, fishing, marine scientific research and other legitimate uses of the high seas, as well as upon the right of innocent passage through the territorial sea.

Article 20

Status of Annexes

The Annexes attached to the present Convention form an integral part of the Convention.

Article 21

Relation to other Conventions

The provisions of the present Convention shall be without prejudice to the rights and obligations of the Contracting parties under treaties concluded previously as well as under treaties which may be concluded in the future, furthering and developing the general principles of the Law of the Sea that the present. Convention is based upon and in particular provisions concerning the prevention of pollution of the marine environment.

Article 22

Revision of the Convention

A conference for the purpose of a general revision of

the present Convention may be convened with the consent of the Contracting Parties or at the request of the Commission.

Article 23

Amendments to the Articles of the Convention

1. Each Contracting Party may propose amendments to the Articles of the present Convention. Any such proposed amendment shall be submitted to the Depositary Government and communicated by it to all Contracting Parties, which shall inform the Depositary Government of either their acceptance or rejection of the amendment as soon as possible after the receipt of the communication.

The amendment shall enter into force ninety days after the Depositary Government has received notifications of acceptance of that amendment from all Contracting Parties.

2. With the consent of the Contracting Parties or at the request of the Commission a conference may be convened for the purpose of amending the present Convention.

Article 24

Amendments to the Annexes and the adoption of Annexes

1. Any amendment to the Annexes proposed by a Contracting Party shall be communicated to the other Contracting Parties by the Depositary Government and considered in the Commission. If adopted by the Commission, the amendment shall be communicated to the Contracting Parties and recommended for acceptance.
2. Such amendment shall be deemed to have been accepted at the end of a period determined by the

Commission unless within that period anyone of the Contracting Parties has objected to the amendment. The accepted amendment shall enter into force on a date determined by the Commission.

The period determined by the Commission shall be prolonged for an additional period of six months and the date of entry in to force of the amendment postponed accordingly, if, in exceptional cases, any Contracting Party before the expiring of the period determined by the Commission informs the Depositary Government, that, although it intends to accept the proposal, the constitutional requirements for such an acceptance are not yet fulfilled in its State.

3. An Annex to the present Convention may be adopted in accordance with the provisions of this Article.

4. The Depositary Government shall inform all Contracting Parties of any amendments or adoption of a new Annex which enter into force under this Article and of the date on which such amendment or new Annex enters into force.

5. Any objection under this Article shall be made by notification in writing to the Depositary Government which shall notify all Contracting Parties and the Executive Secretary of any such notification and the date of its receipt.

Article 25

Reservations

1. The provisions of the present Convention shall not be subject to reservations.

2. The provision of Paragraph 1 of this Article does not prevent a Contracting Party from suspending for a period not exceeding one year the application of an Annex of the present

Convention or part thereof or an amendment thereto after the Annex in question or the amendment thereto has entered into force.

3. If after the entry into force of the present Convention a Contracting Party invokes the provisions of Paragraph 2 of this Article it shall inform the other Contracting Parties, at the time of the adoption by the Commission of an amendment to an Annex or a new Annex, of those provisions which will be suspended in accordance with Paragraph 2 of this Article.

Article 26

Signature, ratification, approval, and accession

1. The present Convention shall be open for signature in Helsinki on 22 March 1974 by the Baltic Sea States participating in the Diplomatic Conference on the Protection of the Marine Environment of the Baltic Sea Area, held in Helsinki from 18 to 22 March 1974. The present Convention shall be open for accession to any other Convention, provided that this State is invited by all the Contracting Parties.

2. The present Convention shall be subject to ratification or approval by the States which have signed it.

3. The instrument of ratification, approval, or accession shall be deposited with the Government of Finland, which will perform the duties of the Depositary Government.

Article 27

Entry into force

The present Convention shall enter into force two months after the Depositary of the seventh instrument of ratification on approval.

Article 28

Withdrawal

1. At any time after the expiry of five years from the date of entry into force of the present Convention any Contracting Party may, by giving written notification to the Depositary Government was notified of the withdrawal.
2. In case of notification of withdrawal by a Contracting Party the Depositary Government shall convene a meeting of the Contracting Parties for the purpose of considering the effect of the withdrawal.

Article 29

Language

The present Convention has been drawn up in a single copy in the English language. Official translations into the Danish, Finnish, German, Polish, Russian, and Swedish languages shall be prepared and deposited with the signed original.

In witness whereof the undersigned Plenipotentiaries, being duly authorized thereto, have signed the present Convention.

Done at Helsinki, this twenty-second day of March one thousand nine hundred and seventy-four.

Annex-I

Hazardous Substances

The protection of the Baltic Sea Area from pollution by the substances listed below can involve the use of appropriate technical means, prohibitions and regulations of the transport, trade, handling, application, and final deposition of products containing such substances.

1. DDT (1,1,1-trichloro-2,2-bis-(chlorophenyl)-ethane) and its derivatives DDE and DDD.
2. PCBs(polychlorinated biphenyls).
3. PCT's (polycholorinated terphenyls).

Annex II

Noxious Substances and Materials

The following substances and materials are listed for the purposes of Article 6 of the present Convention.

The list is valid for substances and materials introduced as waterborne into the marine environment. The Contracting Parties shall also endeavour to use best practicable means to prevent harmful substances and materials form being introduced as airborne into the Baltic Sea Area.

For urgent consideration

1. Mercury, cadmium, and their compounds.
2. Antimony, arsenic, beryllium, chromium, copper, lead, molybdenum, nickel, selenium, tin, vanadium, zinc and their compounds, as well as elemental phosphorus
3. Phenols and their derivatives.
4. Phthalic acid and its derivatives.
5. Cyanides.
6. Persistent halogenated hydrocarbons.
7. Polycyclic aromatic hydrocarbons and their derivatives.
8. Persistent toxic organosilicic compounds.
9. Persistent pesticides, including organophosphoric

and organostannic pesticides, herbicides, slimicides and chemicals used for the preservation of wood, timber, wood pulp, cellulose, paper, hides and textiles, not covered by the provisions of Annex 1 of the present Convention.

10. Radioactive materials.

11. Acids, alkalis, and surface active agents in high concentration or big quantities.

12. Oil and wastes of petrochemical and other industries containing lipid-soluble substances.

13. Substances having adverse effects on the taste and/or smell of products for human consumption from the sea, or effects on taste, smell, colour, transparency or other characteristics of the water seriously reducing its amenity values.

14. Materials and substances which may float, remain in suspension or sink, and which may seriously interfere with any legitimate use of the sea.

15. Lignin substances contained in industrial waste waters.

16. The chelators EDTA (ethylenedinitrilotetraacetic acid or ethylenediaminetetraacetic acid) and DTPA (diethylenetri-aminopentaacetic acid).

Annex III

Goals, Criteria and Measures concerning the Prevention of Land-based Pollution

In accordance with the provisions of Article 6 of the present Convention the Contracting Parties shall, endeavour to attain the goals and apply the criteria and measures enumerated in this Annex in order to control and minimize land-based pollution of the marine environment of the Baltic Sea Area.

1. Municipal sewage shall be treated in an appropriate way so that the amount of organic matter does not cause harmful changes in the oxygen content of the Baltic Sea Area.

2. Municipal sewage shall also be treated in an appropriate way to ensure that the hygienic quality, and in particular epidemiological and toxicological safety, of the receiving sea area is maintained at a level which does not cause harm to human health, and in a way that under the given composition of the sewage no significant amount of such harmful substances as are listed in Annexes I and II of the present Convention is formed.

3. The polluting load of industrial wastes shall be minimized in an appropriate way in order to reduce the amount of harmful substances, organic matter and nutrients.

4. The means referred to in Paragraph 3 of this Annex shall in particular include minimization of production of wastes by processing techniques, recirculation and re-use of processing water, developing of water economy and improvement of qualifications for water treatment. In the treatment of waste water mechanical, chemical biological and other measures, according to the quality of the recipient water, shall be applied.

5. The discharge of cooling water from nuclear power plants or other kinds of industries using large amounts of water shall be effected in a way which minimizes the pollution of the marine environment of the Baltic Sea Area.

6. The Commission will control criteria, objectives for reduction of pollution and objectives concerning measures, including processing techniques and waste treatment, to reduce pollution of the Baltic Sea Area.

Annex IV

Prevention of Pollution from Ships

Regulation 1

The contracting Parties shall, in matters concerning the protection of the Baltic Sea Area from pollution by ships, cooperate.

within the International Martime Organization, in particular in promoting the development of international rules,

in the effective and harmonized implementation of rules adopted by the International Maritime Organization.

Regulation 2

The Contracting Parties shall, without prejudice to Paragraph 4 of Article 4 of the present Convention, as appropriate assist each other investigating violations of existing legislation on anti-pollution measures, which have occurred or are suspected to have occurred within the Baltic Sea Area. This assistance may include but is not limited to inspection by the competent authorities of oil record books, cargo record books, log books and engine log books and taking oil samples for analytical identification purposes.

Regulation 3

Definitions

For the purpose of this Annex:

1. "Ship" means a vessel of any type whatsoever operating in the marine environment and includes hydrofoil boats, air-cushion vehicles, submersibles, floating craft and fixed or floating platforms.

2. "Administration" means the Government of the State under whose authority the ship is operating. With respect to a ship entitled to fluy a flag of any State, the Administration is the Government of that State. With respect to fixed or floating platforms engaged in exploration and exploitation of the sea-bed and subsoil thereof adjacent to the coast over which the costal State exercises sovereign rights for the purposes of exploration and exploitation of their natural resources, the Administration is the Government of the Coastal State concerned.

3. (a) "Discharge", in relation to harmful substances or effluents containing such substances, means any release howsoever caused form a ship and includes any escape, disposal, spilling, leaking, pumping, emitting, or emptying; (b) "Discharge" doesn't include:

   (i) dumping within the meaning of the Convention on the Prevention of Marine Pollution by Dumping of Wastes and other Matter done at London on 29 December 1972; or

   (ii) release of harmful substances directly arising from the exploration, exploitation and associated offshore processing of sea-bed mineral resources; or

(iii) release of harmful substances for purposes of legitimate scientific research into pollution abatement or control .

4. "Nearest land" The term "from the nearest land" means from the baseline from which the territorial sea of the territory in question is established in accordance with international law.

5. The term 'Jurisdiction" shall be interpreted in accordance with international law in force at the time of application or interpretation of this Annex.

6. The term "MARPOL 73/78" means the International Convention for the Preventions of Pollution from Ships, 1973, as modified by the Protocol of 1978 relating thereto.

Regulation 4

Oil

The Contracting Parties, also being parties to MARPOL 73/78, apply in conformity with that agreement the provisions of Annex I to MARPOL 73/78 for the prevention of pollution by oil.

Definitions

For the purposes of this Regulation:

1. "Oil" means petroleum in any form including crude oil, fuel oil, sludge, oil refuse and refined products (other than petrochemicals which are subject to the provision of Regulation 5 of this Annex) and, without limiting the generality of the foregoing, includes the substances listed in Appendix I to this Annex.

2. "Oily mixture" means a mixture with any oil content.

3. "Oil fuel" means any oil used as fuel in connection with the propulsion and auxiliary machinery of the ship in which such oil is carried.

4. "Oil tanker" means a ship constructed or adapted primarily to carry oil in bulk in its cargo spaces and includes combination carriers and any "chemical tanker" as defined in Regulation 5 of this Annex when it is carrying a cargo or part cargo of oil in bulk.

5. "Combination carrier" means a ship designed to carry either oil or solid cargos in bulk.

6. "Clean ballast" means the ballast in a tank which since oil was last carried therein has been so cleaned that effluent therefrom if it were discharged from a ship which is stationary into clean calm water on a clear day would not produce visible traces of oil on the surface of the water or on adjoining shore lines or cause a sludge or emulsion to be deposited beneath the surface of the water or upon adjoining shore lines. If the blast is discharged through an oil discharge monitoring and control system approved by the Administration, evidence based on such a system to the effect that the oil content of the effluent did not exceed 15 parts per million shall be determinative that the ballast was clean, notwithstanding the presence of visible traces.

7. "Segregated Ballast" means the ballast water introduced into a tank which is completely separated from the cargo oil and oil fuel system and which is permanently allocated to the carriage of ballast or to the carriage of ballast or cargos other than oil or noxious substances as variously defined in the Regulations of this Annex.

Control Discharge of Oil

1. (a) Subject to the provision of Paragraph C of this Regulation, any discharge into the sea of oil or oily mixtures from any oil tanker and any ship of 400 tons gross tonnage and above other than an oil tanker shall be prohibited, while in the Baltic Sea Area;

   (b) such ships. while in the Baltic Sea Area shall retain on board all oil drainage and sludge, dirty ballast and tank washing waters and discharge them only to reception facilities.

2. (a) Subject to the provision of Paragraph C of this Regulation, any discharge into the sea of oil or oily mixtures from a ship of less than 400 tons gross tonnage, other than an oil tanker, shall be prohibited while in the Baltic Sea Area, except when the oil content of the effluent without dilution does not exceed 15 parts per million or alternatively when all of the following conditions are satisfied:

   (i) the ship is proceeding en route;

   (ii) the oil content of the effluent is less than 100 parts per million; and

   (iii) the discharge is made as far as practicable from the land, but in no case less than 12 nautical miles from the nearest land;

3. (a) The provisions of Sub-Paragraphs 1 and 2 of this Paragraph shall not apply to the discharge of clean or segregated ballast.

   (b) The provisions of Sub-Paragraph 1 of this Paragraph shall not apply to the discharge of processed bilge water from machinery, spaces, provided that all of the following conditions are satisfied:

(i) the bilge water does not originate from cargo pump;

(ii) the bilge water is not mixed with oil cargo residues;

(iii) the ship is proceeding en route;

(iv) the oil content of the effluent without dilution does not exceed 15 parts per million;

(v) the ship has in operation an oily-water separating system and an effective filtering system, or an equivalent equipment, approved by the Administration;

(vi) the system or equipment is such that it will produce an effluent, the oil content of which does not exceed 15 parts per million, and is provided with alarm arrangements to indicate when this level cannot maintained, as well as a stopping be device which will ensure that the discharge is automatically stopped when the oil content of the effluent exceeds 15 parts per million.

4. (a) No discharge into the sea shall contain chemicals or other substances in quantities or concentration which are hazardous to the marine environment of chemicals or other substances introduced for the purpose of circumventing the conditions of discharge specified in this Regulation.

(b) The oil residues which cannot be discharged into the sea in compliance with Sub-Paragraphs 2 or 3, (b) of .this Paragraph shall be retained on board or discharged to reception facilities.

5. Whenever visible traces of oil are observed on or below the surface of the water in the immediate vicinity of a ship or its wake, the Contracting

Parties should, to the extent they are reasonably able to do so, promptly investigate the facts bearing on the issue of whether there has been a violation of the provisions of this Regulation.

The Investigation should include, in particular, the wind and sea conditions, the track and speed of the ship, other possible sources of the visible traces in the vicinity, and any relevant oil discharge records.

Exceptions

Paragraph B of this Regulation shall not apply to:

(a) the discharge into the sea of oil or oily mixtures necessary for the purpose of securing the safety of a ship or saving life at sea; or

(b) the discharge into the sea of oil or oily mixtures resulting from damage to a ship or its equipment:

   (i) provided that all reasonable precautions have been taken after the occurrence of the damage or discovery of the discharge for the purpose of preventing or minimizing the discharge; and

   (ii) except if the owner or the Master acted either with intent to cause damage, or recklessly and with knowledge that damage would probably result; or

(c) the discharge into the sea of substances containing oil, approved by the Administration, when being used for the purposes of combating specific pollution incidents in order to minimize the damage from pollution. Any such discharge shall be subject to the approval of any Contracting Party in whose jurisdiction it is contemplated discharge will occur.

Special Requirements for Drilling Rigs and other Platforms

Fixed and floating drilling rigs when engaged in the exploration, exploitation and associated offshore processing of sea-bed mineral resources and other platforms shall comply with the requirements of this Regulation applicable to ships of 400 tons gross tonnage and above other than oil tankers, except that:

(a) they shall keep a record of all operations involving oil or oily mixture discharges, in a form approved by the Administration; and

(b) subject to the provision of Paragraph C of this Regulation, the discharge into the sea of oil or oily mixture shall be prohibited except when the oil content of the discharge without dilution does not exceed 15 parts per million.

Reception Facilities of Baltic Sea Area

The Contracting Parties undertake to ensure that no later than 1 January 1977 all oil loading terminals an repair ports of the Baltic Sea Area are -provided wit facilities adequate for the reception and treatment of ail the dirty ballast and tank washing waters from oil tankers In addition all ports of the area shall be provided with adequate reception facilities for other residues and oily mixtures from all ships. Such facilities shall have adequate capacity to meet the needs of the ships using them without causing undue delay.

Regulation 5

Noxious liquid substances

The Contracting Parties, also being parties to ARPOL 73/78., apply in conformity with that agreement the provisions of Annex 11 to ARPOL 73/78 for the prevention of pollution by noxious liquid substances carried in bulk.

Definitions

1. "Chemical tanker" means a ship constructed or adapted primarily to carry a cargo of noxious liquid substances in bulk and includes an "oil tanker" as defined in Regulation 4 of this Annex when carrying a cargo or part cargo of noxious liquid substances in bulk.

2. "Clean Ballast" means ballast carried in a tank which, since it was last used to carry a cargo containing a substance in Category A,B,C, or D has been thoroughly cleaned and the residues resulting therefrom have been discharged and the tank emptied in accordance with the appropriate requirements of this Regulation.

3. "Segregated ballast" means ballast water introduced into a tank permanently allocated to the carriage of ballast or to the carriage of ballast or cargos other than oil or noxious liquid substances as variously defined in the Regulations of this Annex, ' and which is completely separated form the cargo and oil fuel system.

4. "Liquid substances" are having a vapour pressure not exceeding 28 kp/cm at a temperature of 37.8 C

5. "Noxious liquid substances" means any substances designated in Appendix III to this Annex or provisionally assessed under the provisions of Sub-Paragraph 4 of paragraph B of this Regulation as falling into Category A,B,C, or D.

Categorization and Listing of Noxious Liquid Substances

1. For the purposes of this Regulations noxious liquid substances shall be divided into four categories as follows:

(a) Category A—noxiousa liquid substances which if discharged into the sea from tank cleaning or deballasting operations would present a major hazard to either marine resources cr human health or cause serious harm to amenities or other legitimate uses of the sea and therefore justify the application of stringent anti- pollution measures;

(b) Category B—noxious liquid substances which if discharged into the sea from tank c leaning or deballasiting operations would present a hazard to either marine resources or human health or cause harm to amenities or other legitimate uses of the sea and therefore justify the application of special anti-pollution measures;

(c) Category C—noxious liquid substances which if discharged into the sea from tank cleaning or deballasting operations would present a minor hazard to either marine resources or human health or cause, minor harm to amenities or other legitimate uses of the sea and therefore require special operational conditions;

(d) Category D—noxious liquid substances which if discharged into the sea from tank cleaning or deballasing operations would present a recognizable hazard to either marine resources or human health or cause minimal harm to amenities or other legitimative uses of the sea an therefore require some attention in operational conditions.

2. Guidelines for use in the categorization of noxious liquid substances are given in Appendix II to this Annex.

3. The list of noxious liquid substances carried in bulk and presently categorized which are subject to the provisions of this Regulation is set out in Appendix II to this Annex.
4. Where it is proposed to carry a liquid substance in bulk which has not been categorized unser Sub-Paragraph 1 of this Paragraph or evaluated as referred to in Sub-Paragraph 1 of Paragraph C of this Regulation the Contracting Parties involved in the proposed operation shall establish and agree on a provisional assessment for the proposed operation on the basis of the guidelines referred to in Sub-Paragraph 2 of this Paragraph. Until full agreement between the Governments involved has been reached, the substances shall be carried under the most severe conditions proposed.

C Other Liquid Substances

The substances listed in Appendix IV to this Annex have been evaluated and found to fall outside the Categories A,B,C, and D as defined in Sub-Paragraph 1 of Paragraph B of this Regulation because they are presently considered to present no harm to human health marine resources, amenities or other legitimate uses of the sea, when discharged into the sea from tank cleaning or deballasting operations. The discharge of bilge or ballast or other residues of mixtures containing oily substances listed in Appendix IV to this shall not be subject to any requirement of this' Regulation.

The discharge into the sea of clean ballast or segregated ballast shall not be subject to any requirement of this Regulation

Discharge of Noxious Liquid Substances

Subject to the provisions of Paragraph E of this Regulation:

1. The discharge into the sea of substances in Category A as defined in Sub-Paragraph 1 (a) of a Paragraph B of this Regulation, or of those provisionally assessed as such or ballast water, tank washings, or other residues or mixtures containing such substances shall be prohibited. If tanks containing such substances or mixtures are to be washed, the resulting residues shall be discharged to a reception facility which the Contracting Parties shall provide in accordance with Paragraph H of this Regulation, until the concentration of the substance in the effluent to such facility is at or below the residual concentration prescribed for that substance in column IV of Appendix III to this Annex and until the tank is empty. Provided that the residue then remaining in the tank is subsequently diluted by the addition of a volume of water of not less than 5 per cent of the total volume of the tank, it may be discharged into the sea when all the following conditions are also satisfied:

   (a) the ship is proceeding en route at a speed of at least 7 knots in the case of self-propelled ships or at least 4 knots in the case of ships which are not self-propelled;

   (b) the discharge is made below the waterline, taking into account the location of the seawater intakes; and

   (c) the discharge is made at a distance of not less than 12 nautical miles from the nearest land and in a depth of water not less than 25 metres.

2. The discharge into the sea of substances in Category B as defined in Sub- Paragraph I (b) of Paragraph B of this Regulation or of those provisionally assessed as such or ballast water,

tank washings, or other residues or mixtures containing such substances shall be prohibited except when all the following conditions are satisfied:

(a) the tank has been washed after unloading with a volume of water of not less than 0.5 percent of total volume of the tank, and the resulting residues have been discharged to a reception facility until the tank is empty;

(b) the ship is proceeding en route at a speed of at least 7 knots in the case of self-propelled ships or at least 4 knots in the a case of self-propelled ships or at least 4 knots in the case of ships which are not self-propelled.

(c) the procedures and arrangements for discharge and washings are approved by the Administration and shall ensure that the concentration and rate of discharge of the effluent is such that the concentration of the substance in the wake astern of the ship does not exceed part per million.

(d) the discharge is made below the waterline; taking into account the location of the seawater intakes; and

(e) the discharge is made at distance of not less than 12 nautical miles form the nearest land and in depth of water of not less than 25 metres.

3. The discharge into the sea of substances in Category C as defined in Sub-Paragraph I (c) of Paragraph B of this Regulation or of those provisionally assessed as such or ballast water, tank washings, or other residues or mixtures containing such substances shall be prohibited except when all the following conditions are satisfied:

(a) the ship is proceeding en route at a speed of at least 7 knots in the case of self-propelled ships or at least 4 knots in the case of ships, which are not self-propelled;

(b) the procedures and arrangements for discharge are approved by the Administration and shall ensure that the concentration and rate of discharge of the effluent is such that the concentration of the substance in the wake astern of the ship does not exceed I part er million

(c) the maximum quantity of cargo discharged from each tank and its associated piping system does not exceed the maximum quantity approved in accordance with the procedures referred to in Sub-Paragraph 3 (b) of this Paragraph which shall not case exceed the greater of 1 cubic metere of 1/3,0000 of the tank capacity in cubic metres;

(d) the discharge is made below the waterline, taking into account the location of the seawater intakes; and

(e) the discharge is made at a distance of not less than 12 nautical miles from the nearest land and in a depth of water of not less than 25 metres.

The discharge into the sea of substances in Category D as defined in Sub-Paragraph 1 (d) of Paragraph B of this Regulation, or of those provisionally assessed as such or ballast water, tank washings, or other residues of mixtures containing such substances shall be prohibited except when all the following conditions are satisfied:

(a) the ship is proceeding en route at a speed of at least 7 knots in the case of self-propelled ships or at least 4 knots in the case of ships which are not self- propelled;

(b) such mixtures are of a concentration not greater than one part of the substance in ten parts of water; and

(c) the discharge is made at a distance of not less than 12 nautical miles from the nearest land.

Ventilation procedures approved by the Administration, may be used to remove cargo residues from a tank. If subsequent washing of the tank is necessary, the discharge into the sea of the resulting tank washings shall be made in accordance with Sub-Paragraph 1, 2, 3 or 4 of this Paragraph, whichever is applicable.

The discharge into the sea of substances which have not been categorized, provisionally assessed, or evaluated as referred to in Sub-Paragraph 1 of Paragraph C of this Regulation, or of ballast water, tank washings, or other residues of mixtures containing such substances shall be prohibited.

Exceptions

Paragraph D of this Regulation shall not apply to:

(a) the discharge into the sea of noxious liquid substances or mixtures containing such substances necessary for the purpose of securing the safety of a ship or saving life at sea; or

(b) the discharge into the sea of noxious liquid substances or mixtures containing such substances resulting from damage to, a ship or its equipment:

   (i) provided that all reasonable precautions have been taken after the occurrence of the damage or discovery of the discharge for the purpose of preventing or minimizing the discharge; and

(ii) except if the owner or the Master acted either with intent to cause damage, or recklessly and with knowledge that damage would probably result; or

(c) the discharge into the sea of noxious liquid substances or mixtures containing such substances, approved by the Administration, when being used for the purpose of combating specific pollution incidents in order to minimize the damage from pollution. Any such discharge shall be subject to the approval of any Contracting Party in whose jurisdiction it is contemplated the discharge will occur.

Measures of Control

1. The Contracting parties shall appoint or authorize surveyors for the purpose of implementing this Paragraph.

Category A Substances

2. (a) If a tank is partially unloaded or unloaded but not cleaned, an appropriate entry shall be made in the Cargo Record Book;

   (b) until that tank is cleaned every subsequent pumping or transfer operation carried out connection whit that tank shall also be entered the Cargo Record Book.

3. If the tank is to be washed:

   (a) the effluent from the tank washing operation shall be discharged from the ship to reception facility at least until the concentration of the substance in the discharge, as indicated by analyses c samples of the effluent taken the surveyor, ha fallen to the residual concentration specified that substance in Appendix III to this Annex When the required residual concentration has bee achieved remaining tank washings shall continue to be discharged to the reception facility until the tank is empty. Appropriate entries of these operations shall be made in the Cargo Record Book and certified by the surveyor; and

(b) after diluting the residue then remaining in the tank, with at least. 5 per cent of the tank capacity of water, this mixture may be discharged into the sea in accordance with the provisions of Sub-Paragraphs 1 a), b) and c) of Paragraph D of this Regulation. Appropriate entries of these operations shall be made in the Cargo Record Book.

4. Where the Government of the receiving Party is satisfied that it is impracticable ~to measure the concentration of the substance in the effluent without causing undue delay to the ship, that Party may accept an alternative procedure as being equivalent to Sub-Paragraph 3 a) of this Paragraph provided that:

(a) a precleaning procedure for that tank and that substance is approved by -the Administration and that Party is satisfied that such procedure will fulfil the requirements of Sub-Paragraph 1, of Paragraph D of this Regulation with respect to the attainment of the prescribed residual concentrations;

(b) a surveyor duly authorized by that Party shall certify in the Cargo Record Book that:

(i) the tank, its pump and piping systems have been emptied and that the quantity of cargo remaining in the tank is at or below the quantity on which the approved precleaning procedure referred to in Sub-Paragraph (ii) of this Sub-Paragraph has been based;

(ii) precleaing has been carried out in accordance with the precleaning procedure approved by the Administration for that tank and that substance; and

(iii) the tank washings resulting from such precleaning have been discharged to a reception facility and the tank is empty;

(c) the discharge into the sea of any remaining residues shall be, in accordance with the provisions of Sub-Paragraph 3 b) of this Paragraph and an appropriate entry is made in the Cargo Record Book.

Category B Substances

5. Subject to such surveillance and approval by the authorized or appointed surveyor as may be deemed necessary by the Contracting Party, the Master of a ship shall, with respect to a Category B Substance, ensure compliance with the following:

(a) if a tank is partially unloaded or unloaded but not cleaned appropriate entry shall be made in the Cargo Record Book;

(b) until that tank is cleaned every subsequent pumping or transfer operation carried out in connection with that tank shall also be entered in the Cargo Record Book;

(c) if the tank is to be washed, the effluent from the tank washing operation, which shall contain a volume of water not less than 0.5 per cent of the ,total volume of the tank, its pump and piping system are empty. An appropriate entry shall be made in the Cargo Record Book;

(d) if the tank is to be further cleaned and emptied at sea, the Master shall:

(i) ensure that the approved procedures referred to in Sub-Paragraph 2 c) of Paragraph D of this Regulation are complied with and that the appropriate entries are made in the Cargo Record Book; and

(ii) ensure that any discharge into the sea is made in accordance with the requirements of Sub-Paragraph 2 of Paragraph D of this Regulation and an appropriate entry is made in the Cargo Record Book;

(e) if after unloading a Category B substance, any residues of tank washings are to be retained on board until the ship is outside the Baltic Sea Area, the Master shall so indicate by an appropriate entry in the Cargo Record Book.

Category C Substances

Subject to such surveillance and approval by the authorized or appointed surveyor as may be deemed necessary by the Contracting Party, the Master of ship shall, with respect to a 'Category C Substance, ensure compliance with the following:

(a) if a tank is partially unloaded or unloaded but not cleaned, an appropriate entry shall be made in the Cargo Record Book;

(b) if the tank is to be cleaned at ses;

(i) the cargo piping system serving that tank shall be drained and an appropriate entry made in the Cargo Record Book;

(ii) the quantity of substances remaining in the tank shall not exceed the maximum quantity which may be discharged into the sea for that substance under Sub-Paragraph 3 c) of Paragraph D of this Regulation. An appropriate entry shall be made in the Cargo Record Book

(iii) where it is intended to discharge the quantity of substance remaining into the sea the approved procedures shall be complied with and the necessary dilution of the substance satisfactory for such discharge shall be achieved An appropriate entry shall be made in the Cargo Record Book; or

(iv) where the tank washings are not discharged into the sea, if any internal transfer of tank washings takes place from that tank an appropriate entry shall be made in the Cargo Record Book; and

(v) any subsequent discharge into the sea of such tank washings shall be made in accordance with the requirements of Sub-Paragraph 3 of Paragraph D of this Regulation;

(c) if the tank is to be cleaned in port:

(i) the tank washings shall be discharged to reception facility and an appropriate entry shall be made in the Cargo Record Book; or

(ii) the tank washings shall be retained on board the ship and an appropriate entry shall be made in the Cargo Record Book indicating the location and disposition of the tank washings;

(d) if after unloading a Category C substance within the Baltic Sea Area any residues or tank washings are to be retained on board until the ship is outside the area, the Master shall so indicate by an appropriate entry in the, Cargo Record Book.

Category D Substances

7. The master of a ship shall, with respect to a Category D Substance, ensure compliance with the following:

(a) if a tank is partially unloaded or unloaded but not cleaned, and appropriate entry shall be made in the Cargo Record Book;

(b) if the tank is to be cleaned at sea:

(i) the cargo piping system serving that tank shall be drained and an appropriate entry made in the Cargo Record Book;

(ii) where it is intended to discharge the quantity of substance remaining into the sea necessary dilution of the substance satisfactory for such a discharge shall be achieved. An appropriate entry shall be made in the Cargo Record Book;

(iii) where the tank washings are not discharged into the sea, if any internal transfer of tank washings takes place from that tank an appropriate entry shall be made in the Cargo Record Book; and

(iv) any subsequent discharge into the sea of such tank washings shall be made in accordance with the requirements of Sub-Paragraph 4 of Paragraph D of this Regulation;

(c) if the tank is to be cleaned in port:

(i) the tank washings shall be discharged to a

reception facility and an appropriate entry shall be made in the Cargo Record Book; or

(ii) the tank washings shall be retained on board the ship and an appropriate entry shall be made in the Cargo Record Book indicating the location and disposition of the tank washings.

Discharge from a Slop Tank

8. Any residues retained on board in a slop tank, including those from pump room bilges, which contain a Category A or a Category 13 substance, shall be discharged to reception facility in accordance with the provisions of Sub-Paragraph 1 or 2 of Paragraph D of this Regulation, whichever is applicable. An appropriate entry shall be made in the Cargo Record Book.

9. Any residues retained on board in a slop tank, including those from pump room bliges, which contain a Category C substance in excess of the aggregate of the maximum quantities specified in Sub-Paragraph 3 c) of Paragraph D of this Regulation shall be discharged to reception facility. An appropriate entry shall be made in the Cargo Record book.

G Cargo Record Book

1. Every ship to which this Regulation applies shall be provided with a Cargo Record, whether as part of the ship's official log book or otherwise, in the form recommended by the Commission.

2. The Cargo Record Book shall be completed, on a tank-to-tank basis, whenever any of the following operations with respect to a noxious liquid substance takes place in the ship:

(i) Loading of cargo (substances of Category A,B,C and D);

(ii) international transfer of cargo;, (iii) unloading of cargo;

(iv) cleaning of cargo tanks;

(v) ballasting of cargo tanks;

(vi) discharge of ballast from cargo tanks; (vii) disposal of residues;

(viii) discharge onto the sea in accordance with

Paragraph D of this Regulation

3. In the event of any discharge of the kind referred to in Annex VI of the present convention and Paragraph E of this Regulation of any noxious liquid substance of mixture containing such substance, whether intentional or accidental, an entry shall be made in the Cargo Record Book stating the circumstances of, and the reasons for, the discharge.

4. When a surveyor appointed or authorized by a Contracting Party to supervise any operations under this Regulation- has inspected a ship, then that surveyor shall make an appropriate entry in the Cargo Record Book.

5. Each operation referred to in Sub-Paragraphs 2 and 3 of this Paragraph shall be fully recorded without delay in the Cargo Record Book so that all the entries in the Book appropriate to that operation are completed. Each entry shall be signed by the officer or officers in charge of the operation concerned and, when the ship is manned, each page shall be signed by the Master of the ship. The entries in the Cargo Record Book shall be in an official language of the State whose flag the ship is entitled to fly, and, except when the ship is engaged in domestic voyages, in English or French. The entries in an official national language of the State whose flag the ship is entitled to fly shall prevail in case of dispute or discrepancy.

6. The Cargo Record Book shall be kept in such a place as to be readily available for inspection and, except in the case of unmanned ships under tow, shall be kept on board the ship. It shall be retained for period of three years after the last entry has been made.

7. The competent authority of a Contracting Party may inspect the Cargo Record Book on board any ship to which this Regulation applies while the ship is in its port, and may make a copy of any entry in that Book and may require the Master of the ship to certify that the copy is a true copy of such entry. Any copy so made which has been certified by the Master of the ship as a true copy of an entry in the ship's Cargo Record Book shall be made admissible in any judicial proceeding as evidence of the facts stated in the entry. The inspection of a Cargo Record Book and the taking of Certified copy by the competent authority under this Paragraph shall be performed as expeditiously as possible without causing the ship to be unduly delayed.

Reception Facilities

1. The Contracting Parties undertake to ensure the provision of reception facilities according to the needs of ships using their ports, terminals or repair ports of the Baltic Sea Area as follows:

   (a) cargo loading and unloading ports and terminals shall have facilities adequate for reception without undue delay to ships of such residues and mixtures containing noxious liquid substances as would remain for disposal from ships carrying them as a consequence of the application of this Regulation; and

(b) ship repair ports undertaking repairs to chemical tankers shall have facilities adequate for the reception of residues and mixtures containing noxious liquid substances.

2. Each Contracting Party shall determine the types of facilities provided for the purpose of Sub-Paragraph 1 of this Paragraph at its cargo loading and unloading ports, terminals and ship repair ports of the Baltic Sea Area.

Regulation 6

Harmful substances in packaged forms

A. The Contracting Parties shall as soon as possible apply suitable uniform rules for the carriage of harmful substances in packaged forms or in freight containers, portable tanks or road and rail tank wagons.

B. With respect to certain harmful substances, as may be designated by the Commission, the Master or owner of the ship or his representative shall notify the appropriate port authority of the intent to load or unload such substances at least 24 hours prior to such action.

C. A report of an incident involving harmful substances shad be made in accordance with the provisions of Annex VI of the present Convention.

Regulation 7

Sewage

The Contracting Parties shall apply the provisions of Paragraphs A to D of this Regulation on discharge of sewage ships while operating in the Baltic Sea Area.

Definitions

For the purposes of this Regulation:

1. "New ship" means a ship:

   (a) for which the building contract is placed, or in the absence of a building contract, the keel of which is laid or which is at a similar stage of construction, on or after the date of entry into force of the present Convention; or

   (b) the delivery of which is three years or more after the date of entry into force of the present Convention;

2. "Existing ship" means a ship which is not a new ship.

3. "Sewage" means:

   (a) damage and other wastes from any of toilets urinals, and WC scuppers;

   (b) drainage from medical premises (dispensary, sick bay, etc.) via wash basins, wash tubs and scuppers located in such premises;

   (c) drainage from spaces containing living animals; or

   (d) other waste waters when mixed with the damages defined above.

4. "Holding tank" means a tank used for the collection and storage of sewage.

Application

1. The provisions of this Regulation shall apply to:

   (a) new ships certified to carry more than 100 persons from a date not later than 1 January 1977;

   (b) existing ships certified to carry more than 400 persons form a date not later than 1 January 1978; and

(c) other ships, as specified in Sub-Paragraph (i), (ii), and (iii), from dates decided by the Contracting Parties on recommendation by the Commission:

   (i) ships of 200 tons gross tonnage and above;

   (ii) ships of less than 200 tons gross tonnage which are certified to carry more than 10 persons;

   (iii) ships which do not have measured gross tonnage and are certified to carry more than 40 persons.

In the case of new such ships the date shall be not later than 1 January 1979. In the case of existing such ships the date shall be not later than ten years after the date decided for new ships.

2. A Contracting Party may, if it is satisfied that the application of the provisions of Sub-Paragraph 1 b) of this Paragraph with respect to certain ship would necessitate constructional alterations which would be unreasonable exempt the ship from the application until a date not later than ten years after the date of entry into force of the present Convention.

Discharge of Sewage

1. Subject to the provisions of Paragraph D of this Regulation, the discharge of sewage into the sea is prohibited, except when:

   (a) the ship is discharging comminuted and disinfected sewage using a system approved by the Administration at a distance of more than 4 nautical miles form the nearest land, or sewage which is not comminuted or disinfected at a distance of more than 12 nautical miles form the nearest land, provided that any case the sewage that has been stored in holding tanks shall not be discharged instantaneously but, at a moderate rate when the ship is en route and proceeding at not less than 4 knots; or

(b) the ship has in operation a sewage treatment plant which has been approved by the Administration, and

(i) the test results of the plant are laid down in a document carried by the ship;

(ii) additionally, the effluent shall not produce visible floating solids, nor cause discolouration of the surrounding water; or

(c) the ship is situated in the waters under the jurisdiction of a State and is discharging sewage in accordance with such less stringent requirements as may be imposed by such State.

2. When the sewage is mixed with wastes or waste water having different discharge requirements, more stringent requirements shall apply.

Exceptions

Paragraph C of this Regulation shall not apply to:

(a) the discharge of sewage from a ship necessary for the purpose of securing the safety of ship and those on board or saving life at sea; or

(b) the discharge of sewage resulting from damage to a ship or its equipment if all reasonable precautions have been taken before and after the occurrence of the damage for the purpose or preventing or minimizing the discharge.

Reception Facilities

1. Each Contracting Party undertakes to ensure the provision of facilities at its ports and terminals of the Baltic Sea Area for the reception of sewage.

   Without causing undue delay to ships, adequate to meet the needs of the ships using them.

2. To enable pipes of reception facilities to be connected with the ship's discharge pipeline, both lines shall be fitted with a standard discharge connection in accordance.

Regulation 8

Garbage

The Contracting Parties shall as soon as possible but not later than 1 January 1976 or on the date of entry into force of the present Convention, whichever occurs later, apply the provisions of Paragraphs A to D of this Regulation on the disposal of garbage from ships while operating in the Baltic Sea Area.

Definition

For the purposes of this Regulation:

"Garbage" means all kinds of victual, domestic and operational waste excluding fresh fish and parts thereof, generated during the normal operation of the ship and liable to be disposed of continuously or periodically except those substances which are defined or listed in other Regulations of this Annex.

Disposal of Garbage

1. Subject to the provisions of Paragraphs C and D of this Regulation:

   (a) disposal into the sea of the following is prohibited:

(i) all plastics, including but not limited to synthetic ropes, synthetic fishing nets and plastic garbage bags; and

(ii) all other garbage, including paper products, rags, glass, metal, bottles, crockery, lining and packing materials;

(b) disposal into the sea of food wastes shall be made as far as practicable from land , but in- any case not less than 12 nautical miles from the nearest land,

2. When the garbage is mixed with other discharges having different disposal or discharge requirements the more stringent requirements shall apply.

Special Requirements for Fixed and Floating Platforms

1. Subject to the provision of Sub-paragraph 2 of this paragraph, the disposal of any materials regulated by this Regulation is prohibited from fixed or floating platforms engaged in the exploration, exploitation and associated off-shore processing of sea-bed mineral resources, and all other ships when alongside or within 500 meteres of such platforms.

2. The disposal into the sea of food wastes may be permitted when they have passed through a comminuter or grinder from such fixed or floating platforms located more than 12 nautical miles from land and all other ships when alongside or within 500 meters of such platforms. Such comminuted or ground food wastes shall be capable of passing through a screen with openings no greater than 25 millimeters.

Exceptions

Paragraphs B and C of this Regulation shall not apply to:

(a) the disposal of garbage from a ship necessary for the purpose of securing the safety of ship and those on board or saving life at sea; or

(b) the escape of garbage resulting from damage to a ship or its equipment provided all reasonable precautions have been taken before and after the occurrence of the damage, for the purpose of preventing or minimizing the escape; or

(c) the accidental loss of synthetic fishing nets or synthetic material incidental to the repair of such nets, provided that all reasonable precautions have been taken to prevent such loss.

Reception Facilities

Each Contracting Party undertakes to ensure the provision of facilities at its ports and terminals of the Baltic Sea Area for the reception of garbage, without causing undue delay to ships, and according to the needs of the ships using them.

Annex V

Exceptions from the General Prohibition of Dumping of Waste and other Matter in the Baltic Sea Area

Regulation I

In accordance with Paragraph 2 of Article 9 of the present Convention the prohibition of dumping shall not apply to the disposal at sea of dredged spoils provided that:

1. They do not contain significant quantities and concentrations of substances to be defined by the Commission and listed in Annexes I and II of the present Convention; and
2. The dumping is carried out under a prior special permit given by the appropriate national authority, either
   (a) within the area of the territorial sea of the Contracting Party; or
   (b) outside the area of the territorial sea, whenever necessary, after prior consultations in the Commission.

When issuing such permits the Contracting Party shall comply with the provisions in Regulation 3 of this Annex.

Regulation 2

1. The appropriate national authority referred to in Paragraph 2 of Article 9 of the present Convention shall:
   (a) issue special permits provided for the Regulation 1 of this Annex;
   (b) keep records of the nature and quantities of matter permitted to be dumped and the location, time and method of dumping;
   (c) collect available information concerning the nature and quantities of matter that has been dumped in the Baltic Sea Area recently and up to the coming in to force of the present Convention, provided that the dumped matter in question could be liable to contaminate water or organisms in the Baltic

Sea Area, to be caught by fishing equipment, or otherwise to give rise to harm, and the location, time and method of such dumping.

2. The appropriate national authority shall issue special permits in accordance with Regulation 1 of this Annexed inrespect of matter intended for dumping in the Baltic Sea Area:

    (a) loaded in its territory;

    (b) loaded by a vessel or aircraft registered in its territory or flying its flag, when the loading occurs in the territory of a State not Party to the present Convention,.

3. When issuing permits under Sub-Paragraph 1 a) and above, the appropriate national authority shall comply with Regulation 3 of this Annex, together with such additional criteria, measures and requirements as they may consider relevant.

4. Each Contracting Party shall report to the Commission, and where appropriate to other. Contracting parties, the information specified in Sub-Paragraph 1 c) of Regulation 2 of this Annex. The procedure to be followed and the nature of such reports shall be determined by the Commission.

Regulation 3

When issuing special permits according to Regulation 1 of this Annex the appropriate national authority shall take into account:

1. Quantity of dredged spoils to be dumped.
2. The content of the matter referred to in Annex I and II of the present Convention.
3. Location (e.g. co-ordinates of the dumping area, depth and distance from coast) and its relation to

areas of special interest (e.g. amenity areas, spawrning, nursery and fishing areas, etc.)

4. Water characteristics, if dumping is carried outside the territorial sea, consisting of:
   (a) hydrographic properties (e.g. temperature, salinity density, profile);
   (b) chemical properties (e.g. pH dissolved Oxygen nutrients);
   (c) biological properties (e.g. primary production and benthic animals).

The data should include sufficient information oil the annual mean levels and the seasonal variation *Of* the properties mentioned in this paragraph.

5. The existence and effects of other dumping which may have been carried out in the dumping area.

Regulation 4

Reports made in accordance with Paragraph 5 of Article 9 of the present Convention shall include the following information:

1. Location of dumping, characteristics of dumped material, and counter measures taken:
   (a) location (e.g. coordinates if the accidental dumping site, depth and distance from the coast):
   (b) method of deposit; .
   (c) quantity and composition of dumped matter as well as its physical (e.g. solubility and density), chemical and biochemical (e.g. oxygen demand, nutrients) and biological properties (e.g. presence of viruses, bacteria yeasts parasites);
   (d) toxicity;

(e) content of the substances referred to in Annexes I and II of the present Convention;

(t) dispersal characteristics (e.g. effects of currents and wind, and horizontal transport and vertical mixing);

(g) water characteristics (e.g. temperature, pH, redox conditions, salinity and stratification);

(h) bottom characteristics (e.g. topography, geological characteristics and redox conditions);

(i) counter measures taken and follow-up operations carried out or planned.

2. General consideration and conditions:

(a) possible effect on amenities (e.g. floating or stranded material, turbidity, objectionable odour, discolouration and foaming);

(b) possible effect on marine life, fish and shellfish culture, fish stocks and fisheries, seaweed harvesting and cultures; and

(c) possible effects on other uses of the sea (e.g. impairment of water quality for industrial use, underwater corrosion of structures, interference with ship operations from floating materials, interference with fishing or navigation and protection of areas of special importance for scientific or conservation purposes).

Annex VI

Co-operation in combating Marine Pollution

Regulation 1

For the purposes of this Annex:

1. "Ship" means a vessel of any type whatever operating in the marine environment and includes hydofoil boats, air-cushion vehicles, submersibles, floating craft and fixed or floating platforms.

2. "Administration" means the Government of the State under whose authority the ship is operating. With respect to a ship entitled to fly a flag of any State, the Administration is the Government of that State. With respect to fixed or floating platforms engaged in exploration and exploitation of the seabed and subsoil thereof adjacent to the coast over which the coastal State exercises sovereign rights for the purposes of exploration and exploitation of their natural resources, the Administration is the Government of the coastal State concerned

3. (a) "Discharge", in relation to harmful substances or effluents containing such substances, means any release howsoever caused from a ship and includes any escape, disposal, spilling, leaking, pumping, emitting or emptying.

   (b) "Discharge" does not include:

   (i) dumping within the meaning of the Convention on the Prevention of Marine Pollution by Dumping of Wastes and Other Matter done at London on 29 December 1972; or

   (ii) release of harmful substances directly arising from the exploration and associated offshore processing of seabed mineral resources; or

   (iii) release of harmful substances for purposes of legitimate scientific research into pollution abatement or control.

Regulation 2

The Contracting Parties undertake to maintain ability to combat spillages of oil and other harmful substances on the sea. This ability shall include adequate equipment, ships and manpower prepared for operations in coastal waters as well as on the high sea.

Regulation 3

The Contracting Parties shall, without prejudice to Paragraph 4 of Article 4 of the present Convention, develop and apply, individually or in cooperation, surveillance activities covering the Baltic Sea Area, inorder to spot and monitor oil and other harmful substances released into the sea.

Regulation 4

In the case of loss overboard of harmful substances in packages, freight containers, portable tanks, or road and rail tank wagons, the Contracting Parties shall cooperate in the salvage and recovery of such packages, containers or tanks so as to minimize the danger to the environment.

Regulation 5

1. The Contracting Parties, also being parties to the International Convention for the Prevention of Pollution from ships, 1973, as modified by the Protocol of 1978 relating thereto (MARPOL73/78) apply in conformity with that protocol I to MARPOL 73/78 on reports on incidents involving harmful substances. These provisions shall also be applied with regard to significant spillagers, of oil or other harmful substances in cases not covered by Article 8 of MARPOL 73/78.
2. The Contracting Parties shall request masters of ships and pilots of aircraft to report without

delay in accordance with this system on significant spillages of oil or other harmful substances observed at sea. Such reports should as far as possible contain the following data: time, position, wind and sea conditions, and kind, extent and portable source of the spill observed.

3. The master of ship involved in an incident referred to in Paragraph 1 of this regulation, or other person having charge of the ship shall without delay and t~ the fullest extent possible report in accordance with this system and with the provisions of the Appendix to the present Annex.

4. Each Contracting Party undertakes to issue instructions to its maritime inspection vessels and aircraft and to other appropriate services to report to its authorities any observation or incident referred to in Paragraph 1 of this Regulation. Such reports shall as far as possible contain the data referred to in paragraphs 2 or 3 of this Regulation respectively, as well as possible indications on the spreading or drifting tendencies of the spill question.

5. Whenever a Contracting Party is aware of a casualty or the presence of spillages of oil or other harmful substances in the baltic Sea Area likely to constitute a serious threat to the marine environment of the Baltic Sea Area or the coast or related interests of any other Contracting Party, it shall without delay transmit all relevant information thereon to the Contracting Party which may be affected by the pollutant and, as regards ship casualty incidents, to the Administration of the ship involved.

Regulation 6

Each Contracting Party shall request masters of ships flying its flag to provide, in case of an incident, on request by the proper authorities, such detailed information about the ship and its cargo which is relevant to actions for preventing or combating pollution of the sea, and to cooperate with these authorities.

Regulation 7

1. (a) The contracting Parties shall as soon as possible agree bilaterally or multilaterally on those regions of the Baltic Sea Area in which they will take action for combating or salvage activities whenever a significant spillage of oil or other harmful substances or any incidents causing or likely to cause pollution within the Baltic Sea Area have occurred or are likely to occur. Such agreements shall not prejudice any other agreements 'concluded between Contracting Parties concerning the same subject. The neighbouring States shall ensure the harmonization of the different agreements. The Contracting Parties shall inform each other about such agreements.

   The contracting Parties may ask the Commission for assistance to reach agreement, if needed.

   (b) The Contracting Party within whose region a situation as described in Regulation 1 of this Annex occurs shall make the necessary assessments of the situation and take adequate action in order to avoid or minimize subsequent pollution effects and shall keep drifting parts of the spillage under observation until no further action is called for,

2. In the case that such a spillage is drifting or is likely to drift into a region, where another

Contracting Party should take action for purposes as definded in Subparagraph 1 a) of this regulation, that Party shall without delay be informed of the situation and the actions that have been taken.

Regulation 8

A Contracting Party requiring assistance for combating spillages of oil or other harmful substances .at sea is entitled to call for assistance by other. Contracting Parties, starting with those who seem likely also to be affected by the spillage. Contracting Parties called upon for assistance in accordance with this Regulation shall use their best endeavours to bring such assistance.

Regulation 9

1. The Contracting Parties shall provide information to the other Contracting Parties and the Commission about

   (a) their national organization for dealing with spillages at sea of oil and other harmful substances;

   (b) national regulations and other matters which have a direct bearing on combating pollution at sea by oil and other harmful substances;

   (c) the competent authority responsible for receiving and dispatching reports of pollution at sea by oil and other harmful substances;

   (d) the competent authorities for dealing with questions' concerning measures of mutual assistance, information and cooperation between the Contracting Parties according to this Annex;

   (e) actions taken in accordance with Regulation 8 of this Annex.

2. The Contracting Parties shall exchange information of research and development programs and results concerning ways in which pollution by oil and other harmful substances at sea may be dealt with and experiences in combating such pollution.

Regulation 10

The authorities referred to in Sub-Paragraph 1 d) of Regulation 9 of this Annex shall establish direct contact and cooperate in operational matters.

Index